SALEM COLLEGE LIBRARY

GIFT OF PATRICIA TURLINGTON-DEES

Celebrity Performers and the American Public

STARSTRUCK

JIB FOWLES

Smithsonian Institution Press
Washington and London

Designer: Linda McKnight

Library of Congress Cataloging-in-Publication
Data

Fowles, Jib.
    Starstruck : celebrity performers and the
American public / Jib Fowles.
        p.   cm.
    Includes bibliographical references (p.   )
and index.
    ISBN 1-56098-123-7
    1. Motion picture actors and actresses—
Public opinion. 2. Entertainers—Public
opinion. 3. Athletes—Public opinion. 4.
Fame—Public opinion. 5. Public opinion—
United States. 6. United States—Popular
culture.   I. Title.
PN1998.F68   1992
790.2'092'273—dc20   91–23702

British Library Cataloguing-in-Publication
Data is available

Manufactured in the United States of America
99 98 97 96 95 94 93 92   5 4 3 2 1

⊗ The paper used in this publication meets the
minimum requirements of the American National Standard for Permanence of Paper for
Printed Library Materials Z39.48–1984.

★ To

Joy Castronovo Fowles,

Celeste Fowles,

and

Nathaniel Castronovo Fowles

CONTENTS

PREFACE

The word *star,* as applied to entertainment figures, nicely spec-
ifies the subject matter of this book. There are many other kinds
of celebrities—political leaders and creative artists among
them—but here the topic is exclusively that group of people
who have achieved great fame in the United States as performers—Hollywood stars, sports stars, comedy stars, and music
stars.

On two counts stars are rare creatures. They are unprecedented in the expanse of human history: with few exceptions,
stars have occurred only within the past century. And additionally, in any given year during this comparatively short stretch
of time, there have been only a limited number of them—approximately one hundred.

Yet for all their scarcity, stars have an enormous impact
upon our way of life. They are recognized by virtually the entire
American population, who observe them closely onstage and off,
think about them, talk about them, emulate them, even dream
about them. Stardom is an indisputably vital force in our popular culture.

Several questions about the phenomenon of stars motivate

this interdisciplinary study. Why have stars appeared at this point in history, the twentieth century? On what basis do some performers become stars, and others not? What does the role of star look like from the occupant's viewpoint? What functions do stars serve for the public? What is the descent from those high reaches like? Do stars decline and die differently from the rest of the population? Is the existence of stardom a troubling comment on American culture?

It is a commonplace among those who have written seriously about American stardom to note that the study of the star—of the role, its occupiers, and its functions—scarcely exists. Daniel Boorstin, some time before he became the Librarian of Congress, stated in *The Image* that "the literature on the history of celebrities and of celebrity worship is meager."[1] Sociologist Orrin Klapp reflected that stars provide "an important form of leadership, one that has not, I believe, been sufficiently recognized, by scholars at least (the masses, of course, have always recognized it)."[2] Film historian Garth Jowett commented about stars, "We know a great deal about their lives, but very little about the essential nature of their appeal to the public."[3] And in *The Frenzy of Renown*, a monumental chronicle of the concept of fame from the time of Alexander the Great onward, Leo Braudy offered, "We have become immensely sensitive to the subject of fame. Since the late 1960s, its hazards have become obligatory fare in every celebrity interview. But that sensitivity has not brought very much understanding."[4]

These writers are largely correct, and this book has come about partly in response to the lack of a coherent interpretation of stardom. But a literature on the star role, although small and scattered, does exist. These authors themselves have produced much of what has appeared in book form. Beyond this, other serious work in journals and dissertations has occasionally presented insights about the occupation of the star.

My main source of information concerning the job of the American celebrity entertainer, however, is a survey of stars' careers conducted for this book. For a representative group of 100 stars, biographical profiles have been compiled according to a standardized form. Commonalities have been ascertained for such matters as the stars' family backgrounds, pre-star preparation, lengths and sorts of careers, fan interactions, press relations, home lives, post-star years, manner of dying, and so forth. From this material a picture of the norms for those who occupy the star role has been derived. As the first empirical investigation of its kind, this project ("The Study of 100 Stars") represents some headway into the hitherto unsurveyed realm of stardom. Here, alphabetically, are the stars whose lives and careers were examined:

1. Louis Armstrong
2. Fred Astaire
3. Gene Autry
4. Lucille Ball
5. Theda Bara
6. John Barrymore
7. John Belushi
8. Jack Benny
9. Ingrid Bergman
10. Humphrey Bogart
11. Clara Bow
12. Lenny Bruce
13. Richard Burton
14. James Cagney
15. Karen Carpenter
16. Wilt Chamberlain
17. Charlie Chaplin
18. Montgomery Clift
19. Ty Cobb
20. Nat "King" Cole
21. Gary Cooper
22. Joan Crawford
23. Bing Crosby
24. Bette Davis
25. Doris Day
26. James Dean
27. Jack Dempsey
28. Marlene Dietrich
29. Joe DiMaggio
30. Jimmy Durante
31. Duke Ellington
32. Douglas Fairbanks, Sr.
33. W. C. Fields
34. Errol Flynn
35. Henry Fonda
36. Clark Gable
37. Greta Garbo
38. Ava Gardner
39. Judy Garland
40. Lou Gehrig
41. Jackie Gleason
42. Benny Goodman
43. Betty Grable
44. Cary Grant
45. Bill Haley
46. Jean Harlow
47. Rita Hayworth
48. Jimi Hendrix
49. Katharine Hepburn
50. Bob Hope
51. Harry Houdini
52. Rock Hudson
53. Al Jolson
54. Janis Joplin
55. Danny Kaye
56. Buster Keaton
57. Grace Kelly
58. Billie Jean King
59. Ernie Kovacs
60. Hedy Lamarr
61. Gypsy Rose Lee
62. Vivien Leigh
63. John Lennon
64. Liberace
65. Carole Lombard
66. Joe Louis
67. Steve McQueen
68. Jayne Mansfield

69. Mickey Mantle
70. Roger Maris
71. Groucho Marx
72. Glenn Miller
73. Marilyn Monroe
74. Jim Morrison
75. David Niven
76. Gregory Peck
77. Mary Pickford
78. Tyrone Power
79. Elvis Presley
80. Jackie Robinson
81. Ginger Rogers
82. Roy Rogers
83. Will Rogers
84. Mickey Rooney
85. Jane Russell
86. Babe Ruth
87. Peter Sellers
88. Red Skelton
89. Roger Staubach
90. James (Jimmy) Stewart
91. Gloria Swanson
92. Shirley Temple
93. Spencer Tracy
94. Lana Turner
95. Rudolph Valentino
96. John Wayne
97. Lawrence Welk
98. Mae West
99. Ted Williams
100. Babe Didrikson Zaharias

The study (which is described in the appendix) concentrated upon performers whose careers were over, in order to document ends as well as beginnings. To their sagas I have added the reflections of current stars as well. In interviews these newcomers reveal the same opinions about their profession, and the same puzzlements, as those who have gone before.

I have quoted liberally from such interviews past and present throughout the text, generally without source attribution since they were widely disseminated in hundreds of American newspapers via wire services. More substantial and interpretive sources are cited in the Notes section.

It is curious that stars, so committed to their line of work, have such an imperfect overall sense of it. As a general rule, they have little idea of what stardom is or why they were selected for it. Typical is Marilyn Monroe's reflection: "There was a reaction that came to the studio, the fan mail, or when I went to a premiere, or the exhibitors wanted to meet me. I don't know why." To achieve some improvement over this level of understanding is the task of this book.

In the belief that many human relations involve a transaction, I have found it fruitful to ask what we get from stars, and what stars get from us. As it turns out, we give them so much because we get so much in return.

ACKNOWLEDGMENTS

I am grateful to those who read and responded to earlier drafts of this book. George Lipsitz, Bob Aaron, and Dean Scaros reviewed portions. Garth Jowett and Joel Kurtzman critiqued the manuscript in its entirety, and I am very much in their debt.

Appreciation is due to my colleagues in the Popular Culture Association for listening at successive annual meetings to three papers based on material in *Starstruck:* "How Do 'Stars' Die?" in 1986, "The Birth of the 'Star' Role" in 1987, and "On the *Under*compensation of Stars" in 1988.

My personal thanks go to my colleague Roger Bilstein, who introduced me to Smithsonian Institution Press. At the Press, acquisitions editor Martin Williams, director Felix Lowe, editorial director Daniel Goodwin, and editor Duke Johns were especially helpful. My agent, Julie Castiglia, is to be commended for her efforts on my behalf.

My wife, Joy Castronovo Fowles, championed the use of photographs to accompany the text. Mary Corliss and Terry Geesken at the Film Stills Archive of the Museum of Modern Art, and Howard Mandelbaum and Ron Mandelbaum at Photofest, were most cooperative. The Mary Pickford Foundation gra-

ciously granted permission to reprint from its original photograph of a besieged Pickford and Douglas Fairbanks, Sr.

ciously granted permission to reprint from its original photograph of a besieged Pickford and Douglas Fairbanks, Sr.

My home institution, the University of Houston–Clear Lake, kindly provided me with two grants, the first to undertake the initial bibliographic search and the second to pay for the preparation of the manuscript.

The first draft of the book was typed expeditiously by Pam Sisk, and the final draft by Dora Wimbish, whose enthusiasm for the project was greatly appreciated. For last-minute revisions, Denise Vega came to my rescue; her industry and attention to detail were praiseworthy.

My guiding professors in the Media Ecology doctoral program at New York University, Neil Postman and Terry Moran, remain in my memory almost twenty years later for their good humor, tolerance of ideas, and spirit of inquiry. I hope *Starstruck* follows in that tradition.

This book is dedicated to my wife and our daughter and son. Family life has been a source of great pleasure and support for me; without it, I doubt that this research would have been undertaken or the manuscript written. My mother, Jane Finley, has also been supportive of this project from the outset.

Finally, in some way stars themselves are owed thanks for making their private lives more or less accessible to an outsider. It is a virtual requirement of their occupation that they do so, although no star does this easily. By relying on secondary sources I have avoided adding to the intrusion, but even at this remove I occasionally felt I was prying into matters that were no one's business but the star's. Yet absent this feature of near-transparency, the information could not have been gathered to reach sound conclusions about this singular occupation and the individuals working at it.

Anyone who discusses modern culture has to do a great deal of contemplating of the invisible in the obvious.

—O. B. HARDISON, JR.
Disappearing Through the Skylight:
Culture and Technology in the Twentieth Century

☆

INTRODUCTION: THE STAR ROLE

1. ★
STARRING

ate in his career Charlie Chaplin produced the movie *Limelight*, casting himself as an ex-vaudeville comedian, Calvero. The actress Claire Bloom played a recuperating ballet dancer, Terry. Describing to Terry what it means to be a successful comedian, Calvero exclaims gleefully, "To hear that roar go up—waves of laughter coming at you."

"To hear that roar go up"—this is the emotional reward for the entertainer. There is nothing so exhilarating as the exuberant response of an audience. The singer Al Jolson put it this way: "When you have a crowded house, you can feel the electric what-do-you-call-'em surging across the footlights between your audience and yourself, and you know you've got 'em."

"Electric what-do-you-call-'em" must have been what Bette Davis *(photograph 1)* experienced when, as a young actress in a Boston theater, she performed so well that she was called back onstage for her first-ever solo bow: "The theater now shook with applause and bravos. People actually stood on their seats and cheered—for *me*. It was really just for me. Wave after wave of love flooded the stage and washed over me. I felt my face crumble and I started to cry. 'Bravo!' I was alone—onstage and everywhere; and that's the way it was obviously meant to be. 'Bravo!' My first stardust. It is impossible to describe the sweetness of such a moment."

In the view of pitching great Nolan Ryan, "A standing ovation is always a great thrill. It's an emotional thing, a sense of appreciation from people that I've done my job well. But there's a physical sensation, too. Sort of a chill, a climactic feeling that can't really be topped." Rock star Rod Stewart explained, "You've got no idea what it's like to be up there in front of 20,000 screaming fans. It's a hard thing to give up. It's really like a drug."

While entertainment in the twentieth century has shifted in the main from live performance to the channels of mass communication, the response of the audience has lost some of its immediacy but little of its power. Because the audience for television shows, films, and recordings is so large and so appreciative, the acclamation of the star is if anything more ferocious than ever. The wave, the surge, the electric thing that stage performers describe rain upon the media star as well. Through ticket sales, high ratings, and fan mail, the audience makes known its jubilant response to the star's performance. As the recipient of this flow of good tidings, the star is certified in public regard and elevated to a special glory. "Public adoration is the greatest thing in the world," remarked ex-child star Jackie Coogan, Jr.

No wonder Hedy Lamarr felt that "to be a star is to own the world and all the people in it. After a taste of stardom, everything else is poverty."

Considering that their work requires them to display themselves expansively before the eyes of millions, it would seem likely for stars to be extraordinary extroverts by nature. Yet a surprising number of celebrity performers are shy.

The captain of American entertainers, Johnny Carson, confesses to having been withdrawn and shy all his life. And so does his erstwhile replacement, Joan Rivers: "I'm very private. I'm very introverted. I'm very shy, and I find it very hard to deal with strangers." Shyness has been present among the ranks of stars since the beginning; both Mary Pickford and Charlie Chaplin were excruciatingly shy. When Chaplin first reported to the Keystone Studio in Los Angeles, he was so timid he could not bring himself to go in: "The problem of entering the studio and facing all those people became an insuperable one. For two days I arrived outside the studio, but I had not the courage to go in."

In the camp of the shy belong such stellar performers as Fred Astaire, Gene Autry, Ingrid Bergman, Clara Bow, James Cagney, Gary Cooper, Clark Gable, Greta Garbo, Rita Hayworth, Liberace, Joe Louis, Mickey Mantle, Gregory Peck, Elvis Presley, Gloria Swanson, Lana Turner, Rudolph Valentino, and Ted Williams. Marilyn Monroe's comment about first meeting Joe DiMaggio was, "And I could see he was as shy as I was."

Mary Tyler Moore and Martina Navratilova admit to being reserved. Michael Jackson is retiring, and so are two of his intimates, Elizabeth Taylor and Sophia Loren. Even Robin Williams and Mick Jagger are shy offstage. After Robert Redford and Meryl Streep had finished work on *Out of Africa*, Redford observed, "I'm very shy and Meryl's very shy."

In fact, it is probable that shyness is as common among celebrity performers as it is among the general population. An authoritative estimate is that 40 percent of Americans experience significant shyness;[1] in the study of 100 stars undertaken for this book, thirty-four were judged to be markedly introverted. This tallies with the research of Yoti Lane, who reported in *The Psychology of the Actor*, "The players who answered my questionnaire did not seem to be extroverts."[2]

How to account for the fact that, while leading entertainers would seem to be the epitomes of extroversion, many are actually introverts? The answer is that being a star is a social role an individual adopts, a role that can be occupied by an introvert as well as by an extrovert. Every day of our lives, we too take on social roles; we accept the obligations and behaviors of being an employee, a parent, a spouse, and so forth. It is similar with celebrity performers; they wake up in the morning and step into the star role. One who perceived this clearly was Clark Gable: "It's no different from any other job. I start at seven in the morning. When I finish at the end of the day, that's that. I want my own life at home. No pictures, no talk, no nothing. It's a job that I do; I try to do it the best I can. When I come home, it's finished."

Though playing a social role like other roles, the star is at the same time exceptionally different. There are several distinguishing features to the occupation. The work of the star is to play: actors "play" a role, athletes "play" a game, musicians "play" an instrument, comedians "play" a joke. The word *player*, in fact, is a synonym for *performer*. Stars excel in the world of play, the antithesis of the workaday world that consumes most people's efforts.

Playing admirably, stars delight their audiences. A star will act or sing or dance or crack jokes or play ball or even just pose, and do it with such style that we are diverted and refreshed. We follow stars because their performances are so successful at entertaining us.

The ability to entertain is the sine qua non, but there is more to the star role. The performance of the star is transmitted to virtually the total American population by television, radio, films, recordings, videotapes, and other means. Many individuals have the ability to entertain, but only a comparatively few eminent ones are conveyed through the channels of mass communication to a national audience.

Public response to these famous performers can range widely. At moments for certain stars and their captivated followers, the reaction can be manic, as when the Beatles first toured the United States in 1964. One young and rabid fan, Pamela Des Barres, was waiting for the British foursome to arrive in Los Angeles. As she wrote about it later, she and two other devotees resolved to sneak up on the group's rented mansion: "Sweatstained and dirty, we all trudged for hours through the bushes and brambles, our hearts pounding Beatle blood." The house was cordoned off by police, so they hid until the sun had set. "When it got dark, we decided to head across the street, one by one, crawling on our bellies like reptiles. I prayed hard for Paul to glance out his window. I just knew he would see a light shimmering behind the chain link because Pam of Reseda, California, was aglow with incandescent Beatle Love that would never die."[3]

The response to stars can be more temperate—the glint of acknowledgment and nothing more. This is more often the case. The essential factor about stars is not whether the response is frenzied or otherwise, but that they are broadly known. The general renown of celebrity performers was documented in a 1981 survey of 500 randomly selected American adults.[4] The respondents were asked if they could recognize six stars: John Wayne, Robert Redford, Joan Baez, Jane Fonda, Dick Gregory, and Marlon Brando. Awareness varied from a high of 99 percent for Wayne to a low of 94 percent for Redford. In social science research such lofty rates are extremely rare. Little else of cultural significance is shared so universally by the U.S. populace.

Another report on the general fame of celebrity entertainers comes in the form of an annual survey conducted by Marketing Evaluations, Inc., a New York market research firm. This poll investigates the extent to which certain performers are known and are liked by the television audience. It should be emphasized that the respondents are a sample of all Americans above the age of six—so the findings pertain to virtually the entire U.S. population. Here are Marketing Evaluations, Inc.'s familiarity ratings for those television performers recognized by more than 80 percent of Americans in 1985:

95% Lucille Ball	88% Sylvester Stallone
94% Alan Alda	87% Mike Farrell
94% Carol Burnett	87% Jackie Gleason
94% George Burns	87% Robert Redford
94% Bill Cosby	86% Lionel Richie
92% Clint Eastwood	86% Stevie Wonder
92% Bob Hope	85% James Garner
92% Richard Pryor	85% Marla Gibbs
92% Burt Reynolds	85% Robert Guillaume
91% Kenny Rogers	85% Dustin Hoffman
89% Sally Field	85% Paul Newman
89% Sherman Hemsley	85% Robert Wagner
89% Michael Landon	84% Chevy Chase
89% John Ritter	84% Kirk Douglas
89% Tom Selleck	84% Emmanuel Lewis
88% Tim Conway	83% Dom DeLuise
88% Barbara Mandrell	82% George Peppard
88% Harry Morgan	82% Stephanie Powers

81% Art Carney   80% Jack Klugman
80% Nell Carter   80% Dudley Moore
80% Richard Chamberlain   80% Pernell Roberts
80% Brian Keith

Not all stars are included in this survey, but the results are indicative of how widely such performers are known among Americans.

Stars perceive their fame as something odd and quite distinct from themselves. Singer Janis Ian once remarked, "Fame is not a reality of life, it's just a persona or false shell. I'm famous when I work, but then I go home, and I'm not famous." Mickey Mantle's reaction was: "It's like it is happening to someone else—like Mickey Mantle is some other guy." Don Johnson commented about the sudden fame that descended upon him for his role in television's *Miami Vice:* "It isn't reality. It has nothing to do with me."

The final defining aspect of the star role is that at any given time there are few in office. The sum of the performers from all entertainment fields who are recognized by more than 80 percent of Americans is, in any one particular year, going to be about one hundred. This exclusivity, which I believe I can show has come about for historical and cultural reasons, is frustrating in the extreme for the army of aspirants to the star role.

2.
A ROLE IS BORN (AND ENDURES)

tardom is a modern phenomenon. This observation may sound puzzling to someone who recalls Richard Burton in *Hamlet* or Marlon Brando in *Julius Caesar*. But associating historical dramas with stars is misleading. When Shakespeare's plays were originally staged, the actors in those parts were not what we would think of as stars. They were ordinary people, rarely known by name to the spectators. They did not receive billing above the title of the drama. Theatergoers did not ask each other, whenever a new play came along, "Who's in it?"; that is a present-day query.

A few isolated performers of the past did stand out much like contemporary stars. A Roman comedian, Quintus Roscius, achieved renown in the first century before Christ. In the sixth century A.D. Justinian, ruler of the Byzantine Empire, took as his wife an acclaimed mime, Theodora. In eighteenth-century London David Garrick's reputation as an actor ensured the popularity of his Drury Lane Theatre. But individuals like these were very much the exception. For the most part, performers in the past remained anonymous; Roman actors were generally slaves, and Renaissance players likewise occupied a lowly social niche. If an actor did gain fame, it was often because he was a playwright as well, such as the Greek tragedians or Shakespeare. It was not until the last two centuries that an ever-replenishing class of celebrity performers appeared.

The novelty of the role is revealed in the chronicle of the word *star* itself. Words can disclose much through their own histories, as they appear in response to something new, gain currency, and then recede when the need diminishes. For eons there was no call for a word to label special performers who on their own could draw large numbers of spectators, since conditions largely denied such a role. People attended events to see the play or the game, not to see a specific performer. Keeping with the impersonal tone of those performances, in many periods the players wore masks or ritualistic makeup. But as the star role slowly began to surface, a word for it was needed. The borrowed noun *star* was initially used in this sense around 1830. Many other words, old or newly fashioned, might have served, but *star* somehow captured the emerging role. It signaled something removed from the mud of common existence, glowing against drabber surroundings, providing a celestial point of reference.

Previous to this first faint glimmer of the star role in the nineteenth century, the famous were primarily people who wielded social power, such as religious figures, state leaders, or military commanders. They occupied the top rungs of institutional hierarchies, and if they did so with majesty and approval, and were triumphant in their endeavors, then they were heroes to contemporary and succeeding generations. They would be looked up to worshipfully.

For Americans, Andrew Jackson was such a person. President from 1828 to 1836, Jackson was popularly known as "Old Hickory," "Old Chief," or simply "Old Hero." He was admired avidly, being elected and re-elected by the largest pluralities seen since George Washington. His vices, which were considerable, were perceived as virtues. He may have killed men in duels, but for this he was seen as strong, not unlawful. What had Jackson done to elicit such adoration? As the commanding general at the routing of British troops in New Orleans in 1815, Jackson was held to be the savior of the American nation. He had also previously swept the South clear of Creek and Seminole Indians—at that time considered another proud statement of national resolve. His inauguration, at the age of sixty-one, turned into a frenzy of public acclaim. He had electrified Americans because, as a military and political leader, he had exercised power to affirm the nation. In many ways Jackson exemplifies all popular idols before the star role was born.

The British essayist Thomas Carlyle, lecturing in 1840 (in the predawn of the age of the star), sought to set out the varieties of heroes. There were, he declaimed, heroes who were rulers: Cromwell and Napoleon ("our last great man!") were his examples. Of religious heroes, some he classified as prophets (Mohammed) and some as priests (Martin Luther). He held that poets such as Dante and Shakespeare were also heroes, although others might wonder if they met the test of wide popularity in periods of limited literacy. Carlyle could not resist lionizing his own profession as a man of letters, and proposed Samuel Johnson as a representative hero. But even as he celebrated the hero, Carlyle felt the earth moving beneath him: "I am well aware that in these days hero-worship, the thing I call hero-worship, professes to have gone out and finally ceased. This is an age that as it were denies the existence of great men; denies the desirableness of great men. Show our critics a great man, a Luther for example, they begin to what they call 'account' for him; not to worship him, but take the dimensions of him—and bring him out to be a little kind of man."[1] All around Carlyle, the traditional role of hero was ebbing.

In the United States toward the end of the nineteenth century, a transitional form of the hero briefly had its day. This was the man situated at the pinnacle not of an enduring institution but of an organization—and a business organization at that. Through enormous application these men had risen from obscure origins to control sizable enterprises. Andrew Carnegie, Thomas Edison, Henry Ford—these were models of what could be accomplished if one put one's mind to it. With Horatio Alger–like visions in their heads, millions of American boys and men attempted to pattern their lives on the careers of those idols.

But by this time American society's shift of attention away from institutional or organizational heroes and toward entertainment stars was under way. This historic movement is captured in a quantitative study released in 1942 by sociologist Leo Lowenthal.[2] Lowenthal scrutinized the biographies that had been carried in popular magazines over the course of the twentieth century. Editors, he reasoned, printed the biographies that people wanted to read, so changes in the categories of individuals profiled would indicate changes in the types of people Americans admired. Lowenthal found that, from the beginning of this century until 1940, there was a distinctive shift from interest in political and business leaders (such as Teddy Roosevelt and J. Pierpont Morgan) to interest in entertainers (such as Will Rogers, Phil Rizzuto, or the trainer of a dancing gorilla). Political biographies fell off steeply, from 46 percent of the total at the beginning of the century to 25 percent in 1940, and business biographies dropped from 28 percent to 20 percent. As these declines were going on, entertainment biographies more than doubled, from 26 percent to 55 percent. Magazine readers were still interested in political and business figures, but the new reigning cadre was that of celebrity performers.

There were profound differences between the newer brand of notables—stars—and all previous types of heroes. The new elite were paragons of play, not achievement. And instead of occupying a hierarchical seat, they were more lateral phenomena; people felt somehow on a par with stars. While traditional heroes were respectfully deferred to, when stars were encountered the inclination was to step forward and engage them. Mae West *(photograph 2)* was being interviewed in a restaurant when a man interrupted and spoke to her familiarly; after he left, the interviewer asked her who he was and was told she had no idea. "He sounded as if he knew you," the interviewer persisted. "They all do, dear," she responded. Stars were regarded as acquaintances, not figureheads.

The rise of the star role has been noted by social commentators but for the most part has not been greeted with enthusiasm. Historian Daniel Boorstin railed against this new cultural invention when he defined the celebrity as someone "known for his well-knownness." Boorstin disapprovingly contrasted the old and new versions of fame: "The hero was distinguished by his achievement; the celebrity by his image or trademark. The hero created himself; the celebrity is created by the media. The hero was a big man; the celebrity is a big name."[3]

Such derision can be satisfying for the social critic and, in its trenchancy, engaging for a reader. Warmed by Boorstin's indignation, readers can repair to age-old standards. But doing so means missing a great deal, for there is something new under the sun here: society has called into being an unprecedented social role. The twentieth century needs something that prior generations did not need. What is there about us, about our times, that has led to the emergence of the star role?

If asked to reflect on stars, many people let their thoughts go directly to the glamorous era of movie supremacy. In their mind's eye they may see a spectacular parade of Hollywood creatures: sophisticated gentlemen in top hats and tuxedos, sirens in slinky gowns, rough-hewn cowboys, swaggering detectives, blondes in bathing suits, gangsters, moppets, all glittering or glistening. It is a heart-stopping array that can walk down an imaginary runway into the spotlight, to look directly our way and receive the applause.

During the first half of the twentieth century, and more precisely in the second decade, the star role exploded into prominence. Suddenly, as never before, Americans all knew the same few personalities, fell over each other to get to them, made time for them, had their names on their lips and their images in their minds. The public felt close to stars in ways people had never been close to the famous before. Stars' successes became the audience's achievements, their antics became spectators' anecdotes.

Who was the earliest movie star? Although Gilbert Max ("Broncho Billy") Anderson is a close contender, it is generally agreed that the first American film star was Florence Lawrence. She had been the anonymous "Biograph Girl" until her presumptions had exceeded the tolerances of that early studio and she had been released. Then she was hired by an independent producer, Carl Laemmle—a resourceful entrepreneur who had much to do with shaping the nascent industry. Laemmle recognized that one way he could achieve a competitive advantage over the established studios was to publicize his players.

Laemmle's opportunity to herald Florence Lawrence came early in 1910. With a classic publicity stunt he brought her public attention of an intensity rarely seen before and much pursued since. Stories had appeared in the nation's newspapers about the presumed untimely death of Miss Lawrence in a streetcar accident; whether these stories originated with her previous employer, who might well have wished to limit the career of the "Biograph Girl" to the films they already possessed, or whether they came from Laemmle's office, can only be conjectured. But since she was alive and at work in his New York studio, Laemmle seized the opportunity. He announced he would produce her in St. Louis where her worried fans could view her in person. A train journey was arranged, and at every stop news was relayed about her progress to that metropolis at the center of America. By the time she arrived in St. Louis, crowd sentiment had built to a hysteria.

From the station Miss Lawrence was scheduled to visit her fans in two theaters. According to Laemmle's biographer, "On the way to the first theater, they demonstrated their affection by tearing the buttons from her coat, the trimmings from her hat, and the hat from her head."[4] The actress barely made it to safety at the second. Here was the first recorded instance of the frenzy that can befall the leading entertainer; until this point in history, public appreciation of performers had always been more temperate. From that day forward, for occupiers of the star role there has been no avoiding incidents of rabid adulation.

But if the star role with its modern intensity appears first with Florence Lawrence, the sad corollary is that the construct can endure should the tenant be discarded. If she was the first to come into the role, she was also the first to depart: it was not long after the St. Louis event that Laemmle let her go. He did bring her back briefly in 1913, but then she was gone altogether. Interviewed in 1924, Miss Lawrence took the plaintive tone of many others who were to be abandoned subsequently: "It's hard at the age of thirty-one to be left forgotten by an industry you helped so hard to develop." She later died by her own hand.

From today's perspective Florence Lawrence remains a dim prototype, her personal features little recalled. The birth of the star role is thus better represented by another: Mary Pickford, "America's Sweetheart," who is the earliest star that most people can actually picture in the processional of performing artists.

Mary Pickford was born Gladys Smith in Toronto in 1893. It was desperation, not family heritage or unquenchable talent, that drove her into the acting profession at an early age. Her father had died tragically and her mother, trying to support three children, had allowed the young Gladys to go on the stage in response to a chance offer—a boarder at their house was a theater manager and needed a young girl for a part. Her success in this and subsequent roles eventually brought the family to New York City, the center of the theater world. Like a number of other aspiring players at the time, Gladys was forced to find occasional work at the new movie studios. A man who was soon to become one of the world's most famous directors, D. W. Griffith, took a liking to her and began to cast her regularly.

The great difference Mary Pickford (her newly adopted professional name) noticed between her work onstage and in the movies was in the nature of the audience. After her first films were released, people began to approach her familiarly in the street. They were responding to her as a movie actress in ways they never had as a theater performer. But the difference was not just one of kind; it was also of degree, and to an awesome extent. The size of her following grew almost inconceivably large. Producers tried to conceal this from her, but as she recounts in her autobiography, "I was driving up Broadway on the way home from the studio one evening when I noticed that a Famous Players picture of mine, *Rags*, was showing at the Strand. As I passed by the theater I saw lines extending from both sides of the box office."[5] That said it all; Mary had what the public demanded to see. The animated, innocent lass was Americans' hearts' desire.

Why should this lithe figure have found such celebrity when the most popular theater actresses of the day were much more matronly? Some commentators on Pickford's fame have credited her success to Griffith, who seems to have had a personal penchant for young, slight women. But a better answer in all likelihood is that, whatever Griffith's proclivities may have been, in his professional capacity he was simply reflecting the current tastes of the audience. It was ingenues like Pickford and Lillian and Dorothy Gish that the ticket-buying public preferred. Perhaps, as the cultural invention of stardom was crystallizing, if there was a sense in the air that something unprecedented and foreboding was about to happen, it may have felt less ominous for fame to be bestowed on persons who were depicted as sweet and innocent. In his memoirs Adolph Zukor reflected, "The first of the great film stars, Mary's rise had been sensational, and more than a little frightening. . . . We had moved in almost total darkness as Mary led the way upward and across the skies."[6] A child led us into the age of the star.

To the name of Mary Pickford must be linked those of Charlie Chaplin and Douglas Fairbanks, Sr. More than others, these three *(photograph 3)* established the parameters of the star role by 1920.

Chaplin's origins had been even less promising than Pickford's. She at least had one parent; not only was Chaplin's father gone, but his mother was mentally ill and was institutionalized when he was a boy. His first job in the new film industry was little more than a fluke. Comedy producer Mack Sennett hired the British-born Chaplin in 1913, mistakenly thinking the pantomimist was a much older man, able and willing to play a fall guy. A perfectionist dandy, one with airs, did not suit Sennett's plans, and he was about to let Chaplin go when he got a telegram from Keystone Comedy's New York office requesting more Chaplin films. Charlie had found an audience.

And what an audience it was. It outreached any previous actor's following, including Mary Pickford's. The buoyancy of the Little Tramp appealed to the never-say-die spirit of people everywhere. In his autobiography Chaplin recounted a 1916 train trip from Hollywood to New York, where he was to sign a contract for a $10,000-a-week salary plus a $150,000 one-time bonus. The journey was reminiscent of Florence Lawrence's trip to St. Louis six years earlier; this time, however, the popular excitement was not whipped up by adroit publicists, but occurred spontaneously. When the train paused in Amarillo, Texas, the mayor came on board and implored Chaplin to address a gathering throng. Chaplin later wrote, "Then the crowd pressed forward, pushing the mayor into me and squashing us against the train, so that for a moment the welcoming speech was forgotten in quest of personal safety."[7] And so, under the brunt of constant acclaim, the journey continued. "From Kansas City to Chicago people were again standing at railroad junctions and in fields, waving as the train swept by. I wanted to enjoy it all without reservation, but I kept thinking the world had gone crazy."

By telegram the New York City police chief asked Chaplin to detrain one stop early, as a mob was already assembling to greet him. Later at his hotel, in a moment of reflection, Chaplin was to make an observation about the star role that has been much echoed subsequently: "It seemed that everyone knew me, but I knew no one."

Douglas Fairbanks, Sr., was also attracting legions of fans during these years. Fatherless like Pickford and Chaplin, he was the only native-born of the three. After growing up in Denver he journeyed to New York at the age of sixteen to find employment in the theater, and through his energetic acting style rose to the highest rank. In 1915 the lure of a large salary drew him to the new movie colony in Los Angeles, where he quickly began making profitable films. Most other leading stage actors faltered at this transition, but Fairbanks' athletic manner and prodigious feats lent themselves to the new medium. Movie after movie, the audience cherished him in his roles as the cheerful, undaunted hero.

When he and Mary Pickford married in 1920, she reported about the first leg of their honeymoon, to New York, "So dense were the crowds that we didn't dare to set foot out of our suite at the Ritz-Carlton Hotel." In the silent film era their fame was not bound by one language or nation: when the honeymoon continued to Europe, "Our first stop was the Ritz in London. Outside our window we saw them, thousands and thousands of them, waiting day and night in the streets below, for a glimpse of us." Homage of this extent, in which hordes of people turn their daily lives on end simply to catch a peek of a performer, was without precedent.

Late in the previous year the three stars had consolidated their success through the formation of their own company, United Artists. Control in the film industry had shifted from the early producers and distributors to the stars, for it was obvious that stars were the deciding factors in how the public allocated its entertainment dollars. And control, either directly through the ownership of production or indirectly through impudent behavior, was to remain in the hands of stars through much of the 1920s. Gloria Swanson said about this halcyon time for stardom, "In those days the public wanted us to live like kings and queens. So we did—and why not? We were in love with life. We were making more money than we ever dreamed existed and there was no reason to believe it would ever stop."

The compelling force behind it all was the fact that Americans could not get enough of their movie stars. The demand for full-length vehicles was insatiable. A producer at the beginning of the film era, Adolph Zukor, said that as early as 1912, "No matter the supply of material, we could not produce fast enough to satisfy the market." In 1918 Hollywood released 841 feature films, and the total rose with each passing year. Historian Garth Jowett has stated, "By 1923 it was estimated that there were approximately 15,000 motion picture theaters in the United States, with a seating capacity in excess of seven and one-half million."[8] At the close of the 1920s, the average number of tickets sold per week per household crested at three, a peak never approached again. In their zeal to watch stars perform, the 120 million Americans of 1929 bought 90 million seats a week.

By this point celebrity performers had begun to appear in other realms and media. In homes across the nation, radio made boxing and baseball vivid to multitudes of listeners and created national heroes of athletes such as Jack Dempsey and Babe Ruth. Like their colleagues in the movies, these sports figures were the objects of the rapt attention of millions of citizens.

But truly understanding the origins of the star role involves digging deeper. The rudiments of stardom were formed in the years after the Civil War, when the role first became conspicuous.

In the 1870s an increasing number of theatrical companies were streaming out from New York City, crisscrossing the nation, putting on performances in cities and towns of all sizes. There was nothing new about touring companies; what was novel was the swelling volume of productions. The trade paper *The New York Dramatic Mirror* listed forty-nine traveling companies in 1879, and twenty years later acknowledged almost ten times that number. Wherever all these companies went, they found large, expectant audiences for their melodramas. Some troupes simply repeated the same play over and over; *Uncle Tom's Cabin*, arguably the most popular drama of the times, was presented to ceaselessly appreciative crowds by companies known as "Tommers." Other troupes were formed specifically to take a single new Broadway show on tour, then were disbanded when the tour was complete.

A side effect of the growth in touring companies was the

demise of resident stock companies. These ensembles, stationed in one theater in one city, had been the mainstay of theatrical production for centuries. They would give a play and then another on through a season, regroup and come back the next year with old favorites and new productions. In 1870 there were fifty resident theater companies in the United States, but by 1900 they had nearly disappeared.

What did the flourishing touring companies have that the resident companies did not? In a word, stars. These traveling troupes, known in the entertainment business as "combination" companies, were a hybrid of two earlier types. The few theatrical stars earlier in the century—often imported from England—had journeyed lightly, without fellow actors or props. When they reached a new engagement, they would hire on for a few evenings' work whatever local talent was available. Also touring at the same time were larger companies without famous players—in a sense, resident companies on wheels. After the Civil War these two types merged into companies featuring proven stars, numerous supporting players, props and costumes, and appropriate staff. A visiting actress observed in 1870 that "with all their ardent love for theatrical amusements, I have no hesitation in saying that the Americans care much more for the actors than for the merits of the play itself. This predilection is constantly accompanied by a regard less to a perfect ensemble than to the excellence of the 'star' of the evening."[9] Because these troupes were well practiced at setting off their stars to full advantage, the combination companies flourished.

Benjamin McArthur, a historian of the acting profession, recounts that the players of this period "overshadowed the play. Edwin Booth, Joseph Jefferson, Minnie Maddern Fiske, Maude Adams, David Warfield, E. H. Sothern, the Barrymores: the great players ruled the stage, dwarfing the roles they played. The public needed stars and lots of them."[10] When Booth came to town to play one of his Shakespearean roles, or Joseph Jefferson recreated his *Rip Van Winkle*, or William Gillette appeared as Sherlock Holmes, the citizens turned out in droves. The star would be regally entertained in private homes until, a few days later, it was time to move on.

The combination companies created a national—as opposed to local—audience for a small number of talented players. The actor's fame, established long before he or she arrived in town, would be easily rekindled with advance publicity. These few celebrated players enticed an extraordinary number of patrons into the theaters of the day. Because they clearly were the drawing cards, the stars of the combination companies were able to command high salaries, as much as half the receipts. Yet there is no evidence that such remuneration posed any threat to the financial condition of the circuit. Just the opposite: the grander stars became, the larger an audience they seemed to attract, and the greater profits grew.

The increasing public appetite for stars created an opportunity for impresarios who could, in the course of a matinee or evening performance, offer up a number of leading performers, each in a setting appropriate to the individual's talents. Variety shows had been around for some time but had never previously risen above low-grade entertainment. In the late 1880s a new form of stage show, vaudeville, began to appear in eastern cities. For the following two decades vaudeville was the dominant form of urban diversion, aimed at the broad middle strata of city folk, and at women and children as well as men. Although the performances became saucier as the years went by, nothing overtly licentious was ever permitted. If people wanted something more risqué, they could go to a burlesque house down the avenue. Vaudeville stayed firmly within the bounds of conventional taste and so held its middle-class audience. As such, it was the first mass entertainment medium.

A typical vaudeville bill contained eight or nine acts: perhaps two comedy skits, an animal act, a magician, acrobats, a pair of dancers, a singer, juggler, and a one-act play. In smaller theaters the program would be repeated twice a day, and in cities it often ran continuously. There were two main booking circuits in the United States and numerous lesser ones; they dispatched vaudevillians to theaters from shore to shore.

Since a number of vaudeville stars went on subsequently to star in other media, many of their names remain familiar: W. C. Fields (juggler), James Cagney (dancer), Cary Grant (acrobat). Vaudeville was an especially fertile training ground for comedians: Fred Allen, Jack Benny, Edgar Bergen, Milton Berle, George Burns and Gracie Allen, Eddie Cantor, Charlie Chaplin,

Bob Hope, Buster Keaton, the Marx brothers, Red Skelton, Mae West. In addition to home-grown talent, vaudeville raided the combination companies for performers in its playlets. Ethel Barrymore did a stint, as did Alfred Lunt, Sarah Bernhardt, and many others. Given the variety of performance types possible within the vaudeville format, it is not surprising that Albert McLean would write in *American Vaudeville as Ritual*, "The channels to stardom were many, and sometimes mysterious."[11] But once a star was established with the vaudeville audience, then the rest of the bill would be constructed suitably.

The audience for vaudeville stars was huge—a 1911 Russell Sage Foundation survey found that in New York City alone 700,000 tickets were sold weekly. Although ticket prices were cheap—as low as five cents—the total gate was immense. A number of producers became extremely wealthy; it has been estimated that there were no millionaire showmen in 1890, and more than a dozen by 1910. The stars became richer still: Harry Houdini, the seductive Eva Tanguay, and comedian Harry Lauder were conspicuous millionaires by 1910.

Over the opening decades of the twentieth century the combination companies, vaudeville, and the upstart film industry coexisted, albeit uneasily. The ascendancy of the cinema was slow-paced chiefly because of the initial absence of stars. Until 1909 American film production consisted largely of one-reelers without identified players. The first crop of producers and directors, aware of how the competition for stars was driving up the salaries of theater performers, saw it was economically advantageous to leave their players unnamed. They wanted to limit actors' popularity and thus their bargaining power. For the same reason D. W. Griffith refused at first to let Mary Pickford know how much mail she was receiving. In an unproven industry moviemakers wanted to control their costs and limit their risks.

It is also true that the performers themselves frequently preferred to be anonymous. Within the acting profession films were perceived as a lesser art. Playing in them was often considered something to tide a person over until a theater engagement came along. Like others, Pickford left moviemaking as soon as she was able to return to the New York stage (only to change her mind again, once she saw how the new wind was blowing). Performers did not press to have their names connected with films, because they thought it would damage their stage careers.

At the outset movies more closely resembled vaudeville acts than the dramas a combination company might stage. Nickelodeon films were about ten minutes long, roughly the same length as a vaudeville "turn." One-reelers, in fact, often ran on a vaudeville bill. When the vaudevillians' union went out on an ill-advised strike, theater owners simply ran more movies and watched the ticket sales mount. The audience for vaudeville became the audience for film.

Once identified stars were added to the movie formula, the format of films changed in the direction of longer melodramas resembling those produced by the combination companies. After 1910 the proportion of feature-length films climbed steeply. The greater length showcased the performances of the stars and deepened the moviegoers' experience.

First the combination companies and then vaudeville began to succumb to the competition from movies. Total capitulation did not occur until the film industry had absorbed all the lessons it could from the theater business about how to entertain early twentieth-century audiences. Because movies lacked the rapport with live spectators, it was onstage where different types of performers, brands of comedy and melodrama, and themes were tried out. By 1920 the transition was over and the cinema had emerged as the uncontested champion, the new medium of the stars whom the audience worshiped.

What had happened is clear enough: in the period between 1870 and 1920, first slowly and then with quickening ardor, Americans had become fascinated with entertainers. This fascination grew so intense that a group of performers obtained a historically unique degree of conspicuousness. Why did it happen? What was going on in the United States that can account for the phenomenal birth of the star role?

The social changes that followed the Civil War can be encapsulated in a word: cities. According to the Bureau of the Census, the U.S. population was 20 percent urban and 80 percent rural in 1860; by 1880 it was 28 percent urban, and by 1900 40 percent urban.[12] The pace of urbanization continued steadily in the twentieth century, and in the second decade the United States crossed the line separating a chiefly rural society from a chiefly urban one. This decade can be seen as the hinge of U.S. history; it is no coincidence that the star role materialized then.

There were two wellsprings of the large numbers congregating in towns and cities. Many were Americans who had been raised on small farms or in villages only to turn their backs on that way of life. Other millions were migrants from Europe and elsewhere. In 1862 less than 100,000 immigrants were counted, but over 400,000 arrived in 1872, and 800,000 in 1882. Immigration peaked in 1914 when 1,218,000 new citizens entered, the majority taking up residence in urban settings. Whether their previous experiences had been rural or not, once they reached this country they tended to stay in metropolitan areas.

What these droves of new arrivals sought and found in the exploding cities and towns was employment. The fertility of the newly opened Great Plains, together with the increasing mechanization of farming, meant that less labor was required to feed the nation efficiently. Correspondingly, after the Civil War the manufacturing sector of the economy began to grow by leaps and bounds. Individuals found that their best employment opportunities lay in the new urban factories, foundries, plants, and mills. Situated at these transportation hubs, other business enterprises grew in size and complexity, creating more jobs. This was the period when the large business organization became increasingly prevalent, eventually dominating the economic landscape. Over several decades of pell-mell change, America was transformed from a nation of self-sufficient small farmers to a nation of urbanized wage earners.

Although these changes were uneven and at times bitterly conflictful, it is clear from the present vantage point that in the long haul the people caught up in the transformation materially benefited and had steadily more wealth at their disposal, at least up to the onslaught of the Great Depression. Census Bureau data reveal that in constant (1914) dollars the average annual income for a nonfarm employee was $375 in 1870, $395 in 1880, $519 in 1890, and $573 in 1900.[13] This climb continued, reaching $607 in 1910, $672 in 1920, and $834 in 1930. As wages rose, the average hours of weekly work in manufacturing industries dropped slowly but steadily: in 1890, the first year for which government data on this topic were reported, the average was sixty hours; this figure fell to fifty-one in 1920 and forty-two in 1930.

Increasingly, then, city dwellers were people with coins in their pockets and time on their hands. The majority of the population enjoyed a modicum of leisure. James A. Garfield, in his 1880 presidential campaign, declaimed, "We may divide the whole struggle of the human race into two chapters: first the fight to get leisure; and then the second fight of civilization— what shall we do with our leisure when we get it?"

Some of the development of leisure activities occurred in the public domain, such as city parks and libraries. But much of it beckoned entrepreneurs. Entertainment and amusements of every sort and for every price sprang up. Much free time and loose change were absorbed by the budding saloon industry. Besides the combination companies, vaudeville shows, and eventually moving pictures, there were also circuses and Wild West extravaganzas, "museums" (collections of oddities) and minstrel shows, amusement parks, and horse races. In contrast to the austerity of the preceding two centuries of American history, the variety of diversions was astounding.

Baseball as a spectator sport also came into its own after the Civil War. Originally a village pastime, baseball was brought to urban centers by the new arrivals. As cities prospered and began to rival each other, they started to contest on the baseball diamond. At first the teams were composed of amateurs, but when the Cincinnati Red Stockings were humiliated by the touring Washington Nationals in 1867, local partisans resolved it would not happen again. The Red Stockings were reconstituted the following year as the first team with salaried players. In the 1869 season they competed without defeat, winning fifty-six games and tying one. Other municipalities began to follow suit, and soon interurban leagues were forming. In cities nationwide an increasing number of enthusiasts began to troop out to the ballpark in fair weather to cheer their local team.

If this growing urban population was gaining more per capita wealth, more free time, and more engaging diversions, then what might it have been losing? This, it turns out, is the key question.

In moving from farms and small villages to towns and cities, individuals were undertaking a radical shift from one kind of social existence to another. The lower the human density had been in rural areas, the stronger the social emphasis had been upon conventionality, fellow feeling, and cohesion. But in cities, the higher the density became, the greater was the extent of impersonality and normlessness. The social sanctions prevailing in rural areas or back in home countries may have imposed uncomfortable strictures upon the individual, but they had also brought personal definition. Religious and community pressures had lent sure guidelines to beliefs and behavior. But once individuals had joined the urban throng, they were stripped of these supporting prescriptions and left to their own devices. For the new urbanites the abiding question became one of self-definition.

City folk were alone in ways more profound than country folk had ever experienced. Urban individuals had to determine their own economic locus; no longer did one follow in the footsteps of a parent, or search through just a handful of potential occupations. Employment options proliferated. One's private life was also increasingly of one's own making, rather than being handed to a person. If marriages had previously been arranged or at least guided, now everyone was on his or her own. Gone were the rigid behavioral precepts of rural Protestant creeds. Gone was any single, uncontested set of standards. As people flowed into metropolises from all walks of life and all corners of the globe, the chances of any one ethos prevailing could only decline.

Previous to this period, a premium upon the individual had received much philosophical endorsement in Western civilization, especially in the United States and particularly at the time of the American Revolution. In those feisty days, the Founding Fathers advocated a faith in the stalwart independent figure who bowed to no external authority. Visiting the country early in the nineteenth century, the French nobleman Alexis de Tocqueville observed that "'individualism' is a word recently coined to express a new idea." That new idea took on a hard edge in Ralph Waldo Emerson's 1841 essay "Self-Reliance": "Society everywhere is in conspiracy against the manhood of every one of its members," he wrote, and "Who so would be a man, must

be a nonconformist." When the poet Walt Whitman later published his famous volume *Leaves of Grass*, the first line was "I
celebrate myself."

It was one thing for social philosophers and poets to uphold
the ideal of the autonomous individual, but it was quite another
for that ideal to become an actuality in the lives of numerous
disconnected city dwellers in the last third of the nineteenth
and first third of the twentieth centuries. The reality was not
half so pleasant as the concept. A new peril had emerged: to be
lost in the crowd, to forfeit emotional grounding. One outcome
of the transformation from the close-knit human fabric of the
countryside to the loose-knit one of the city was a general manifestation of anxiety and mental distress. This development had
been foreseen by James Bruce, a British lord and historian who
visited the United States in 1876. He noted that "the urban type
of mind and life" was coming to predominate, and predicted
that "it will tend to increase that nervous strain, that sense of
tension, which Americans are already doomed to show as compared with the more sluggish races of Europe."[14]

As individuals left behind the highly prescriptive Protestant
ideology of rural America, historian Jackson Lears relates, they
left behind a sturdy framework of purpose, sliding into anomie
and psychic discomfort. He traces the rise of what was variously
called the "American nervousness," "nervous prostration," and
"neurasthenia," and observes, "By the early twentieth century,
the problem seemed general; references to 'our neurasthenia epidemic' proliferated in the established press."[15]

Among the many antidotes for the widespread malaise of
anxiety and depression was a growing number of self-help manuals and behavioral guides. Until the turn of the century, the
majority of these exhorted individuals to strengthen their "character"—to bolster their resoluteness and inner strength. Devoid
of meaningful support, individuals had to tighten the screws on
their resolve. At a certain point, however, this kind of self-help
book began to lose favor, and a second brand with a different
emphasis started to catch on. According to Warren Susman's
scholarly scrutiny of these manuals, instead of emphasizing
"character" the replacements explained how to develop "personality."[16] The individual, in the face of a strident and traceless

urban environment, had temporized. Rather than forcing his or her will upon this new world, and perhaps battering oneself senseless in the process, a person was now to take a more accommodating path, one that emphasized personal charm. Honey was to be used instead of vinegar as the social lubricant; the goal was to attract. In order to endure and find purpose, the individual needed to develop his personality and get others to like him.

Personality was never an issue until the sense of identity was called into question. Previous to the urban explosion, Americans had little difficulty in knowing who they were; the very dilemma would have seemed absurd to most of them. Within the confines of cultural heritage, family tradition, community, church, political persuasion, and profession, they were sharply defined. But shorn of these supports and isolated in the new urban milieu, their identities had to derive from inside, not outside. To establish the self called for establishing one's personality.

The stream of humans leaving old modes of existence and pouring into a new one needed models of personality—models of worldly, successful, attractive people free of "neurasthenia." Where were such models who could help in defining the individual against the backdrop of urban anonymity?

They were—it was increasingly if unreflectingly felt—on stage, on screen, and on the playing fields. Stars seemed to exude the perfected, confident behavior that unanchored city dwellers coveted. As performers acted and reacted in emotionally charged dramas, as they became decisive or adorable, their performances seemed to reveal purified feelings within, and to issue from harmonious personalities. How to be a whole and resolved person, what the peerless male or ideal female was like: this is what spectators thought they were viewing. Performers offered various models of the well-integrated self, at a time of excruciating need, and when other well-wrought exemplars were not forthcoming. In a most revealing word choice, celebrated actors came to be called "personalities."

Chaplin once tried to describe why his early comedies had so decisively surpassed the Keystone reels in popularity. He explained that the Keystone films always built to an extended chase scene, and that "personally I hated a chase. It dissipates one's personality; little as I knew about the movies, I knew that nothing transcended personality."

Chaplin, Pickford, and Fairbanks were the particular personalities most generally appreciated, for good reason. Despite their differences, there was much they had in common. All three were slight of stature and brimming with a compacted, radiant energy. Their slightness emphasized their youthfulness—an important empathetic feature for an audience of newcomers to a new culture. The stars' small bodies, moving with practiced grace, suggested uncorrupted souls. All three demonstrated tenacity and pluck in their roles; they were never undone for long. They would overcome the forces of evil, authority, and tedium, and would venture forward as intact, happy individuals. They were resolute but never stiff; a liberal dose of comedy made their roles delectable—more so in the case of Chaplin, but humor was never absent for Fairbanks or for Pickford, who once commented, "I always tried to get laughter into my pictures." As well as beating the opposition, these idols pursued love and were sure to end up in exalting unions. For a moment, unsure urban viewers could experience exaltation, too. Here, in these three protostars, they found their inspiration for coping with a strange new world.

The star role thus arrived at the time when ancient institutions—ones that had helped lend each individual a sense of personal identity—were slackening. While the changing nature of social organization after the Civil War accounts in a general way for the unprecedented interest in performing artists, the actual delivery of stars to the American public has to be seen as a technological achievement, or a series of such achievements. Without these technologies the star role would never have taken shape. Technologies fulfilled the culture's mandate for stars.

What this sequence of technical advances accomplished was the circulation of performers' images to an ever-widening audience. By allowing a large number of people to focus on a small number of performers, these technologies fashioned the crucible of extensive public attention from which issued the star role.

The technological side to the story of the star role actually began before images could be easily circulated. Immediately after the Civil War it was the performers themselves who were circulated; the technologies responsible were the newly developed railroad and telegraph systems. Absent these transportation and communication lines, organized baseball with its star players would never have come into existence. To set up a season's schedule, make travel arrangements, keep in touch with touring teams, and relay messages back to the home stand, the telegraph was indispensable. (The telephone was largely restricted to local calls until the turn of the century.) The telegraph was also an important implement of the growing clan of sportswriters, who were spinning out column after column of baseball stories for a fascinated readership. "Box scores, betting odds, and all kinds of messages were relayed from one city to another; and by 1870 daily reports were published in many metropolitan newspapers," states historian John Betts. "Sport had emerged into such a popular topic of conversation that newspapers rapidly expanded their coverage in the 1880s and 1890s, relying in great part on messages sent over the lines from distant points."[17]

What the readers of the sports pages principally wanted to learn about were the achievements of the starring players. Conveyed to a national audience by the railroad and the telegraph, certain players began to stand out from the rest. One of those was Cap Anson, who played for eight years before becoming manager of the Chicago White Sox in 1880, and then continued both to play and manage for another nineteen. Writing about Anson's long career, baseball historian Harold Seymour states, "During that time, his name became a household word—better known, it was said, than that of any statesman or soldier of his time. The fans in Chicago flocked to cheer him. On the road they came out in equally large numbers to jeer."[18]

Just as the railroad and telegraph helped to create a following for baseball players, they also built a national audience for certain actors and actresses. Without these technologies the combination companies could not have toured so readily, and vaudeville acts could not have been booked and been transported so efficiently. Events would have proceeded at the horse-and-buggy pace of earlier times; schedules would not have been half so tight; and the extent of the players' exposure would never have been sufficient to create celebrities. With the railroad and telegraph systems in place, performers could be rotated rapidly through the populace, and some of them would catch and hold the regard of a large audience. Telegraphed accounts of new performers, which appeared in journals and newspapers, produced initial familiarity, and publicity wired ahead brought out ticket-buying customers.

Although the railroad and telegraph initiated the closer relationship of player and public, they were quickly proven less than adequate. The audience's need for stars was deeper than the ability of these technologies to satisfy. The stars could not be in all places at all times, but suddenly their images could. As the technologies of photography and photographic reproduction advanced, they were swiftly put to the purpose of disseminating stars' pictures, particularly of their faces. Photographs of baseball players and other sports figures were circulated widely in the 1880s and 1890s. Pictures of stage performers, especially actresses like Maude Adams and Ethel Barrymore, came into vogue at the same time. The public wanted to get closer to the players they had seen in the theater or on the playing field; they wanted to hold their likenesses in their hands.

Then something cataclysmic happened: the pace of the technologized distribution of star images turned furious with the advent of motion pictures. It was this technology, above all others, that ushered in the age of the star. When Thomas Edison combined several existing and arriving inventions to construct the system of movie camera, film stock, and projector, it was an epochal advance. Photography's advantage for the wide and rapid distribution of the star's image was combined with the theater's advantage at presenting the star in performance.

The ability to provide people across the nation with virtually simultaneous exposure to a star was an important feature of the movies. No longer did years have to pass before a performer and a sizable audience got to know each other. Because many prints would be made and distributed, the star could be seen by millions of people within months or even weeks. When Americans left farm and village life, they had sacrificed a commonality of experience; now here was something new to be shared by all: the celebrity performer whose image was flushed through the culture upon a movie's release.

Beyond distribution, the other star-creating feature of film technology was that audiences could now see not a static image of a performer, as in a photograph, but the performer in motion. The star's behavior could now be observed. Behavior defines a social entity and reveals the person within, and it was the person within that Americans were most curious about and most receptive to.

Above all, the technology of the cinema permitted audiences to concentrate on the faces of the performers. The close-up shot, conveying visages and excluding all else, eradicated the distance between viewer and actor, and so represented a great improvement over traditional proscenium theater. It was even an improvement over real life: moviegoers could stare at those famous faces unabashedly and study every feature, every tic of feeling.

The close-up shot, so simple in its execution and so profound in its consequences, was the greatest gift of the new entertainment form. There is no exaggerating the importance of this cinematic technique in providing the audience with what it desired. Although probably apocryphal, the tale goes that when early directors like D. W. Griffith were first experimenting with the close-up, some theater-trained producers scoffed, arguing that patrons expected to see the entire performer top to bottom, not just the head. In any case, it quickly became clear that a camera shot tightly framed around the face had majestic properties and captured attention as nothing else. It was not long before leading performers were fighting for close-ups and demanding the camera operators, lighting specialists, and makeup experts who were gifted at them. These masters could create close-ups of bewitching brilliance and appeal.

Of all portions of the human body, the face is the primary one to go unclothed, unshielded. It is via the face that privacy is broached and humans enter into contact with each other. Behavioral science research has demonstrated that in face-to-face communication, words count for less than 10 percent of what is exchanged. The real messages are carried in the tone of voice (38 percent) and in facial expressions (55 percent).[19] The face discloses the fundamentals of affect; the close-up enthrones this primal language and prohibits irrelevant clues.

The face in a close-up may be emoting or it may be responding. But whether it is acting or reacting, it is still the avenue to the soul, the inner personality of the star. Everything else about the movies of the early twentieth century—the plots, the dialogue, the direction, the cinematography, the supporting characters—existed to highlight these luminous personalities. While closeness to others was diminishing in urbanized life, here was first-rate intimacy. If identity was in question, here were personalities to try on.

The proximity of star and spectator was further narrowed by the advent of sound reproduction, coming to movies late in the 1920s. Now the audience knew leading performers through their voices as well as their images. Studios responded to the new familiarity by providing publicity of a less fantastic nature; stars were now represented as being similar to other mortals. They were shown as domesticated, with spouses and children. Kitchens cropped up in publicity stills.

The arrival of sound precipitated pronounced changes in the movie industry and in the way stars were delivered to Americans. Sound movies cost over twice as much to produce as silent films, so the industry was required to recapitalize. Financial resources did come to Hollywood's aid, but with them arrived a new breed of movie executives who realized that the likelihood of a proper return on investment could be improved only by controlling what everyone recognized was the central element of movie production: the stars. Stars could no longer be permitted to ride roughshod, their inflated egos wrecking production schedules. The need to exert control was hastened by the onset of the Great Depression. As the economic straits worsened, the volume of ticket sales entered its first major reversal. When unemployment climbed to one-third of the labor force, many Americans had to forgo their weekly visits with their star friends. At home a competing new medium was waiting to take up some of the slack. Radio might not have had pictures, but it offered everything else: it delivered comedy and sports stars for free, at a click of the knob. All these factors increased the pressure for the close corporate rule of the movie business.

The upshot was the "star system," by which a degree of orderliness and predictability was brought to the rambunctious film industry. Since stars were what the movies were selling, stars would have to be carefully cultivated and regulated. Only in this way could the eight major studios meet their annual combined production quota of three to four hundred films. The development of stars was systematized to the extent possible: each studio would present a crop of new aspirants to the public, largely in B movies; the less successful would be weeded out, and the more successful would be put to work on a regular basis. Seven-year contracts became standard throughout the industry. By regularizing the process of star selection and use, studios diligently worked to stabilize themselves in turbulent times.

From the celebrity actor's point of view, the star system brought both advantages and disadvantages. The pressures for regularity steered most stars into stereotyped molds. There was little leeway for experimentation in roles. Some, like Bette Davis, chafed against this restrictiveness, but most accepted it without comment, if not willingly. The standardizing of their image brought them steady work, and indeed longer careers than stars had previously enjoyed. Once a studio had gone to the expense of developing a star, it had every inclination to employ the person as long as possible. The average star career in the silent movie period has been estimated at three to five years; under the star system it could be six to eight times longer.

As the 1930s wore on and movie attendance continued to drop, cost-cutting measures became prevalent in Hollywood. Popular but expensive performers were released by studios like Paramount and Universal in an attempt to reduce burdensome financial commitments. As Leo Rosten explains the results of this maneuver, "The 'sensible' businessmen did cut their movie costs by letting high-priced stars go—but they cut their profits (or increased their lack of profits) even more. And the stars which Paramount and Universal dropped—or who were lured away by Warner Brothers or MGM—kept bringing the big money into the coffers of the studios for which they worked."[20] Again it was demonstrated that, above all, stars were what the public wanted. Even in times of extreme exigency, when studios cut stars they hurt themselves.

It was not until the Depression and World War II were over that the 1929 high of 90 million tickets sold weekly was again reached. But even though attendance had slumped, Americans had not been losing their commitment to stars. Other indicators suggest that fan devotion remained high over the 1930s. People who could not afford ticket prices were buying postage stamps and mailing in their pledges of adoration. It has been estimated that at the beginning of the 1930s more than 30 million letters were sent to stars each year. The studios were in danger of being swamped by this outpouring. Moviegoers organized themselves into fan clubs to more powerfully display their affection. In 1934 there were 535 recognized clubs, with a combined membership of 750,000—a horde of devotees. According to Alexander Walker's tally, Joan Crawford and Jean Harlow each had about fifty clubs, and Clark Gable had over seventy.[21] The burden on the studios to handle this star worship became onerous, and new clubs had to be discouraged.

Matters continued in this vein until mid-century, when a new technology arrived that did yet better at distributing star images. This was accomplished by delivering the imagery directly into homes.

While the star role had its incubation period in the nineteenth century and its explosive birth during the heyday of the movies, it has been since 1950 that its period of maturation has set in. Mid-century marks the closeout of cinema supremacy and the start of the television era. Over the 1950s the proportion of American households with television sets shot up past 80 percent. The technology diffused with a rapidity unseen before, and among its many consequences was a substantial impact upon the nature of stardom. First, it radically altered the conditions under which celebrity entertainers were viewed. Before 1950 people set off to a movie palace or theater to observe stars. Removed from their mundane routines, spectators were receptive to the outsized and fantastic. The stars were larger than life on the screen and in the imagination. They were expected to be grand, Olympian, and in these halls of dark enchantment they often were.

After 1950 the stars came right into American living rooms. They were made to fit into household activities, somewhere between doing the laundry and getting a dish of ice cream. The room was never as darkened as a theater, the ambience never as mysterious or transporting. Viewers no longer tilted their heads up to the screen; what in the movie theater was looked up to was now subjected to a more or less level gaze.

Under these changed viewing conditions, stars changed as well. As Edgar Morin put it, "The star has actually become familiar, and familial."[22] The new stars had to be people who were acceptable in the home. An air of unapproachable mystery, for example, might have worked well in the older medium, but not in the newer. The gradual publicity buildup of the Hollywood star system no longer operated. In the television era the star had to be someone the audience liked immediately, or the series would be soon gone from the airwaves. These instant stars, once elevated, were then exposed week after week until, not too many seasons later, viewers grew weary of them. While the tenure of movie stars could last for decades, the tenure of television stars, who were first familiar and then overfamiliar, was measured in a few short seasons. Where is Robert Culp now? In several senses television celebrities were slighter creations than their cinematic predecessors.

As television swept into American life the film industry eroded. The average weekly audience for movies had regained its all-time peak size in 1948 at 90 million and then began a precipitous decline to 15 million in 1970—one-sixth the former magnitude—before plateauing at the current figure of about 20 million. The studios initially fought back, forbidding their performers to work in the newer medium. Shortly thereafter they lost control of the acting corps entirely, as they could no longer afford to pay their contract players. "The care and maintenance of artists not earning their keep, and having to be paid contract fees from dwindling box-office receipts, gave them their independence more speedily than any previous acts of defiance or supplication," reports Alexander Walker.[23] The studios stumbled, lost their economic foundation, proved inept at consolidating, and descended into a time of troubles.

The B movies that made up the bottom half of double feature bills were no longer produced, since television had become the champion of B-grade entertainment. The decline of the B movies spelled the end of the star system: they had been the training ground for new talent, the opportunity for aspirants and the audience to see if they could strike up a relationship.

Now the development of new performers no longer happened in a systematic way. Stars obviously were still around and new ones were still appearing, but the apparatus of star development was gone. Once the role was firmly established, it seemed, a delineated restaffing operation was no longer mandatory.

The movies were not the only star arena to be trampled by the arrival of television. Live baseball too suffered mightily at the hands of the new medium, and again it was the system for the preparation of new stars that was buffeted the most. With televisions in their homes people stopped attending the local minor league games, and the farm system began to crumble. Baseball still developed starring players in sharply curtailed minor leagues, but the extensive apprenticeship programs of past years died out.

Not only was the player development structure damaged, but baseball itself was threatened by the imperatives of the new medium. Baseball, many observers felt, was particularly suited to radio. The linearity of the game, with one thing happening at one time, lent itself to verbal description. The announcer's words, necessarily tardier than the action, filled many empty moments in the slow-paced sport. In televised sportscasts, however, the game's sluggish rhythm became a great liability. It was also difficult for the cameras to be positioned in a way to capture both the field broadly and the battery. The visual medium underscored the fact that much of the time nothing dramatically visual was happening.

Another sport lent itself better to television. The rise of professional football has often been credited to the incursion of telecasting. A sidelines camera could capture the action; the notion of opposition as the two teams lined up play after play was visually explicit; the aggression was graphic; the action was better paced and easier to anticipate on each play. The gridiron was where a new squad of stars emerged over the 1960s and 1970s, as football bypassed baseball to become Americans' favorite spectator sport.

More recently basketball has also come to the fore courtesy of television. Millions of viewers in their cozy living rooms can enjoy a tempo that rarely slackens, as the cameras frame the half-court play or track a fast break. Americans have grown to admire the power and grace of basketball players, and to hallow a few truly exceptional ones, the stars. David Stern, commissioner of the National Basketball Association, commented in 1989 that "I think the players today have been helped tremendously by the enormous growth of the media. Today's players are more widely known than ever before. Players are coming into the NBA today much more fully developed as media personalities. By the time Larry Bird and Magic Johnson came into our league, they had played in a very well publicized Final Four, and in their case, a Final Two." These standouts receive the extraordinary salaries of celebrity performers because of the huge television audience that the networks can deliver to advertisers for large revenues.

Off-network television is currently bringing other sorts of stars home to Americans, and broadening the reputation of these performers. The sensational rise of the rock star in post–1950 America occurred through live concerts and recordings, but now broadcasts and rock videos are creating an even wider audience. In addition, cable television's need for relatively inexpensive programming has encouraged the resurgence of a traditional sort of entertainer—the stand-up comedian.

The number of celebrated performers per year has most likely remained about the same in the movie and television eras. The count, however, is being partitioned differently as media evolve. In the 1930s most stars were still found in the movies; there was a much smaller contingent of radio stars and recording stars. Today film stars are fewer in number and are equaled by television stars; famous athletes are more common; rock stars and other music stars are conspicuous.

One thing has not changed: from the performer's perspective, films still represent the preferred medium. In the absence of a systematic way of developing movie stars these days, many players who have achieved fame in another entertainment field feel drawn to try their luck in Hollywood. Jim Brown, Joe Namath, and O. J. Simpson left the football field and auditioned for film roles—in their cases, with lackluster results. More successful were two singers: Liza Minnelli and Barbra Streisand. Country and western music contributed Dolly Parton. Ever since the days of Elvis Presley, rock stars have been potential movie performers: David Bowie, Madonna, Sting. Rock stars have the advantage of achieving fame with a young audience that overlaps significantly with the audience for films. Television remains the biggest feeder into the truncated movie industry: James Garner, Robert Wagner, Goldie Hawn, Chevy Chase. As Arnold Schwarzenegger has demonstrated, even bodybuilding can be a path to Hollywood stardom—or bodyguarding, as with Mr. T. It hardly makes any difference what one does, just as long as national attention is focused on a person. The person will then try to cash in that fame for a film career. The paths may be more varied than before 1950, but the goal is still the same.

Why is it that, well into the television era, films still form the high point of a star's career? This situation in many ways parallels the movie era, when the theater was felt to be the most prestigious form of entertainment. (To some extent it still is: Cher does a stint on Broadway and, although playing to a minuscule audience, must feel virtuous.) In the history of media, the contemporary dominant medium always seems common and a little vulgar (perhaps because it is) while the earlier medium with its smaller audience seems more exclusive (because it is). Prestige being a subjective value and easily directed by nostalgia, it tends to attach itself to older media. Thus movies are prestigious today, and those who have already found fame and fortune in one field and are looking for the next rung on the career ladder gravitate to films. The day will come when network television will be passé and so more esteemed.

Films also remain the favored vehicle of celebrity performers because there is still a great deal of money to be made in them. Stars remain such a key ingredient of film success that, in lieu of high salaries, they have since the 1950s been able to get a percentage of the returns, just as their theatrical forebears did in the nineteenth-century touring companies. Jack Nicholson reportedly made $10 million for his role in *One Flew Over the Cuckoo's Nest* and $20 million from *Batman*. The chance of striking it rich has spurred other stars to produce their own films, which some have done with remarkable success, Clint Eastwood and Sylvester Stallone among them.

But while movies remain the stars' favorite medium, television is the usual way that Americans see their celebrated performers. It is not until a new film is broadcast that the bulk of the population makes renewed contact with a leading player.

Through televised movies, series, games, and rock videos, people stay in touch with stars. As the years go by, the nation is spending more and more time at this pursuit. Average television viewing time has been steadily rising since 1950, with only an occasional breathing spell. The Nielsen ratings disclose that in the typical household the set is now on over seven hours daily. The individual watches less than this—how much less is in debate, but apparently the mean is about three and one-half hours a day.

Beyond convenience, there is another reason for the popularity of television: it is the close-up medium par excellence. The television screen carries more head shots than the movie screen ever did. One explanation is the tendency of the medium, whose resolution and focus are not yet the equal of film, to use reduced visual stimuli in the interest of better communication. Another is that reliance on close-ups diminishes the need for expensive location shots or elaborate sets. Once the star has been hired, it is cheaper to focus on his or her face as much as possible. But the fundamental reason is the audience's eagerness for those faces. The close-up comes into the living room at a pleasing proportion, not much larger than real-life heads and at proper proximity.

So the American public, thanks to television, has been spending even more time with stars, and seeing more of each in close-ups. The limits of our star needs have not yet been approached, nor are they soon to be. The star role promises to continue as a mainstay in our way of life.

☆
CREATING STARS

3.
ASPIRANTS

t is the maturing young who are most in need of personality models, as they slowly develop the attributes that will permit them to function as adults in the modern world. Adolescents find in celebrity entertainers highlighted exemplars of temperaments and appearances. Elaine Barrie, who would subsequently marry movie idol John Barrymore, wrote about being young and star-crazy in the 1930s: "My being stage-struck and movie-mad was hardly peculiar in my generation. With the possession of high heels and Tangee lip rouge, the teenagers on the West Side of Manhattan, along with the rest of the country, suddenly turned into a multitude of girls resembling Joan Crawford, Diana of the goddesses. Her arched eyebrows, surprised eyes, and torn pocket mouth were easily imitated, and the vestal virgins of the Loew's Eighty-third Street copied her shamelessly."[1] Children in the 1980s who sprouted spiky hairdos in imitation of punk rock stars were continuing in this emulative line.

Even those who went on to become stars in their own right received inspiration when young from the celebrities who captivated them. The lass Clara Bow idolized Mary Pickford. The lad Elvis Presley styled his hair and his mannerisms after the

Tony Curtis he had viewed on a Memphis movie screen; a year or two later, he was thinking of himself as a Rudolph Valentino successor. Mary Wilson (who would find fame with the Supremes) adored Doris Day and spent hours in her Detroit home imitating her heroine. Martina Navratilova as a child in Prague saw *The African Queen:* "From then on I wanted to be like Katharine Hepburn." O. J. Simpson worshiped James Brown. The boyhood idol of rock star Keith Richards was Roy Rogers, while for David Bowie it was James Dean.

Since the young fix on stars, the occupation of the celebrity entertainer is, of all occupations, the most visible to them. Boys and girls repeatedly attend to the recorded or live performances of their favorite stars, follow up by reading about them, and converse about them with their peers. Adolescents are likely to know more about the work of stars than about the work of their own parents. Other more conventional occupations are shadowy in young minds, or absent altogether.

Being a star is more than the most visible career to the young; it is also the most admired. All the torment and distress of teenage years are seen as wonderfully remedied in the personage of the star. While adolescents may feel their own identities to be shaky and ill-formed, the identities of stars are perceived as solidly established. Their traits and attributes are harmoniously set, and their appearances are defined, not experimental. On top of this, stars radiate confidence; there appears to be no indecision or insecurity in their behavior. They are always ready to step up and bat, step up and sing, step up and emote. They never seem to be plagued by uneasiness or awkwardness.

Beyond having sure identities and behaviors, stars display another quality of great importance to the young: they are popular. Certainly within the precincts of stardom they are going to share in boundless companionship and romance. Aren't they always seen playing golf or tennis with each other, or exiting functions arm-in-arm? No specter of rejection there. Further, they are popular in the eyes of the nation; everyone knows and cherishes them. Being well-known was what attracted the young Katharine Hepburn *(photograph 4)* to the profession: "When I started out I didn't have any desire to be an actress or to learn how to act. I just wanted to be famous."

The thought of being widely celebrated for simply being

oneself is bound to be grandly enticing to the young. The idealized star seems to suffer none of the painful missteps that can
accompany maturation. Free of the possibility of error, a star is
encouraged to stay just as he or she is. There is no compulsion
to adjust, and no need to endure the pain of chastisement by
adult authority. The unbridled ego is allowed to flare.

So in the eyes of the young, freedom and license can be the
gift of stardom. The star is lifted out of the setting where there
is an uneven match between oneself and the world, where one's
personality is sometimes short of the mark and sometimes too
flagrant. The star dwells on a plane devoid of exhortation and
reproof, and is allowed to sail along, doing exactly as he or she
wishes, applauded all the while. Compared to adolescence, stardom inevitably looks idyllic.

Is it any wonder that so many young people, setting out on
their life's course, are drawn to this singular occupation? Stars
appear to frolic in a world more familiar to the adolescent—the
world of play, of games and stories. This domain can look quite
inviting for someone being released from childhood. Otherwise
what looms ahead is the forbidding, indistinct world of work.

Moreover, from a youthful point of view it can seem almost
easier to become a star than to become anything else. Other jobs
call for apprenticeships, for working one's way up a ladder on
which youth and inexperience are liabilities. But for stardom
youth is an asset. The baseball player, the rock star, the television actor will play their youth like a trump card. It is a glorious
attribute in this line of work.

Where is the young woman or man, distant from the halls
of fame, going to turn to learn more about this career? To the
media, of course. Those are the channels that open directly
upon the performance of stars. But nowhere in the mass media
is there anything like an evenhanded description of the struggle
to achieve stardom. Just the reverse—wide-eyed youngsters
witness only the winners in the scramble to the pinnacle. The
American audience does not want to see failures in its entertainment; it far prefers success stories. So the arduous road to stardom is viewed not at all, and the destination is seen only in a
glorifying light. Under these conditions reality is unlikely to in-
trude on a young person's dream of celebrity, and the initial inclination will be endlessly reinforced. Soon an aspiring youth

may join the countless others, like schooling fish, who aim at entering the most prominent occupation of the twentieth century.

Once committed to this career, the usual aspirant now draws on his or her stock of ambition and determination. At a school assembly where each student was asked in turn what his future profession might be, sixteen-year-old David Bowie solemnly announced, "I want to be a pop idol." A woman who had dated Frank Sinatra in 1940, at the outset of his career, reflected, "I always knew that he was going to be a great success someday because he was absolutely determined to be a star. He had amazing confidence in himself." Drive and persistence are needed in abundance to propel the hopeful along. As a result of her series of interviews with aspiring comedians, Betsy Borns concluded, "In order to rise above competition, a comic must have blind faith in himself—or at least enough confidence to ignore others' work and continue his own." [2] Of the scant number of scholarly studies that have covered performers at this initial stage of their careers, one was conducted by researcher Alfred Golden in 1940. [3] Comparing drama students to other collegians, he administered personality tests and questionnaires to both groups. What he found conspicuous among the novice actors was "a determination that is excessive when compared to the prospective members of other professions."

For aspiring athletes, determination cannot be limited to game days. Religiously they must go out onto the football field or basketball court or baseball diamond and practice the motions that may bring them notice. If not there, then to the weight room. When scouts come by to check their abilities, the hopefuls must be prepared to run dashes against a stopwatch, undertake agility tests, do some paper-and-pencil work. As well as possessing talent, they will have to be dogged and steadfast to survive the long years of apprenticeship—season after season as college football or basketball players, years in the minor leagues of baseball. The life in the minor leagues that awaits all baseball aspirants was described by one disgruntled wife: "Down there you're pretty much on the end of a string. You're like a yo-yo; if they want you there, you go there, if they want you here, you go here. I feel like, I don't know, just like a piece of meat that's sold over a counter sometimes."[4] Only the most determined are likely to endure.

Just as rookie athletes must strive and strive if they are going to have a chance of succeeding, so must young actors. Most who want to become celebrity entertainers get themselves to one of the centers of dramatic production in the United States—either New York City or Los Angeles—and study acting. In 1968 and 1969 sociologist Anne Peters lived at the Hollywood Studio Club while doing research on aspiring actresses. Eighty were in residence at that time, and Peters interviewed twenty-eight intensively.[5] Seventy percent of these young women said their objective was to become stars; would the percentage have been higher still if modesty had not intruded? Surely few would have refused if the opportunity had beckoned. All twenty-eight had taken acting lessons, and a number were maintaining a full schedule of classes.

One of the questions Peters asked these ambitious actresses was whether or not they believed that sexual liaisons with influential men in the industry would boost their careers. One theory about the path to stardom is that some aspirants may rise through their sexual antics: by making love with the right people, and doing it with skill and vigor, they would be able to ratchet their way upwards. Peters reported, "Answering with extreme candidness, they generally agreed that getting involved with a man who has some power over their careers is dangerous." Also answering with extreme candidness was Marilyn Monroe, who held the opposite view, believing that sexual encounters with the right executives could open doors. It cannot do everything, she told an interviewer late in her career, "But it helps. A lot of actresses got their first chance that way."

Another answer to the question of whether sex can help a newcomer's career, probably a more balanced response, came from anthropologist Hortense Powdermaker, who in the 1940s studied the moviemaking industry. She observed that sleeping around was a common if not universal practice in Hollywood. It did not hurt anyone's carer, but perhaps because it was so unremarkable it did not help much either.[6]

Some aspirants do find themselves in uncomfortable sexual situations. One who eventually made it to stardom, Goldie Hawn, recounted, "I had to decide whether to 'use' the casting couch a couple of times very early in my career. I was in New York a couple of months, and not very savvy, let me tell you. I had really thought I was in those offices for honest reasons." One who did not make it to stardom, Pamela Des Barres, had this Los Angeles experience: she read for a part, and the director said that her voice was too high but that he would give her instruction. He asked her to lie down on a couch and close her eyes. "I heard a strange buzzing sound and peeked through my eyelashes to see him fiddling with a small vibrating machine and heading in my direction. [He said,] 'The lower I go, the lower you go.' When the vibrator was humming into my crotch area, I jumped up and announced I was late for an appointment." Her deduction: "It was tough trying to break into show business."[7]

Having arrived in New York or Los Angeles, begun to take acting lessons, and resorted or not to sexual wiles, the typical aspirant conscientiously searches for work. A resume of performance credits, real or conjured, has to be assembled and printed. These will be bundled with a portfolio of professionally produced photographs that show one off to best advantage.

If aspirants do not like what they see in the photographs, they may elect to alter a few things. Changing hair styles and getting colored contact lens is a beginning, but many go on to have cosmetic surgery, minor or major. Marilyn Monroe, whose face at the start was far from classically beautiful, had her teeth pulled in, her nose bobbed, her jawline changed. At the same early point in his career, Liberace had his teeth filed down and capped. Joan Crawford had her back molars removed to give her hollow cheeks and high cheekbones. Tyrone Power and Rita Hayworth *(photograph 5)* raised their hairlines through electrolysis. According to writer Penny Stallings, nose jobs were had early in their careers by Dean Martin, Peter O'Toole, George Hamilton, Joel Grey, Sissy Spacek, Raquel Welch, Marlo Thomas, and the Gabor sisters.[8] Sculpting one's body in the hopes of finding fame is not limited to Hollywood performers; athletes who munch on steroids and pump barbells are also trying to make themselves look more impressive in the eyes of potential coaches and team owners.

If an athlete ultimately does make it onto a professional

team, he or she will be invited to join the players' union. Most do join, since the union noticeably acts on their behalf, establishing working conditions and salary guidelines. In Hollywood, however, the aspirant's experience with a union is going to be quite different; there the union serves as a major obstacle in the fledgling actor's search for work. To land any part in a movie, the novice must belong to the Screen Actors Guild (SAG). But SAG will not accept new members unless they already have a role. It sounds like an insuperable conundrum—you cannot get a part without being a member, and you cannot be a member without having a part—but it is remarkable how rapidly aspirants figure out how to circumvent this stumbling block. By finding work, however inconsequential, in commercials or in the theater, and joining the appropriate union there, the novice is then able to transfer membership to SAG.

After joining SAG, the next step normally is to acquire an agent. If casting directors were to consider people not represented by agents, there would be an unmanageable number of applicants for any role. Newcomers are unlikely to win representation from industry giants like the William Morris Agency or Creative Artists, whose clients are largely proven professionals, so the resumes and photographs are sent to the smaller agencies. Jack Rose, head of a firm with fifteen agents, said in 1985 that each month about 2,000 separate portfolios arrived in the mail. Of these a chance for an interview was extended to about twenty people, or roughly 1 percent. "And of that number we may sign two as clients." The remaining 1,998 aspirants who were not picked must try to catch on with another agency.

Many beginners find that the effort to secure an agent is the hardest test of their resolve. The actresses whom Anne Peters interviewed at the Hollywood Studio Club said there was just one conceivable stratagem for dodging normal channels. This was to show up at dawn, long before an agency's protective cordon of receptionists and secretaries had arrived, and try to buttonhole the agents who were coming in early to work.

After joining the union and landing an agent, aspirants must press on, now more than ever. Agents are good for giving direction and handling contracts, but they are not much help at actually getting the work. As M. K. and Rosemary Lewis wrote,

"An actor's true vocations are selling and job getting: his avocation is acting."[9] Trying to become known in the industry, to curry favor with producers, and to win assignments, young actors will embark on a perpetual round of auditions. They will go to one place and read aloud from a few pages of a script just handed to them, then go to another place and read from another new and unstudied script. They will spend far more time at these readings than they ever will before the cameras. A veteran agent observed to writer Mark Litwak, "Cold readings are very difficult to do and I'm not sure they have anything to do with acting, but they determine if you get the job."[10]

Meantime, between roles, aspirants have to sustain themselves. Usually this entails menial jobs of one sort or another. Marilyn Monroe labored in a wartime defense plant where she packed parachutes until she tired of that, then sprayed dope on target planes. The Hollywood Studio Club actresses took part-time jobs, although as Peters learned, "A few have inheritances."

The Los Angeles work force is filled with young and talented people waiting for their chance at the big time. One observer who has taken note of this is writer Tom Shales. A media critic for the *Washington Post*, Shales is often given to a jaundiced view of the entertainment industry. Yet on a visit to Los Angeles, what struck him was the abounding energy and optimism. "In Los Angeles, the idea of upward mobility still thrives. People believe they are headed for a better lot in life. They think they will land an acting job and quit waiting on tables at Hamburger Hamlet," he wrote. "We're all going to make it, the city says; you're going to make it, too."

And sometimes wonderful things do happen. In decades past, it might have been a superlative screen test. Director George Cukor recalled about Katharine Hepburn's first test, "I suppose I thought right away, 'She's too odd. It won't work.' But at one moment in a very emotional scene she picked up a glass. The camera focused on her back. There was an *enormous* feeling, a *weight* about the manner in which she picked up the glass. I thought she was very talented in that action. David Selznick agreed. We hired her." Producer Hal Wallis took a look at a screen test by a young singer: "I felt the same thrill I experienced when I first saw Errol Flynn on the screen. Elvis [*photo-*

graph 6], in a very different, modern way, had exactly the same power, virility, and sexual drive. The camera caressed him."

So many people ache to become celebrity entertainers that the situation presents a grand opportunity for fraud. When supply exceeds demand to the extent that it does for this occupation, it is as if a signal has gone out to all those who like taking unfair advantage of others. In the Los Angeles entertainment industry there is a netherworld of exploiters who wring exorbitant agent fees from aspirants, sell them needless lessons and overpriced beauty and career consultations, divert them into the pornography business, and otherwise prey on their goodwill and high hopes.

The exploitation of those who would be stars extends far beyond Los Angeles. It is a nationwide industry of sorts. Every city offers modeling schools and beauty instruction and photography sessions to those who dream of being the dream of everyone else. Promoters who say they are based in Los Angeles will tour the United States and at every stop conduct high-priced seminars on how to break into the entertainment business. Or they will issue a call for all local performers, for a small fee, to have their photos included in a volume that is claimed to be distributed to Hollywood agents. Sometimes the exploitation is not so innocuous. In 1984 a man murdered a string of attractive women whom he had picked up in shopping malls by simply stating that he was a photographer and saw in them the possibility for becoming famous.

This large corps of eager and sometimes vulnerable aspirants—somehow it has to be whittled down. While not more than a half dozen new stars appear in any given year, hundreds of thousands of young Americans set that career goal for themselves, whether as athletes, actors, musicians, or comedians. By one means or another the very many who are called are narrowed down to the very few who are chosen. The winnowing process could hardly be more ruthless.

A sense of this culling can be gleaned from the statistics out of the world of sport. Annually just under 2 million high school students suit up for athletic contests, while slightly over 2,000 individuals play in the leading three professional sports. Thus the odds are roughly 1 in 1,000 that a young athlete can beat the competition and become a pro football, baseball, or basketball player.

Of all high school varsity football players, only 6 or 7 percent will demonstrate the strength and agility that permits them to play on a college team. From this sharply reduced pool, a mere 3 percent will be drafted to play in the National Football League. And for every ten of those carefully scouted draftees, just three will actually make it onto the roster of a professional football team. To put this another way, every year 1 million young men play high school football; every year only 100 new players become professionals. Of those who finally get to perform in the National Football League, only a handful will have the extraordinary ability and the staying power in the minds of fans to be considered genuine stars.

The same pitiless winnowing goes on in the other two major sports. In baseball the minor leagues take in about 1,200 new players each year, while the major leagues will incorporate about 100. Not all the 100 will stay on, and of those the great baseball stars that the average fan can readily recall may be less than two dozen. A basketball player has even slimmer chances than a minor leaguer of playing professionally. Just one-sixth of 1 percent of eligible college players find a place on a National Basketball Association team. The indisputable stars in basketball are correspondingly few in number.

This paring process is no less acute in the case of actors. From the time of the Civil War onward, the acting profession has been notoriously oversubscribed. In the twenty years from 1880 to 1900, the number of professional actors rose from under 5,000 to nearly 15,000—a number increasingly greater than the proliferating touring companies could accommodate. According to theater historian Benjamin McArthur, the rate of unemployment among actors at that time was the highest of any American profession.[11] This has remained a conspicuous feature of the occupation throughout the twentieth century. Some sort of frenzied extreme of oversupply may have been reached during the heyday of child stars, suggests Diana Cary: "When the child star craze was at its height—roughly between 1925 and 1945—an estimated one hundred children poured into the Hollywood marketplace every fifteen minutes. The ratio of those who in an entire year earned so much as a single week's expenses from movie work was reckoned at less than one in fifteen thousand."[12]

The new arrivals in Los Angeles nowadays face a grueling rivalry against legions of other aspirants, and bleak prospects. Cathy Smith, the woman who was later accused of administering a lethal injection of narcotics to John Belushi, came to the West Coast from Toronto: "Los Angeles, despite the constant parties and relentless sunshine, quickly began to reveal itself as a tough city to crack. On the one hand I felt that I had finally landed in the absolute center of all the things I cared about. But this also meant that the competition was fantastically intense."[13] Vanna White, who eventually fared better, had initially the same observation: "I was used to rejection, but I didn't realize you had to be much more tough-skinned to make it in Hollywood."

The Hollywood newcomers who manage to get into SAG may feel that they have overcome a major barrier and are in line for work before the cameras. But the number of SAG members is far larger than the industry can employ, and so the paring down continues. The actor quickly learns that SAG is hardly an exclusive fraternity; there are 60,000 other members who are just as determined as he or she is to land one of the roughly 100 roles that are to be cast each week throughout the industry.

While SAG has grown from 8,000 members in 1953 to 60,000 now, the number of roles available has remained about the same. The result has been to sharply increase the competition among members, and to decrease each actor's opportunities for work. It has been estimated that at any given moment 90 percent of the membership is unemployed. Sociologist Muriel Cantor, who studied the guild in the 1970s, believes that over half the membership goes year after year without ever landing a part.[14]

The statistics on the earnings of SAG members are equally grim. Over 75 percent of the membership earns less than $3,000 annually at their chosen line of work. About half of Hollywood's professional performers earn under $1,000 each year. At the other end of the scale, about 1 percent (or 600 individuals) earn over $100,000 at television or movie acting. Those who receive the millions of dollars in salaries associated with stars are obviously few in number.

Why has the membership of SAG been permitted to grow so large in relation to the opportunities for work? Cantor believes there are several reasons. SAG itself benefits from the excessive number of members because it collects dues from each individual. Hollywood producers benefit both because they have a large pool of actors to pick from, and because the size of the pool has a generally dampening effect upon wages. But most of all, she explains, the oversized guild is the result of the ambitions of many, many people to achieve stardom. She writes that "all actors have the possibility in their work lives of becoming 'stars' and gaining great financial success and acclaim. The star system preserves the large labor force of underemployed and unemployed actors in proportion to the work available."[15]

Since so many people are striving to become stars, and since so few will make it, the typical aspirant's work life is a ceaseless round of rejection and exclusion. The forces of the winnowing process are constantly bearing down. He or she may attempt to maintain motivation with visions of ultimate stardom, but the daily experience of trudging from audition to audition is one of devastating repudiation. George C. Scott commented about acting, "I think it is a psychologically damaging profession, just too much rejection to cope with every day of your life."

At a certain point along the way, most aspirants will recognize that they are no longer in the running. They have been dissuaded. The statistics on this lack of success are so incontrovertible that a principle can be formulated: the person setting out to be a star is guaranteed, with near absolute certainty, to fail. The vice president of a film company observed, "It's the myth of success that brings the prettiest boys and girls from high schools across the country to Hollywood to become stars. They end up pumping gas and making sundaes and contributing to the most incredible gene pool in the country."

Yet one or two do make it. In the study of 100 stars undertaken for this book, information was collected on the backgrounds of the minuscule number who have risen to become indisputable celebrities. What generalities emerged about their family life and preparation from stardom? When aspirants, did they as a group share features that distinguished them from other aspirants?

It helps if the star-to-be is a male, although this observation sounds callous. But the indisputable truth is that the majority of stars are men. Virtually all starring athletes are male, as are most comedians and the greater proportion of screen performers. In the study for this book, 67 percent were males.

Some states have produced more stars than others. In the study sample, New York contributed thirteen, followed by California with seven and, at six each, Illinois and Pennsylvania. To succeed at this American occupation, it is not at all necessary to be native-born. Seventeen percent of the 100 stars were born outside the United States, including Ingrid Bergman (Sweden), Errol Flynn (Tasmania), Bob Hope (England), Hedy Lamarr (Austria), and Vivien Leigh (India). Of the eighty-three stars born in this country, seventeen were born on a farm or small town, while sixty-six were from urban settings.

Stars are likely to be the firstborn in their families. Of the 100 in my study, fifty-five were firstborn—a rate almost double what would be expected if star births reflected the normal distribution through the birth order. From the outset, stars are in the lead.

A stereotype exists about the families of stars: the father is either absent or inconsequential, while the mother pushes the performer on to glory. This stereotype does receive some confirmation in the study results. Twenty-one of these stars had no male parent around during most of their childhood. For Louis Armstrong, Jackie Gleason, Steve McQueen, and Jackie Robinson, the father was either missing or dead. Mary Pickford noted in her autobiography, "I know positively that I would not have been in the theater if father had lived." The father was present only intermittently for another twenty-four: John Barrymore, Jack Dempsey, Ernie Kovacs, Ted Williams. And the father was present but was an essentially weak or minor figure in their childhoods for yet another twenty-three: Gene Autry, Bing Crosby, Cary Grant, Gregory Peck, Mae West. It does seem to be the case, therefore, that stars are likely to originate in families where there is no strong father figure. This is not always true—Karen Carpenter, Duke Ellington, and Grace Kelly, along with twenty-nine others, had forceful fathers—but it is to a marked extent.

As for the other half of the stereotype, that of the dominating, ambitious mother, the evidence is not quite so decisive. A mother's vigorous support for the performer was clear in only thirty-seven careers. Stars like Harry Houdini, Jean Harlow, Judy Garland, and Lucille Ball were propelled forward by their moms. Thirty-four mothers were deemed to be positive toward their children but neutral about their work in the limelight: John Belushi's, Montgomery Clift's, Henry Fonda's. Some mothers, being mentally deranged, were largely oblivious to their son's or daughter's career, such as Cary Grant's or Marilyn Monroe's. And a few mothers, like Clara Bow's or Grace Kelly's, were simply opposed.

Most human beings experience a childhood with both stable and unstable aspects to it. But a large percentage of stars do seem to have suffered a decidedly unstable life during their formative years. Fifty-one of the study sample's 100 stars endured childhoods marred by parental deaths, extreme poverty, or constant relocation. Richard Burton, James Dean, Judy Garland, John Lennon, Babe Ruth, and John Wayne survived unsettled lives as youngsters. Stable early lives were enjoyed by Ty Cobb, Henry Fonda, Duke Ellington, and Billie Jean King, but this group has to be balanced against the experiences of people like Joan Crawford, Rock Hudson, Douglas Fairbanks, Sr., and Marilyn Monroe. A disproportionate number of stars have apparently emerged from rocky childhoods.

In order to gain a broad sense of the socioeconomic background of stars, each performer in the study of 100 stars was assigned to one of three categories, depending on family circumstances: poor, middle class, or privileged. The resulting allocation was skewed toward the lower end of the social spectrum. In a nation where the majority of the population can be classified as middle class, half the stars emerged from families that could only be labeled poor. These included Wilt Chamberlain, Glenn Miller, Clara Bow, and Elvis Presley. Forty-one stars, such as Jimi Hendrix, Ty Cobb, and Ingrid Bergman, enjoyed a middle-class ambience in early life. And nine—including Humphrey Bogart, Grace Kelly, and Gary Cooper—came from privileged families.

Is there any advantage in growing up in families connected to the entertainment business? For only eight leading players in the study was there a strong performance background. John Barrymore and Tyrone Power were the products of theater pedigrees. The parents of Buster Keaton, Rita Hayworth, Mickey Rooney, and Peter Sellers had been vaudeville teams. Lenny Bruce's mother was an aspiring comedienne, and Charlie Chaplin's mother had performed onstage when she was in good health. But in general terms, being the descendant of performers is of limited benefit to aspiring stars.

At what age did the desire for stardom first well up in these young people? The average in the study was thirteen; the range of ages, however, was wide. The desire occurs to some stars when they are very young, and for others not until they are into their twenties. Some who felt they had always known they wanted to be stars were Jayne Mansfield *(photograph 7)*, Peter Sellers, and Judy Garland. The late bloomers included Henry Fonda, Bing Crosby, Jimmy Durante, and Janis Joplin *(photograph 8)*; those who do not decide to be stars until after they are twenty are apparently at no disadvantage.

The study made it possible to induce the typical educational level of celebrity performers. Given how early their career goals are set, this level is perhaps higher than might be expected: on average the highest year of education completed by stars is the eleventh grade. Included in this figure are a number who were college graduates or the equivalent: James Stewart, Roger Staubach, Jim Morrison *(photograph 9)*, David Niven. Also included are stars from much earlier in the twentieth century when educational norms were lower (Charlie Chaplin and Mary Pickford received few if any years of schooling), so it is probably safe to say that the average star nowadays is a high school graduate.

What about their training? Do people become stars because they take lessons and special classes that help them perfect their performances? Marilyn Monroe thought so, but in fact the majority of the stars in this study—seventy-two out of 100— were not found to have taken any extensive instruction. Most stars, such as Steve McQueen, John Belushi, Babe Ruth, and Nat "King" Cole, simply picked up their skills as they went along. Chaplin wrote, "I have never studied acting, but as a boy

I was fortunate in living in an era of great actors, and I acquired an extension of their knowledge and experience." Often the star-to-be closely studied the performances of others who were already successful, then went on to best them. Cary Grant recounted about his behavior when he was a fifteen-year-old trouper, "At each theater I carefully watched the celebrated headline artists from the wings, and grew to respect the diligence it took to acquire such expert timing and unaffected confidence, the amount of effort that resulted in such effortlessness." It was a commitment to practice, or an ability to take direction, that was decisive—and not lessons. The parents who bring their children to performance class after performance class may be disappointed.

On the other hand, twenty-eight stars did undertake substantial study and believed it made a difference—these included Duke Ellington, Richard Burton, and James Dean. Betty Grable took every kind of performance class being offered in her native St. Louis, and benefited from them.

Summarizing these statistics, and rendering some injustice to the rich variety of personalities, the basic profile of those who have become stars is this: they are likely to be male, firstborn, from a poor, unstable, fatherless family with a strong mother. Although this typical star-to-be knows before the age of fourteen what his occupational goal is, he does not necessarily take performance lessons, and does finish high school. But these are just general tendencies; many who depart from this profile do become stars. And more important, of all those who do match the profile, only a few will catch the public's eye.

These findings agree generally with those from another research project on famous people that was conducted by Mildred George Goertzel and Victor Goertzel, together with their son, Ted George Goertzel. Published in 1978 under the title *Three Hundred Eminent Personalities*, the Goertzel study did not focus exclusively upon stars, but upon notable people in general, from such arenas as the political, literary, and artistic. They selected everyone who had been treated in a biography or autobiography available to them and published between 1962 and 1977. Their reasoning was that, if a publisher sensed there was sufficient interest in a person to warrant bringing out a book, then that person was eminent.

As in this book's study, the 317 individuals included in the Goertzel study were predominately male—74 percent. New York was the most common state of origin in both studies. The percentage of firstborn (including only children) in the Goertzel study was 47 percent—slightly lower than in the study of 100 stars, but still greater than what it would be if the eminent were distributed normally through the birth order. Home life for the two groups was remarkably similar—the missing fathers in the study of 100 stars are echoed in the Goertzel study, where 36 percent of the subjects were raised by their mothers alone. For 40 percent of the Goertzels' eminent, the father was an erratic provider. Just as with stars, the eminent experienced unsettled households: "Many of the homes are quite troubled by quarreling parents, divorce, financial ups and downs, and parental inability to cope with the children's delinquencies, school failures, and what seems to be a wrong career choice."[16] Average length of schooling was revealed in both studies to be the same: a high school education.

But there were three major differences in backgrounds between the Goertzels' subjects and those in the study of 100 stars. The eminent were voracious readers as children, the Goertzels note time and again; stars were not. Stars when young were kinetic and sportful, not cerebral. Second, 51 percent of the eminent had rural origins, while only 20 percent of the stars did. Stars are urban creatures for an urban age. Third, and perhaps most telling about the distinction between these two groups of celebrities, social locus was conspicuously dissimilar. Eighty percent of the eminent came from middle-class business and professional households, but stars tend to come from impoverished backgrounds. Stars are forged from base material.

Determination would seem to be the prime characteristic of those performers who advance from the aspirant level to the journeyman stage and on to stardom. Yet many who are strongly resolute simply do not become celebrities. The woman who dated Frank Sinatra in 1940 thought he was singularly determined, but many other aspirants who fell by the wayside were equally so.

Moreover, some performers who become stars possess no driving ambition of their own. Betty Grable and Rita Hayworth

are two examples; others forwarded their careers. And occasionally someone will be yanked into stardom willy-nilly, as if by
accident. Mr. T hardly knew what hit him when fame descended.

Some of those who lack outright determination yet become
stars anyway are said to be "discovered." The theme of discovery
is a durable element in the mythology of stardom. An attractive
proposition, it appeals to every dreamer's desire to be recognized and applauded for the pure, private person concealed
deep within. Like Cinderella, a "discovered" person is presum-
ably singled out and ennobled without any special effort on his
or her own part.

The career most frequently held to exemplify the lore of discovery was Lana Turner's *(photograph 10)*. The persistent story
was that she was tapped for celebrity while sitting at the lun-
cheon counter of Schwab's drugstore in Hollywood, sipping a
chocolate malted. There is a kernel of truth to this tale. When a
15-year-old student at Hollywood High, she skipped classes one
afternoon and went out for a soda. Buying a Coca-Cola, she happened to meet the publisher of the *Hollywood Reporter,* W. R.
Wilderson. He sent her to the agent Zeppo Marx (who had earlier performed as one of the Marx brothers). Though the tale has
her rocketing to fame at this juncture, Zeppo Marx actually
could not find her any work and turned her over to another
agent, who turned her over to yet another. Eventually she signed
on with a studio for the grand sum of $50 a week. In her first
film she played a scene at a soda fountain, and this was probably the origin of her discovery legend. The main beneficiary of
the fable was no doubt Schwab's drugstore, since during its existence it was a mecca for Hollywood hopefuls. There was even
an agreed-upon Lana Turner stool that starlets elbowed each
other to perch on.

While Turner's start was not an authentic example of instant discovery, it did occasionally happen to others. Ava Gardner was one. At age eighteen the strikingly attractive North Car-
olina native went on vacation to visit her sister in New York
City. The sister's husband was a commercial photographer, and
he took several shots of his sister-in-law. These photographs
eventually found their way to the talent department of Metro-
Goldwyn-Mayer, which summoned her to Hollywood for a

screen test. She had never done any acting before and spoke with a heavy regional accent, so the test was a silent one. The verdict of the MGM executive in charge of new talent was, "She can't act, she can't talk, but she's a terrific piece of merchandise." On the spot she was offered a contract.

So although most aspirants to stardom do exhibit determination, this quality turns out to be hardly the sole criterion for elevation. After he had finally found fame as the star of the television series *Hill Street Blues*, Daniel J. Travanti commented, "If success only took good thought and will power, I'd have had no problem. But there are two many forces at work beyond us. I spent seventeen years being frustrated and drinking a lot because it wasn't happening." Of course many others fiercely aspire for seventeen years, and then for another seventeen years, and still are never invited inside the starry portals even for a visit. In deciding who enters stardom and who does not, clearly factors other than determination are at work.

4.★
STAR VILLAGE

O f the crowd of applicants pressing against the gate to stardom, only a few will be granted admission. By what mechanism are these few selected? Who picks?

The ultimate answer, of course, is that the public selects. Bette Davis put it simply: "The public makes stars. No one else." The viewing audience anoints this one and ignores all those others. It is only reasonable that stardom should happen this way, for it is the public that the star serves. In a real sense the star is employed by the spectators, who in turn reward the star handsomely. The audience ought to have the privilege of hiring those who work for it, and in the last analysis it does.

Are stars selected on the basis of their talent as performers? Are they the most artful of the aspirants? Talent clearly does count for something. When exposed to a player without any flair for the work, an audience will quickly notice that something is missing. A number of movie stars, however, have had little conspicuous dramatic skill. As Jean Harlow said at the peak of her career, "If audiences like you, you don't have to be an actress." Clark Gable remarked, "I'm no actor and I never have been." John Wayne's performances struck many critics as stilted and repetitious, but he boasted, "I play John Wayne in every part regardless of the character, and I've been doing okay, haven't I?" Vanna White receives little praise for her acting abilities, but has become a star nonetheless.

Clint Eastwood once observed that "a lot of damn good actors are passed by. The public recognizes their work as good, but they don't run out to see them with their three dollars for a ticket. The public goes to see the stars. I didn't invent those rules, that's just the way it is." So being a polished performer is one thing, and being a star is quite another.

Talent will certainly mean more among sports stars than among the Hollywood variety. One does not rise to the stature of a Wilt Chamberlain or a Roger Maris without being able to play exceptionally. But an unusual study conducted during the 1951 baseball season raised questions about the relationship between talent and success in professional sports. A battery of tests was administered to both a group of minor league players and a group of major league players. The differences between the big leaguers and those who wanted to be big leaguers were found to be factors other than talent or skill—factors like dedication and compatibility.[1]

If talent is an advantage but not a requirement for stardom, then perhaps some other attribute is decisive. What about physical attractiveness? Is it the case that males must be handsome and females must be beautiful? Obviously there is much truth to this idea. The proportion of celebrity performers who are good-looking, with striking features and trim silhouettes, is much greater than the proportion of highly attractive people in the population at large. Stars like Joan Crawford and Catherine Deneuve, or Cary Grant and Robert Redford, are certainly attractive by prevailing standards, and so comeliness must figure large in the attributes for stardom.

And yet for all the importance of physical appearance, further reflection leads to complexities and to exceptions. A surprising number of stars are plainly not beautiful or handsome. Take sports stars—this is not a standard usually applied to them. No beauty contests could be won by the likes of Babe Ruth or Martina Navratilova. Similarly, comedians may owe part of their success to looking peculiar rather than attractive—

one thinks of W. C. Fields, Buster Keaton, Groucho Marx, Rodney Dangerfield, and Woody Allen. The public came to view singers like Frank Sinatra and Mick Jagger as mesmerizing, but a dispassionate analysis would reveal them to be physically unattractive. "I've got a head like a walnut," Sinatra once conceded.

Even many Hollywood legends do not measure up to high standards for a captivating appearance. If known only through their photographs, Humphrey Bogart or James Cagney or Dustin Hoffman would not be thought of as handsome. Bette Davis was not conventionally beautiful, yet she could rightly claim that "for a long period I brought more people into theaters than all the sexpots ever." Jane Fonda inherited her father's pronounced jawline and Carol Burnett had the opposite feature (until she had her chin rebuilt), but both have attracted enormous audiences and enjoyed long careers. Two of the greatest female stars of recent decades—Liza Minnelli and Barbra Streisand—represent considerable challenges to the prevailing stereotypes for beauty. Many actresses who found plentiful work in the 1970s and 1980s, such as Goldie Hawn, Shelley Duvall, Sissy Spacek, Sally Field, Debra Winger, and Meryl Streep, did not have the flawless features that might be expected of a movie star.

The public exhibits a preference for certain disproportionate attributes in its movie stars. Compared to the general female population, many leading ladies—including Marlene Dietrich, Joan Crawford, Marilyn Monroe, and Kathleen Turner—have had unusually large heads. Why this should be the case is not known, although it has been pointed out that this feature resembles that of infants, the implication being that Americans prize immature stars. Another possibility is that an outsized visage enhances facial expression, which is what the audience ultimately wants to see.

This preferred ratio of head size to body size might be part of the reason that a number of male stars are short of stature. While the beau ideal of handsomeness may be someone well over six feet tall, Marlon Brando and Robert Redford both measured five feet six inches, and Sylvester Stallone five feet nine inches. Moviegoers have flocked to see Dustin Hoffman (five feet six inches) and Michael J. Fox (five feet two inches). Dudley Moore (five feet two inches) once cracked, "I was offered the part of Attila the Hun but it was too much of a stretch."

Not only are many occupiers of the star role not gorgeous, but many who are gorgeous find it impossible to enter stardom. Fashion models both male and female whom magazine readers think stunning will often discover that the audience responds indifferently when they appear in dramatic roles. Vera "Veruschka" Lehndorff, Jean Shrimpton, Suzy Parker, and Shelley Hack had spectacular careers as mannequins but were greeted with yawns when they tried to make the transition to Hollywood. Therefore, although attractiveness is an important criterion, just as talent is, neither is decisive in the public's selections.

Something else is going on. The audience looks beyond facility at performance, beyond the superficialities of appearance, to what it infers is lurking within. The audience gauges the personality of the performer, and on this basis makes its decision. As Katharine Hepburn noted, "Show me an actress who isn't a personality, and I'll show you a woman who isn't a star."

Personality is an amalgam of inner drives, feelings, traits, and attitudes as these become evident to others. If a spectator is asked to describe the personality of an entertainer, this often proves difficult to do, since these interior attributes are vague and elusive. But for all their mystery they are acutely felt by the fan, who despite an inability to specify the pieces will have a strong sense of the whole. Even if a performer has a great talent, it has to be appraised within the context of the entire personality; sometimes ingenuousness is going to be more appreciated. Similarly, perfection in appearance can lend an attractive gloss to one personality, while flaws can add a becoming quality to others. Marlon Brando's standing with the audience rose after Jack Palance had accidentally struck and broken his nose while the two were performing a scene. Brando's biographer wrote that "his broken nose gave him that brute, Humphrey Bogart sexuality that separates the men from the Tyrone Power pretty boys."[2]

Marilyn Monroe was one of the most popular stars of the century, although few would claim she was a superlative actress. Nor, upon close and disinterested inspection, was she extraordinarily pretty. But she was fervently adopted by an audience who chose to see her as adept and beautiful. What they had really latched onto was a certain kind of archetype: the audience of the time wanted a female who was both sexy and innocent, flagrant and vulnerable, earnest and funny, and they found all these elements in her complex personality.

Yet in spite of how major a star Monroe was, the public was not content to adore her alone, nor to see a whole galaxy of Monroe look-alikes. Americans in the 1950s, as at any point, wanted more than one type of star on view. The same nation that prized Monroe also prized Doris Day and Debbie Reynolds. For every James Dean there was a Fred MacMurray. The public demands—and this is the key provision in an understanding of stardom—an array of contrasting personalities.

Any attempt to isolate even one particular trait—much less one sort of personality—common throughout stardom is doomed to failure. Isn't it necessary for a star to possess at least the psychic energy to project his or her personality? Not at all. A number of stars have been noticeably reticent and sullen: Greta Garbo, James Dean, Bob Dylan. Isn't it a universal requirement that a star have a complex personality? No on this count, too. Some have been renowned for their one-dimensionality: Ty Cobb, Jayne Mansfield, Mr. T. Rather than commonalities among the personalities of stars, it is the rich variety that stands out.

An ironic twist of grand proportions becomes apparent here. Stars are considered to be epitomes of individualism, but they do not take on their full meaning until they are considered in the aggregate. The star, singular, is best understood in the context of stars, plural. Stars are selected not so much to uplift one personality all on its own, but to fill out the full formation of personalities that altogether the public likes to observe.

The composition of this array has an appreciable order and structure to it, and so resembles a community. Let's call it Star Village.

Star Village constitutes a grid into which starring personalities fit: a mythic community composed of the different types of people whom the American public wants to observe.

Social science, hard put to fathom the real world, has little if anything to offer about the makeup of Star Village. But close observation can lead to some tentative conclusions. The first thing to be said is that it is small. If stars are defined as those performers recognized by 80 percent or more of the populace, then in any given year Star Village will have about 100 individuals in residence. Its population remains at this level no matter what the extent of talent or resolve among the aspirants. Nothing is going to make it larger.

Cary Grant's name for Star Village was "A Streetcar Named Aspire": "I see Hollywood as a precarious sort of streetcar. Call it Aspire. There's only room for so many, and every once in a while, if you look back, you'll see that someone has fallen off. When Tyrone Power got on it meant someone was left sprawled out on the street. Ronald Coleman sits up with the motorman. Gary Cooper is smart, he never gets up to give someone his seat."

Star Village is overseen by a managing officer, a sort of prime minister. This manager has little coercive power, but he still can get things done. His job is to cast a watchful eye, to preside at functions and shows, to handle introductions, to snub bad apples, and generally to establish decorum and set tone. He also welcomes new residents and helps them fit in—this is an important task but not a time-consuming one, since the number of inductees each year is never more than ten and usually much less. Before this post was filled by Johnny Carson, it was Ed Sullivan's job.

Star Village also has its reigning couple, who model what it is to be a star for the others. All the trappings of celebrity are associated with them: the glitter, the glamour, the unending public fascination. The initial king and queen, who established the mold, were Douglas Fairbanks, Sr., and Mary Pickford. More recently the leading lady has been Elizabeth Taylor, and the leading man Frank Sinatra, the "Chairman of the Board." They are seen at all the benefits, although (as suits their imperial station) not together.

The residents can be grouped into certain general categories. Preliminary research for the study of 100 stars (see the appendix) broadly indicates the proportions of divisions within Star Village: 51 percent of the celebrities are actors, 18 percent musicians, 15 percent comedians (in all media), 14 percent athletes, and 2 percent miscellaneous (Gypsy Rose Lee, for example). The approximately fifteen starring athletes now in Star Village are drawn from the five or six sports that are widely broadcast. Most are presently active, but a few are retirees who so engaged the imagination of fans that interest in them has not abated: Joe DiMaggio *(photograph 11)*, Arnold Palmer. Most of the athletes are males, but not all; some women tennis players are present.

Slightly more than half the openings are filled by Hollywood performers. These can be sorted into a variety of types. Some of these types will be occupied by just one person—as today's aristocratic female, Meryl Streep has little competition—but other types are in such demand that at any one moment up to a half-dozen nearly identical artists will be in residence. The prime example is the male aggressor; we know him most often by his brandished pistol, although a rifle, knife, staff, or bare fists will serve as well. From the days of "Broncho Billy" Anderson to the present, through the cycle of cowboy and crime dramas, Star Village has seen a string of these tough weapon-toting hombres. During the 1970s and 1980s the two actors who triumphed most notably at this portrayal of vicious manhood were Clint Eastwood and Sylvester Stallone. But they were hardly alone in Star Village. At one time or another they were crowded by Charles Bronson, James Coburn, Chuck Norris, Arnold Schwarzenegger, Mr. T, et al.

Another type that has endured through the history of stardom, to be filled by a succession of performers, is that of the young, available woman ripe for love. From the sultry Theda Bara to the steamy Kathleen Turner, Hollywood has never failed to staff this position amply. This personage is trim, alert, wide-eyed, receptive, with limbs and chest barely half-draped.

A rich variety of other types fills out the ranks. Actresses portray the independent type, the bitch, the girl next door. Actors are cast as the strong type, the lover, the rebel, the sophisticate, the low life. Or the playboy: "The public has always expected me to be a playboy, and a decent chap never lets his public down," explained Errol Flynn *(photograph 12)*. These archetypes have greater validity and staying power than the individuals occupying them. Occupants come and go while the type lives on. Once a performer has found his or her niche and personalized it with a particular image, he tends to be fixed there if he wants to remain a star. An exception is the one type which encourages flagrant changes in image, a jester of sorts; presently this niche is occupied by David Bowie.

Most stars find they enjoy little tolerance in the matter of their public persona. Leo Braudy, in his history of fame, refers to this as "an embalming above ground."[3] Debbie Reynolds said resignedly, "I think no matter how old I get, I'll be the oldest living Tammy." It is only natural for stars, after a while, to become restive and begin to think of playing characters at odds with their types. But as Clint Eastwood despaired, "The idea of purposely setting out to change your image is a futile effort on the part of most actors, who have become stars on the basis of what they do best." Sylvester Stallone concurred: "The image is forever. As much as I'd like to be broadening the field, I have to be realistic. I'm caught in a certain persona. People see me in a certain way. It's a blessing, it's a curse, but it is something very rare. I can't fight it."

When a performer does play a role at variance with his or her image, something may happen that further indicates the importance of type above actor: the public will simply ignore the deviation and continue to think of the star in the same old way. Mary Pickford's audience gladly paid to see her as a slip of a lass again and again, but blithely disregarded her other performances. Clark Gable's *(photograph 13)* enormous following stayed away when he attempted a patrician character, and returned when he came back to his more earthy roles. Claiming "I don't want to be thought of as wholesome," Julie Andrews tried to enlarge her dramatic repertoire, even appearing with bared breasts in one role, but the public remained determined to identify her with the saintly sylphs from *The Sound of Music* and *Mary Poppins*.

Into these fifty-plus Hollywood slots go the variety of personalities that individualize and animate the positions. Some are giving people, others are taking. Some are effusive, others reserved. Some are sexually electric, while others are not. Some control, others cannot be controlled. Some toil, others tarry. The entire arrangement is under a constant process of adjustment so that Star Village does not consist in too much of one trait or too little of another. The dynamics of this process, which maintains the total lineup of personalities that the public appreciates, involves dropping old stars and adding new ones as time passes.

In sum, the requirements of the overall array—the slots and the personalities filling them—are more decisive in the selection of stars than whatever the individual performer might offer. These covert prerequisites for types and traits have more influence on who gets to be a star and who does not at a given time than any intrinsic quality of the aspirant.

If this were all there was to the constitution of Star Village, the game could still be mastered by performers striving to get in. Petitioners could take the measure of the celebrated community, determine what type was underrepresented or about to go underrepresented, and plan accordingly. Anticipating the death of David Niven *(photograph 14)*, an aspirant could have readied himself as the urbane type. But comprehending the array of types and traits is only half the challenge. Star Village confounds most observers' ability to read it because the categories themselves are in constant flux. Old slots disappear: the David Niven type was not refilled; the singing cowboy, which when incarnated by such performers as Gene Autry, Roy Rogers, and Tex Ritter brought them untold popularity, vanished in a puff of smoke.

And new slots come into being. If a new type crashes into the framework of Star Village, it is often an explosive affair, with repercussions throughout the tiny town. When the antihero type—Marlon Brando *(photograph 15)*, James Dean, Montgomery Clift—thundered in during the 1950s, established stars hardly knew what to make of it. The principle behind the creation of new types is that whatever is unresolved deep in the culture will eventually be projected upon the ranks of Star Village. New slots appear, displacing old ones, in response to something profoundly troubling to the spirit of the times. New performers are lifted into these slots because whatever they personify is somehow relevant to these unsettled concerns.

The antihero type apparently was the result of two fundamental developments in postwar American culture. The first was nothing less than the formation of a new stage in the life cycle. In a period of rising prosperity, extended education, and a reconfigured job market, the teenager emerged as a significant new social phenomenon. The term itself was a recent coinage, to label a then-novel condition. Before World War II adolescents had been either employed or assiduously preparing themselves for their lives' work; after the war the pressure was off. The responsibilities that had previously constrained adolescent sensibilities were now removed, and a flood of difficult emotions was let loose. The fluctuating moods and frequent resentments of young men found their personification in the brooding, temperamental antiheroes. Teenagers went to their movies and thought, "They act like I feel."

But teenagers were not the only ones to find their feelings addressed by the antiheroes. Older males paid to see those stars, too. American society had steamed into a period of thoroughgoing domesticity and conformity, and men everywhere were being squeezed into rigid roles as good husbands, fathers, and citizens. The behavioral norms were so stringent that it is not surprising many males would, in their fantasy lives, toy with the opposite deportment. Identifying momentarily with the antihero, they experienced the chance to be self-absorbed and brash. The side of their self that had to be repressed found its catharsis.

Thus the antihero came into being at a time when younger American males needed to identify their confused feelings and older males needed to discharge their resentful ones. The antiheroes were also found attractive by American women; perhaps it was the prevailing maternal spirit that led them to imagine themselves caring for these personalities. If they sensed that Montgomery Clift was a committed homosexual, or that James Dean was at least bisexual, it did not prevent their outpouring of affection.

Elsewhere, another new type was appearing. Teenage women in the 1950s, newly come into their own as a discernible group, lived in a highly charged, ambivalent atmosphere. On one hand a carnal climate of fertility abounded; the baby boom generation was being bred. On the other, young women were remonstrated to hold their libidinous energy in check; if anything were to go wrong it would be considered their lifelong fault. Along came a rock-and-roll star who knew what ailed them. His music circumvented their reserve, his manner egged them on. Millions of girls—their screams of ecstasy one of the more remarkable exhibitions in the history of American entertainment—greeted the arrival of Elvis Presley. Bing Crosby groused that Elvis "never contributed a damn thing to music," so pained was the crooner by the size of his successor's reception. The entrance of Elvis was not simply the induction of a new personality, but of a brand new type with a performer installed. This type—the rock star as a sex symbol for young women—has been filled numerous times since.

A sense of the fluctuating layout of Star Village can be gained from studying the top ten box-office attractions as they have varied over the years. Since 1932 these lists have been compiled annually through a poll of film exhibitors. This is not a highly scientific survey, but as a record of the intuitions of industry insiders it does shed light on the public's shifting preferences. The change that stands out in highest relief is the ever-growing proportion of men. In the 1930s a typical list was 50 percent male stars, but more recently it has averaged 90 percent male. Additional evidence of this remarkable bias comes from a research project conducted by sociology and marketing professor Irving J. Rein. A total of 122 adults were asked to name their three favorite celebrities. Rein reports that "none of the men selected a female celebrity as one of their top three favorites, while in contrast, 59 percent of the females polled selected a male."[4]

The heightened interest of American women in male stars may be partially explained by the demographics of marriage peculiar to the 1970s and 1980s. American males tend to court and marry women who are two or three years younger than themselves. This works out well when the older group of males is the same size as the younger group of females. But as the first half of the baby boom aged and entered into the marrying years, each older group of males was surpassed in size by the younger group of females—a trend paralleling the expanding number of births decades earlier. The result was that the group of marriageable females was always larger than the group of marriageable males. This situation put competitive pressure upon women, who logically want to learn more about the opposite sex in order to increase their chances of successfully finding partners. The upshot was an expanded demand for male stars.

Meanwhile, men too have been giving more attention to male stars. American men have been threatened by the ongoing redefinition of gender roles and the challenges to their conventional power and status. This epochal transformation has produced much uneasiness on their parts, and has prompted them to seek out more male performers. To help males vent the resentment and hostility brought about by these changes, actors who personify aggression are in demand. Said Clint Eastwood shrewdly, "I see my films as first aid to the modern male psyche. Masculinity is becoming obsolete. Most jobs today can be held by women. Many men have become defensive and enjoy being taken to another time, another period, where masculinity was important to survival." Other sorts of male stars are also needed, so that Americans can shop for behaviors. Bill Cosby and Jack Nicholson and Woody Allen and many others have to be kept in view during this transitional era.

While male stars are up and female stars are down, another brand of star has been abandoned altogether, according to a review of the top ten box-office draws over the decades. Americans used to want to see a lot of this type, and now apparently do not care if they see any. Child stars reigned supreme in Star Village for seven straight years, from 1935 to 1941. After that they have never appeared in the top ten again, with the exception of Tatum O'Neal in 1976, who made it to eighth place on the basis of her performance in *Paper Moon*.

For four years running, from 1935 to 1938, the performer all America doted on was Little Miss Shirley Temple *(photograph 16)*. She became the centerpiece of Star Village at a time when the Great Depression seemed endless, when hope for better times was at its lowest point. So forlorn was the population, and so gloomy about their prospects, that the birth rate had plummeted. As an antidote for this infertile spell the public clutched at the cute moppet. Americans ached for something cheerful and buoyant, and Shirley supplied it. The affection of audiences for the little actress was nearly boundless. It has been estimated that at her peak her fan clubs had enrolled 4 million members. Her dimples, her curls—every feature was known and adored by the entire country. A debate raged concerning whether she had fifty-four or fifty-six ringlets. Her mother was contacted on this important point, and she announced solemnly that indeed fifty-six was the correct figure. There was no mystery about the nature of Shirley's attraction; it was even acknowledged by

President Roosevelt, who observed that "it is a splendid thing that for just fifteen cents an American can go to a movie and look at the smiling face of a baby and forget his troubles."

But in 1939 her soaring flight faltered. With attention turning from the Depression and toward the menace of war, other stars were needed. Another child star, Mickey Rooney, served as a transitional figure, and thereafter public regard centered on adults. The perils of the 1930s had been navigated, and the cherub niche was discarded.

While there is great definition to Star Village, then, there is also great flux. No wonder aspirants can feel so frustrated.

Viewed within the context of the twentieth century's eruption of metropolitan living and machine production, the star phenomenon can be seen to have resulted from two historical imperatives. The need of uprooted city dwellers for personality models was compelling enough, but a second force—related yet distinct—was also at work.

Throughout history the dominant and sustaining mode of human existence has been village life. Histories of ancient civilizations may be misleading about how the bulk of the people lived, for only the smallest fraction of those populations ever inhabited urban areas. At the time of the first U.S. census in 1790, as industrialization was about to dawn, just 5 percent of Americans dwelled in cities or in towns with more than 2,500 residents. The other 95 percent lived as people always had. They lived in villages or, if further out in the countryside, they lived with access to villages' churches and markets.

For millennia village life had provided humans with their sense of locus, of community, of participation with others. Within the framework of a village people could find their place and be integrated into the human enterprise. In 1957 Lura Beam tried to describe what life in a small town, so recently the standard sort of existence for Americans, had been like: "There were 227 people in the hamlet, according to the United States Census of 1900, of whom the writer remembers 216 by looks, name, home, family setting, and reputation; they lived in fifty-one households, all of which I had visited. Most of the people of the hamlet lived together so closely that the collective feeling was like that of the tribal clan or the British regiment. The average American never gets a chance now to know a population unit so deeply homogeneous. Schisms and feuds made convolutions within the larger unity, but everyone knew everyone else: what he did, what he had, what he paid, what had happened to him, how he met good or ill."[5]

The vortex of industrialization eradicated this communal sensibility. It sucked people into urban cores and relegated village life to memories. But the cities could do little to replace villagers' traditional sense of belonging. Survival in the crush required wariness and withdrawal. People avoided contact, averted their eyes, kept others at arm's length. The net of community frayed, and individuals began to feel detached and stranded.

What came into the breach as the century advanced was a surrogate community. As the nexus of the traditional village receded into the background, Star Village rose to occupy the foreground. The nation's attention turned to a small population of celebrity performers with intriguing personalities, perhaps more intriguing than those any village ever had. And people could stare at them intensely, as they could not stare at their urban compatriots without jeopardizing the fragile tissue of close-packed city life. In the ways that citizens used to observe their neighbors, they now observed the stars. Instead of sitting on their front porches or looking out their kitchen windows, Americans peered into screens. There entertainers could be seen at work on the sound stage or the athletic field, much as townsfolk used to be noticed at work. Spectators could catch sight of the residents of Star Village supposedly off duty too, when the players appeared in interviews or on talk shows, just as fellow villagers had been spotted after hours.

These ways in which stars constitute a village explain why there are not thousands of stars, or only a handful: Americans need the right number to recreate village life—the most universal of human communities, bred into their cultural bones. And to make this hamlet interesting, the public needs a certain variety, not a sameness, among its members.

It does not make any difference whether in real life stars consort together or not. The nation has it firmly in mind that they do. And the purveyors of star information are happy to oblige, stressing the occasions when stars work together or go out together or romance each other. People want to read about how Elizabeth Taylor marshaled the Star Villagers to fight the AIDS epidemic, and do not want to read Joan Collins's deflating opinion that stars cannot possibly know anything about AIDS and should desist. The populace insists on the idea that stars all pull together. If this stellar fraternization is not the rule, the public is just as happy not to know.

Americans have come to treat celebrity entertainers as they used to treat fellow villagers. They apply the same brand of bantering communication to them; they gossip about stars just as they used to gossip about their neighbors. They seek out information on stars and pass it along. To friends and family members they comment on what is good or bad about a star. They mention the latest achievements, the latest contretemps. They exclaim about the prowess of a starring athlete, lament the drug problems of a leading actress. They transmit rumors, sometimes vicious ones, even ones they recognize are unlikely to be true: "Paul McCartney is dead" or "Burt Reynolds has AIDS." In gossiping about the people of Star Village, Americans are carrying on the age-old brand of personal communication that weaves lives together and ties individuals into the whole.

Americans have called Star Village into being and peopled it in order to restore the sense of belonging that was crushed by the colossus of industrialization. A mobile people, we move around while Star Village provides a powerful illusion of fixity and continuity. It is our thoroughly make-believe, and thoroughly satisfying, settlement; people feel settled when they are in the imaginary company of its residents.

A question lingers: what is the role of publicity in the passage to stardom? Isn't it possible that a performer can be foisted upon the public through adroit publicity?

This concern invokes shades of conspiracy: somehow, fraudulently, the gatekeeping prerogatives of the audience may be abrogated, and someone will be snuck into Star Village via a secret path. Through publicity hype, supposedly, neophytes may be so vividly and craftily promoted that the public will come to embrace them without much reflection.

Such delicious tales of skulduggery are readily spread. Reciter and listener feel they are privy to secret machinations, are in the know. But the power of publicity is a sharply curtailed one, and essentially unsensational. While publicity is certainly relevant to the ascension of those destined for stardom, it cannot actually create stars. As Pia Zadora observed on the basis of experience, "You can't thrust something on the public is what I've learned."

Just as with other aspects of the star phenomenon, publicity buildups have received little attention from scholars. One study undertaken by Thomas Harris and published in 1957 examined the studio campaigns for Grace Kelly and Marilyn Monroe.[6] Publicists, he learned from his research, found it easiest to work with genuine facts from the young actresses' backgrounds as they constructed an image for each. Thus publicity for Grace Kelly emphasized her Philadelphia family to complement the patrician image being created for her, while for Marilyn Monroe it was conversely the stated lack of family that lent itself to an appearance of being loose, sexy, and available. The job of studio publicists, Harris observed, was to take each new film role of the actresses and integrate it into the image that was forming, in order to advance the case for stardom—successfully in these two instances.

Harris's study is informative about the work of publicists as they delineated personality niches for these star candidates, and of the raw material—both personal history and new roles—that was woven into their images. But the study may be deceptive in that it conveys the impression that studio publicity alone was capable of fashioning stars. Of the hundreds of actors and actresses who were boosted by publicity exactly like the treatment Harris describes for Kelly and Monroe, only a handful rose from the ranks of journeymen players into stardom. The trumpeting of publicists could do nothing for the also-rans.

Richard Griffith maintains that the first and last time a star was created by ballyhoo was in the callow period of the silent film era, with Theda Bara.[7] The Fox studio took Theodosia Goodman of Cincinnati and transformed her into an exotic vamp, casting her in forty films in just three years. By the closing months of 1916 an estimated 400,000 Americans were viewing a Bara film every single day. Bara herself, though, saw it the other way around—that her fame was due not to the studio but to the marveling audience. She commented, "Never have I liked being a vampire and never, of course, have I believed there was any such animal, but since the public did and liked to see me as one, I agreed to become one."

What is sometimes represented as the most calculated celebrity creation, and the most flagrant promotion of it, occurred more recently, in the television era. In 1965 the Monkees were formed and marketed to the American audience. They were together for three years, had several popular television seasons, and released a total of nine profitable albums. While their success can be interpreted as a bit of publicity razzle-dazzle, it is also the case that the Monkees never would have survived if the Beatles had not just previously won extraordinary general acclaim. The Monkees were closely modeled on the Liverpudlians and exploited their remarkable popularity. Americans were willing to accept a tamer, cuter version of the Beatles, one which suited the broadcasting medium and its vast audience.

The "pull" element in the formula for stardom—the draw of the audience's needs—is thus much more influential than the "push"—the promotion of the aspirant. This is vividly illustrated by abundant cases of performers who have foundered in spite of strenuous efforts to palm them off. These are sad tales of entertainers being dangled like dainty morsels before the eyes of the public, which deigns not to bite. All the mechanisms of publicity may be lunging and plunging, but nothing happens.

Sometimes the miscalculation occurs with sports figures who are blazoned shamelessly but simply fail to live up to the billing. Fans expected great things from ex–Notre Dame quarterback John Huarte and from running back Marcus Dupree, but they failed to excel. Mark Fidrych had an outstanding pitching season, was the darling of the baseball press, and then entered a precipitous decline, leaving rooters with an unpleasant aftertaste. The history of sports is littered with stars manqué who have been oversold to a public always anxious for winners.

Even more revealing are the tales from Hollywood. Stories of unavailing publicity invariably feature a magnate and his lovely charge, the near-miss star. A prototypical account is that of wealthy publisher William Randolph Hearst, who for years tried to advance the career of his companion, Marion Davies. All who knew her in person agreed that she was a delightful, impish lady, the very best company. She stuttered, however, and when she tried to control it for the camera (as she did not bother to for normal conversation), she became studied and wooden. Despite all the efforts of Hearst and his newspapers to stir up public fervor, her movies lost money and more money.

Sometimes moguls reached all the way to Europe to find their protégées. In 1932 the famous producer Samuel Goldwyn brought Ukrainian actress Anna Sten to Hollywood, apparently in an attempt to unseat Greta Garbo. He is reputed to have spent a million scarce dollars in the effort to promote her and to overcome public resistance to her thick accent. After three money-losing productions, Goldwyn was forced to concede that she had been rejected by the audience. Another similar episode also involved a Hollywood executive and a heavily accented East European actress, but in this case the promotional effort was gargantuan, enduring not for three films but for twenty-six. The participants were Herbert J. Yates, president of Republic Pictures, and his love, Vera Hruba Ralston.

Born in 1880 in Brooklyn, Yates had been a successful marketing executive in the tobacco industry before he entered the film laboratory business in 1915. Again he found success, organizing companies and masterminding mergers. In 1935 he created Republic Pictures Corporation out of four predecessor firms. Ticket sales were falling during the Depression and it was not an auspicious time to start a new studio, but Republic found a place in the industry by making low-budget films that were distributed largely to small-town theaters. Roy Rogers and Dale Evans were two of Yates's biggest stars. When he first met Vera Hruba in 1939, he was fifty-nine years old, in a marriage of many years' duration, and the father of four children.

Hruba's background had been strikingly different. She was born in Prague forty years after Yates. In the 1936 Olympics she took second place in the women's figure skating competition, behind Sonja Henie. Like Henie she came to the United States and soon was skating with the Ice Capades. Since this touring show proved popular, Yates contracted to translate it to film. At this point he spotted, and became enamored of, the young skater. She might have had an ample figure by American standards, and a decidedly foreign way of pronouncing her adopted language, but Yates saw starring potential in her. The plotless *Ice Capades* was released in 1941, to be followed by *Ice Capades Revue* in 1942. In 1943 Yates signed her on a long-term contract for Republic Pictures.

She first needed to change her name, since Hruba was mangled by Americans to "Rhubarb" or "Rhumba." "Ralston" was her choice because the breakfast cereal was one of the things she liked about the United States. Next she required diction lessons. A year of those and Yates felt she was ready. She made her dramatic debut in 1944 in *The Lady and the Monster,* costarring Erich von Stroheim. This mystery picture received better-than-average reviews, but Vera Ralston did not. The *New York Times* called her performance "too lethargic."

From 1944 until 1958, Yates inserted Ralston into the leading roles of twenty-four movies. She was presented in a variety of looks, with her hair darker and lighter, and in a variety of wardrobes. She was committed to the skills of a variety of directors. She appeared in Westerns, spy films, murder mysteries, musicals, skating movies, foreign intrigues, romances, courtroom dramas, adventure films, war movies, crime dramas, and a volcano epic. Nothing seemed to work. It was asserted, and never repudiated, that only two of her movies ever recouped their costs.

Apparently there were just two constants over these various films. The first was her middle European accent, which she confessed in 1973 was "something I just couldn't lose, no matter how hard I tried."[8] In some of her movies the accent was explained by crediting her character with a French background; in others it went untraced, which lent her an odd if not precarious aura. The second constant was her mediocre acting, which was variously described over the years as "wooden," "restrained," "impassive," "bored," "inept," and "implausible."

These recurring defects were not apparent to Yates, who remained infatuated with Ralston. Out of love for her, he put her family and friends to work for Republic Pictures too. Her mother, who had come with her to the United States, went on the payroll first, and then her brother when he resettled in this country. Her Ice Capades roommate, Bobbie Dorree, was hired as her stand-in and stayed at Republic as long as Vera did. (Her father visited after the war but had misgivings about her relationship with Yates, and returned to Europe.) In 1947 Yates separated from his wife of over thirty years, and in 1952, at the age of seventy-two, he married Ralston. The first Mrs. Yates must have been a remarkable woman, for she was one of the two witnesses at the small, private wedding.

But while Yates embraced Ralston the rest of Hollywood did not—not for personal reasons, since she was an altogether pleasant woman, but because she created such disaster at the box office that others wanted to avoid being associated with her projects. One of the few John Wayne movies to lose money paired him with Ralston in *Dakota*, her sixth film. Wayne is reported to have told people beforehand that he would never do a movie with her, but in a closed-door meeting with Yates he was persuaded otherwise. It did not end there for Wayne. Perhaps in return for his first opportunity to act as a producer, Wayne was enticed by Yates to costar with Ralston a second time, in *The Fighting Kentuckians*. This film also fared poorly, and the two never worked together again.

It was not just the moviegoing public and the film industry that was resistant to Vera Ralston. Stockholders in Republic Pictures began to take issue as well. In 1956 two stockholders filed suit in New York Supreme Court alleging that "since 1942 Mr. Yates for personal reasons had used and continues to use company assets to promote as a star Mrs. Herbert J. Yates, also known as Vera Ralston, to the loss and detriment of the company." A similar suit was filed in 1958, and shortly after that Yates resigned from the company. What was to be Ralston's last film had been distributed just weeks before.

She and her husband lived a quiet life until he died in 1966 at the age of eighty-five. Soon afterward she suffered a nervous breakdown, and later commented, "For a year I was in such a state of shock that I couldn't walk or stand." He had been her mainstay, she had been his pet. But for all his support he could not secure her a place in Star Village. The millions of dollars invested in the twenty-six films and the attendant publicity had made her an oddity, not a celebrity. The public had voted against her.

Maintaining that publicity cannot fabricate stars is not to say it is completely unavailing. Clearly it can do something: the elevation of a performer from the aspirant level to a middle echelon, the journeyman stage. Publicity can thus make candidates for stardom. There are tens of thousands of aspirants, and only hundreds of journeymen, so providing access to this tier is not an inconsequential service. The performer who makes it to this stage will be exposed to a national audience.

A publicity stratagem enabled Rita Hayworth to advance to the journeyman rank. In 1939 her husband employed a man who was to become one of the best-known Hollywood publicity agents: Henry Rogers. Rogers's reputation rests in part upon his success at promoting Hayworth. For her he conjured an award—"best-dressed actress off-screen"—from a bogus Fashion Couturiers Association of America. In his press release he proclaimed that although she was just a starlet she spent $15,000 yearly on her wardrobe. The notice sparked interest, and soon thereafter she was approached by *Look* magazine, which did a ten-page layout on her, featuring her on the cover as well. Her publicity had worked.

From the pool of journeyman players displayed to them, Americans make their selections for Star Village. The public looked at tens of beautiful young women in the magazines and films of 1940, and picked Rita Hayworth. During World War II her pinup photograph was the second most desired, a popularity that no amount of drumbeating could have occasioned. With her auburn tresses and sultry manner, she complemented the wholesome blondeness of first-ranked Betty Grable.

As well as ushering some novices into the group of journeyman players being offered to the public, the other function of publicity is to certify star selections once they have been made. Press release after press release will flutter about the new personage. Some of this activity is the result of publicists' tardy efforts to take credit for the event; in his biography of Grable, Doug Warren notes about her abrupt fame, "When the studio finally awakened to what they had, their publicists gave her the full-star treatment."[9] But much of the explanation for the post-induction publicity barrage rests with the audience's large appetite for reading matter about its new favorite.

Creating journeymen and certifying choices are important tasks, but in magnitude they pale when compared to the momentous enterprise of the public's final selection for stardom. Jack Nicholson said, "Only that audience out there makes a star. It's up to them. You can't do anything about it, or I never would've got anywhere. Stars would all be Louis B. Mayer's cousins if you could make 'em up."

5.
INDUCTION

The ascension of some players into Star Village resembles a short and soaring flight. Lauren Bacall's very first movie, *To Have and Have Not* with Humphrey Bogart, put the twenty-year-old's name on the lips of millions of Americans. At the beginning of 1963 the Beatles were just another local band, and by the end of the year they were known worldwide. Moses Malone, rejecting college seasons, went directly from high school to prominence in the National Basketball Association. For such performers the journeyman period hardly existed.

Other stars experience a longer but still apparently effortless rise. By virtue of his family legacy, John Barrymore *(photograph 17)* can be said to have been born in Star Village; it was only a matter of time before he was a leading actor. Olivia de Havilland and Doris Day were two performers whose mothers seemed to do the hard work of striving for them. Roger Staubach's success as a quarterback at the Naval Academy promised inevitable fame in the National Football League.

But for most celebrity entertainers the journeyman stage is both prolonged and arduous. The results of their assaults upon the summit of popularity are always in doubt. Just as most as-

pirants never manage to become journeymen, so most journeymen are unable to parlay their brief moments of national exposure into greater fame. Writer Leslie Raddatz, who profiled
many young actresses for national publications, began to wonder some years later about the outcomes: "I don't know what
has happened to most of the women I wrote about. Where are
Shirley Yelm, Suzi Cornell, Kanala Devi, Miyoshi Umeki, Bek
Nelson, Little Larraine Egypt, Antoinette Boner, Sigrid Valdes,
Sallie Brophy, Sharon Claridge, Jan Davis, and all the others?"[1]
For all their publicity, they had never made it into Star Village.
Stumbling at this point in their careers may have been more
painful than if they had never received any notoriety at all; the
goal of stardom had been within sight, and the descent and
landing were bound to be harder.

Typical journeyman performers behave much as aspirants
do, continuing to exercise the trait that they believe has brought
them to the midpoint: an unflagging determination. Because
the only element in the star-making process over which they
have any influence is themselves, their sole option is to apply
themselves ever more steadily and tenaciously to their goals.
Someone who knew Frank Sinatra at this stage of his career
said about him, "He was a pusher but polite." This remark captures the ingratiating but determined behavior of most journeymen.

At this juncture in a career the performer will normally
have linked up with a personal manager or agent. The earnings
of a journeyman are insufficient for retaining anyone's exclusive
services, however, and so representation is likely to be spotty.
Performers are thus largely left to their own devices in making
career decisions—something in which they are still inexperi-
enced. An agent will give a baseball player advice on whether to
accept this salary offer or those performance stipulations, but
the final judgment rests with the athlete. Should an actor undertake a particular role at certain terms? It is hard to know.
Being confused, journeymen are prone to switching agents. Elvis left his previous manager at this point and signed on with
Col. Tom Parker. Vanna White found she was not getting enough
work in Hollywood to suit her, and "so I changed agents."

What the journeyman is hoping for are "breaks"—opportunities for performing before the national audience. An athlete is

called up to a major league baseball team; a comedian signs for a season on "Saturday Night Live"; an actress lands a role on a soap opera. Each player sees the media exposure surrounding such performances as stepping-stones on the path to celebrity.

In the popular lore regarding stardom, the break is a signal event. It is an interesting word choice: "break" suggests a fracture in the wall of public indifference, a fleeting chance to reach stardom. The word implies a sharp distinction between being a star and not being a star. It also reveals an intuition that external circumstances figure substantially in the formation of stars.

In prototypical accounts a young star-to-be secures the leading role in a production, rises to the occasion, and receives the wild approbation of the audience. A representative version of the break story is the young Katharine Hepburn's first starring role on Broadway, in *The Warrior's Husband* in 1932. A theater executive recalled, "The audience responded to her immediately. This was a star! You could smell it, you could feel it! It was all around you—the perfume of success!"

Often the break is depicted as a casting happenstance. A vehicle for an established star is developed, but the star does not take advantage of it for one reason or another, and the replacement is catapulted to glory. Steve McQueen rejected a role in *Butch Cassidy and the Sundance Kid,* and Robert Redford became a top star. Frank Sinatra was supposed to play *Dirty Harry,* but he broke his wrist and opened the way for Clint Eastwood. Montgomery Clift rejected the James Dean part in *East of Eden* and the Marlon Brando part in *On the Waterfront,* lending them both handholds toward stardom. Jack Nicholson took over from Kirk Douglas in *One Flew Over the Cuckoo's Nest.* Audrey Hepburn's first starring role, for which she won an Oscar, came about when Jean Simmons was unavailable for *Roman Holiday.* Sean Connery became James Bond after Richard Burton and James Mason had turned the role down for salary reasons. Shirley Temple could not be obtained for *The Wizard of Oz,* so Judy Garland was recruited.

These engaging tales aside, however, rarely is it that any single break makes a star. A large number of performers receive breaks, but of these only a fraction will become stars. Rather than one break, the star-to-be normally receives a series of breaks. The commentator on *The Warrior's Husband* may have believed he had witnessed a star's birth, but Katharine Hepburn's career entered the doldrums a few short years later when her first Hollywood films flopped. More breaks led to a resuscitation before another slump occurred, and then it was several additional breaks before she was finally and firmly a movie star.

The typical journeyman performer is thrown about in a blanket toss of opportunities granted and opportunities denied, of public response present and then absent. It is an unsettling time, quite different from the steadier journeyman periods in the careers of most Americans. A baseball player is sent down to the minors and then recalled to a major league team, only to be sent down again. An actor works regularly in supporting roles and then for no discernible reason cannot secure another part. After Michael J. Fox had left his Canadian home and moved to Los Angeles, he was fortunate enough to land a series of roles and to be lodged firmly in journeyman status. But at age twenty he was out of work and $30,000 in debt. "Then my phone suddenly stopped ringing. I'm sure it happens to every actor, but I'd never planned for it."

For all its turbulence, the journeyman period has its constructive side, for this is when the performer can hone a well-defined public image. Shrewder performers will attentively apply themselves to the task of becoming whatever it is the public seems to want from them. Each time out they compel themselves to be highly aware of audience response, and then to adjust their performance and image accordingly. It took David Bowie ten years of trial and error before he arrived at a stable persona approved by a wide audience. Part of this effort involved studying the press accounts of his shows, noted biographer Henry Edwards: "David read every work printed about him. The press always offered clues to what he needed to say and do in order to fulfill the expectations of his audience."[2] George Hamilton commented about this to-and-fro between performer and audience: "When you realize you had success with a character, he becomes a little bit of you." In Hamilton's view of the construction of a star persona, "It's done by some form of confirmation, whether it be a mirror or an audience or some sort of incident that works as a catalyst for you. If you are lucky enough to live long enough, you become a sort of spiraling manifestation of what was originally some sort of little vine, which has now become the trunk of a tree. Hopefully."

The apprenticeship of comedian Paul Reubens illustrates this searching effort by journeyman performers. For years on the improvisational comedy circuit he had tried out a number of characters, and although he had some success and a small following, fame eluded him. But finally one of his creations clicked. "The audience's connection was so immediate it was obvious from the beginning that I was onto something." What he was onto was Pee-wee Herman, the permanently preadolescent goof. Subsequent appearances on the "David Letterman Show" and MTV led to a number of sold-out concert performances, an HBO special, a movie all his own, and even a television series. A nerd slot was opening in Star Village, and Reubens was able to identify and fill it. From that point on he refused to play any other character; he was careful never to be seen by photographers without his Pee-wee makeup on. (A professional nightmare occurred in 1991 when he was arrested for exposing himself in an adult movie theater, rocking his career.)

At a certain magical point in a star-to-be's career the pull of popular acceptance becomes greater than the push of the individual's ambition and drive. As basketball star Michael "Air" Jordan described it in 1987, "You wake up one morning and all of a sudden you've got more money and more attention than you ever dreamed of, more people who want a piece of you than you ever dreamed possible." Now situated in Star Village, the performer suddenly finds that the opportunities that were so infrequent during the journeyman days come in torrents. Daniel J. Travanti remarked, "In the old days when I was drinking and thinking I had to make things happen for myself, I ran so hard in place that I ended up in a deep hole. Then it all got better. Jackie Gleason said the same thing. You try your best to get the work and nothing happens. Then all of a sudden it comes to you. Now I just go along and watch."

Throughout the twentieth century the moment of ascension has been clearly marked in a particular way: letters begin to arrive in volume (photograph 18). This is the certifying event. When enough people go to the trouble to search out an address and to sit down with pen and paper and unabashedly state their affection, then another blessed event has occurred in Star Village. Lana Turner, a featured player at age sixteen, describes this occasion: "Meanwhile letters from fans were beginning to arrive at Warner's—just a trickle at first, but before long, a tide. What a thrill!" When the Beatles arrived in New York in February 1964 there were thirty-seven sacks of mail waiting; one of the letters was from Lyndon B. Johnson. The same year fans began to write to the Rolling Stones, especially to Mick Jagger and Brian Jones. Jones's girl friend later recounted, "There was tons of fan mail pouring in and Brian sitting there and reading it and saying 'Did Mick get more than me this week?'" He was acknowledging this measure of star status.

Although the journeyman has worked strenuously in the hope of becoming a star, when it does happen the usual reaction is one of puzzlement, even incredulity. Celebrity entertainers truly do not understand why they have been elevated at a certain point above all their peers. As the Beatles flew to their rapturous American reception in 1964, George Harrison was left to ponder, "They've got everything over there. What do they want *us* for?" Asked to explain his newly acquired mass popularity, Bob Dylan responded in 1965, "I really have no idea. That's the truth." According to Farrah Fawcett, "Suddenly, when I was doing 'Charlie's Angels,' I was getting all this fan mail, and I didn't really know why. I don't think anyone else did either." Reflecting on the reasons for his rise to stardom, Michael J. Fox commented in 1987, "There are no answers to that that make any sense to me."

Not having a sensible explanation on tap, the new inductee into Star Village can do little more than weakly cite luck. Clark Gable's most profound thought about his elevation was, "I'm just a lucky slob from Ohio who happened to be in the right place at the right time." In Boris Karloff's version, "You could heave a brick out of the window and hit ten actors who could play my parts. I just happened to be on the right corner at the right time." George C. Scott's explanation was, "I think it comes down to meanness, perseverance, and a lot of luck—possibly in that order." Performers are so obsessed with themselves and their own careers that they rarely attempt to view the whole process from the audience's perspective. A star is not likely to perceive that the public has pulled him or her into Star Village for reasons of its own—to complement the existing array or to establish a new position.

Once in Star Village, newly established celebrities must leave the rest of the journeymen behind. They may look wistfully over their shoulders at their old comrades, but the distance between them has grown too great. After actress Teri Garr had suddenly come into demand in the 1980s, she reflected, "I have some friends who lately I don't call anymore. I feel badly that I'm working and they just never are. There's no difference in ability in my mind between us. But I went to another level and they're working in a bank. And they were just as tenacious, just as competitive as I was." Marilyn Monroe told about trying to revisit the starlets at Hollywood's Schwab's Drugstore: "When I starred in my first movie, I went back to Schwab's. I had the idea it would help their confidence to see someone who had gotten a break. But no one recognized me and I was too shy to tell anyone. I was a misfit there!"

A particularly representative rise to stardom was that of Betty Grable. Born in St. Louis in 1916, she had a highly devoted and ambitious mother. The two of them moved to Hollywood when Betty was thirteen, leaving her father behind to tend his business. By lying about her age, Betty was quickly able to get hired for a movie chorus line. Through the 1930s Grable attempted to find her way into entertainment's higher echelons. Appearing in a number of supporting roles, she worked for a total of four studios. Each dropped her when she failed to elicit a response from the audience. To the extent she had any following at all, it was for her performances as a coed—a curious role, given her almost complete lack of formal education. Then at the end of the decade she received in quick succession three opportunities for wider publicity—her breaks. In 1937 she married ex–child star Jackie Coogan and received some of the spotlight that had lingered on him. Two years later she divorced him and found prominence again by starring in a Broadway play, *Du-Barry Was a Lady*. Then, when the leading blonde musical star of the day, Alice Faye, became ill and could not take part in the 1940 Darryl Zanuck movie *Down Argentine Way*, Grable had her first opportunity at the kind of song-and-dance role in which the public came to love her.

By her own admission Grable was not an especially talented performer. She modestly appraised her singing voice as "just a voice" and conceded that her dancing was "average, maybe just a little bit below." Neither did she profess to have the glittering personality of other stars. She once remarked, "You know, Lana Turner and Joan Crawford, they really deserve to be stars. I don't. They know how to act the part. Whey they go out, they're all dressed up, and I hate to dress up. I've seen Lana at parties with little diamonds in her hair—and Crawford always looks so beautiful. I just feel uncomfortable."

None of this mattered. For several years she was indisputably the grandest star in Hollywood. In 1943 she shot up in popularity, from the eighth-ranked attraction to the first. In 1945 and 1946 she was the highest-salaried woman in the United States, earning almost a quarter of a million dollars annually. "Box-Office Betty," as she was called in the industry, never made a film that did not show good returns on investment. The answer to the often-asked question, "Does Betty Grable have talent?" was, according to studio publicists, "Could millions of moviegoers be wrong?" The best-known remembrance of Grable is the publicity shot of her in a bathing suit, looking back over her shoulder at the camera, hand on hip, a fetching look on an otherwise innocent visage *(photograph 19)*. Requests for this pinup picture, which was first available from Twentieth-Century Fox late in 1942, reached 20,000 per week. Of all the Hollywood stars her photo was by far the most sought after by military personnel; 5 million copies had been distributed by the war's end.

What had Grable, who had been such a minor performer during the 1930s, done to win such popularity during the 1940s? She had stepped into a new niche that had appeared in Star Village. The war had caused hundred of thousands of young men to be distanced for an unknown duration from the young women of America. This wrenching dislocation created a yearning that Betty's image symbolically answered. For young males she personified the 1940s ideal of a partner-to-be. As they envisioned her from her series of song-and-dance roles and from the studio publicity, she seemed deliciously pretty, energetic, warm, obliging, and uncomplicated. To young men stationed around the world, she was the heartthrob they were fighting for.

The women in the moviegoing audience felt close to her

also, finding in her a model of the lovable person they would like to become. She was sweet, accessible, "regular"—the girl down the street, a person to trade makeup with. In Grable's strong marriage to bandleader Harry James they foresaw their own lives. History had produced a major separation between the sexes, and Grable addressed the rift by providing a longed-for image of adorable American womanhood.

Her own private personality did not diverge radically from the type she played in Star Village, but neither was it identical. In person Grable possessed a quick and saucy wit that was never an ingredient in her movie roles. Her real-life saltiness would have been sure to mar the pleasant screen character. Her greatest recreational pleasure was to gamble heavily, especially at the horse races, but there was little space in films for her to reveal a penchant for taking chances or enjoying small thrills. Her edges had to be rounded off for her to play the sweet lass. It was a professional adjustment she made readily.

Once the war was over, the troops were home, and lads were finding their lasses, Grable's popularity began to slip. The wholesome-girl-back-home slot in Star Village started to dissolve as marriage vows were taken and the emphasis in American relationships began to change. Innocence gave way to oomph, and Marilyn Monroe's fame began to eclipse hers. The two worked together on *How To Marry a Millionaire,* and on the set Grable is reported to have told her successor, "Honey, I've had it. It's your turn now. Go and get it."

In the transformation to stardom, many performers engage in an act that could hardly be more symbolic of the passage from a common to a superordinate state. Somewhere along the way they will change their name. In doing so, they shuck an old identity ceded at birth and are reborn as the transfigured entertainer. Asked about his renaming, David Bowie remarked, "I was someone else before that." A few entertainers select literally starry names: Frederick Austerlitz became Fred Astaire, and Richard Starkey became Ringo Starr.

This metamorphosis is strikingly illustrated in the tale of the person who was named Lucille Faye LeSueur at her birth in 1906. She was known as Billie Cassin, however, during most of her childhood. When she arrived in Hollywood in 1925 she was again calling herself Lucille LeSueur. Then, in a publicity tour de force engineered by Metro Studios, the magazine *Movie Weekly* conducted a "name-the-star" contest for her, and in 1926 she was dubbed Joan Crawford *(photograph 20)*. Although the publicity people at Metro surely bear the responsibility for the choice, in appearance it was the public who effected the renaming. After two tries, no pedestrian name would suit her; only a glorious one would serve when she made her entrance into the glittering stratosphere.

The business of taking on a new name is somewhat different for sports stars, but it still occurs after a fashion. The celebrity player is often saddled with a nickname; these tags help spectators feel more familiar with the athlete. They used to arise more or less spontaneously: "Cap" Anson, "Babe" Ruth, "Casey" Stengel, "Yogi" Berra. More recently they are likely to have been manufactured: "Catfish" Hunter, called Jim by all who really knew him, was given his sobriquet by team owner Charley Finley. Nevertheless, nicknames remain a distinct component of the baseball world: "Boog" Powell, "Goose" Gosage, Dennis "Oil Can" Boyd. They occur in football and basketball as well: Thomas "Hollywood" Henderson, William "Refrigerator" Perry, Julius "Dr. J" Irving, Earvin "Magic" Johnson.

But Hollywood performers are more likely to indulge in renaming. The most conspicuous tendency is to render names less ethnic, and thereby to situate them in the mainstream of American life. Thus the Spanish-sounding Margarita Cansino became Rita Hayworth, the Russian Natasha Gurdin was changed to Natalie Wood, the Polish Charles Buchinski gave way to Charles Bronson. Italians frequently anglicized their names: Tony Benedetto, Vito Farinola, and Dino Crocetti passed into stardom as Tony Bennett, Vic Damone, and Dean Martin.

If Dean Martin could do it, so could Jerry Lewis, who had been Joseph Levith. Many performers with strongly Jewish-sounding names chose to discard them. Isidore Demsky disappeared and was replaced by Kirk Douglas. New York's Bernard Schwartz turned into Hollywood's Tony Curtis. Betty Joan Perske liked Lauren Bacall better, Eugene Orowitz became Michael London, Allen Stewart Konigsberg turned into Woody Allen, and Robert Alan Zimmerman became Bob Dylan.

There is a terseness to the names of many stars, perhaps in

the interest of memorability, and thus many cumbersome pre-
star names are shortened. Rodolpho Alfonso Raffaelo Pierre Fi-
libert Guglielmi di Valentina d'Antonguolla settled for Rudolph
Valentino. By the time someone said William Claude Duken-
field, they could have said W. C. Fields twice. Anna Maria Pier-
angeli became Pier Angeli, and James Bumgarner was happier
as plain James Garner.

The shrinking of Bumgarner to Garner introduces another
consideration in the adaptation of star names: aesthetics often
dictate. Thus Maurice Micklewhite decreed himself to be the
more euphonious Michael Cain. There is nothing wrong with
Doris von Kappelhoff, but Doris Day sounded better. Mickey
Rooney thought his star name was an improvement over Joe
Yule, Jr. William Beedle chose the stauncher William Holden,
and Leonard Slye became Roy Rogers. Frances Gumm could
not wait to become Judy Garland.

Male stars, if their original names seemed other than unambiguously masculine, have been quick to rectify them. Who
could survive as a cowboy star named Marion? Not John Wayne,
who left behind Marion Morrison. Leslie Hope wanted laughs
but not smirks, so he changed his first name to Bob. Was Gwyl-
lyn Ford male or female? Glenn Ford made it clear.

Female stars sometimes resort to alliteration in the search
for mellifluous, feminine names. Norma Jean Mortenson took on
Marilyn Monroe, while Camille Javal transformed herself into
Brigitte Bardot.

With some performers it is not all clear what the reason was
for the star name selected, or what the gain might have been.
Why did John Sullivan choose to become Fred Allen? Was Es-
telle Thompson any worse than Merle Oberon? Was Patsy Cline
an advance over Virginia Hensley? What is wrong with Jayne
Palmer, that she had to become Jayne Mansfield? But perhaps
such questions miss the point. The important thing about selecting a star name may not be matters of ethnicity or aesthetics
or gender, but rather the very fact that an entertainer has
elected to shed one identity and take on another.

Indeed, there is so little consensus about what constitutes
an improvement that one star will keep a name that another
discards. David Jones was content to remain Davy Jones of the
Monkees, while another David Jones was not happy until he

turned himself into David Bowie. Jean Peters stayed Jean Peters (until she married Howard Hughes), but Jane Peters chose to become Carole Lombard.

Some stars go completely against the grain, selecting names others might cheerfully discard. A man with the dignified name of William Henry Pratt became Boris Karloff. Gerry Dorsey found fame as Engelbert Humperdinck. And nice-sounding Caryn Johnson achieved world renown as Whoopi Goldberg.

Other stars enter into this ritual of transformation a bit tentatively and change only one or the other of their names. Those who altered just their last names include Greta Gustafsson, who became Greta Garbo, and Joe Barrow, known to the world as Joe Louis *(photograph 21)*. Others do not choose to change their surname but feel free to play with their given names. Frank James Cooper became Gary Cooper, and Edward Kennedy Ellington was Duke Ellington. Classmates of Lana Turner at Hollywood High had known her as Judy. And Meryl Streep had once been Mary Louise.

Some, it should not be forgotten, do not change their names at all. They march right along as Clara Bow, Henry Fonda, or Elvis Presley. Even some who by all rights might want to change their name do not: Humphrey Bogart, Marlon Brando, and Barbra Streisand (who merely dropped an 'a' from Barbara). In the study of 100 stars fifty-four had made no appreciable change. Still, forty-six did, and any profession in which almost half the practitioners have consciously altered something so personal as their names has to be reckoned extraordinary.

The forty-six stars who did something more than use a diminutive of their given name were these:

STAR NAME	NAME AT BIRTH
1. Fred Astaire	Frederick Austerlitz
2. Theda Bara	Theodosia Goodman
3. Jack Benny	Benjamin Kubelski
4. Lenny Bruce	Leonard Schneider
5. Richard Burton	Richard Jenkins
6. Nat "King" Cole	Nathaniel Adams Coles
7. Gary Cooper	Frank James Cooper
8. Joan Crawford	Lucille Faye LeSueur
9. Bing Crosby	Harry Lillis Crosby

10. Bette Davis	Ruth Elizabeth Davis
11. Doris Day	Doris von Kappelhoff
12. Jack Dempsey	William Harrison Dempsey
13. Duke Ellington	Edward Kennedy Ellington
14. Douglas Fairbanks, Sr.	Douglas Elton Thomas Ulman
15. W. C. Fields	William Claude Dukenfield
16. Greta Garbo	Greta Gustafsson
17. Judy Garland	Frances Ethel Gumm
18. Cary Grant	Archibald Alexander Leach
19. Jean Harlow	Harlean Carpenter
20. Rita Hayworth	Margarita Carmen Cansino
21. Jimi Hendrix	Johnny Allen Hendrix
22. Bob Hope	Leslie Towns Hope
23. Harry Houdini	Erik Weisz
24. Rock Hudson	Roy Harold Scherer, Jr.
25. Al Jolson	Asa Yoelson
26. Danny Kaye	David Daniel Kaminsky
27. Buster Keaton	Joseph Frank Keaton
28. Hedy Lamarr	Hedwig Eva Maria Kiesler
29. Gypsy Rose Lee	Rose Louise Hovick
30. Vivien Leigh	Vivian Mary Hartley
31. Carole Lombard	Jane Alice Peters
32. Joe Louis	Joseph Louis Barrow
32. Jayne Mansfield	Vera Jayne Palmer
34. Groucho Marx	Julius Henry Marx
35. Marilyn Monroe	Norma Jean Mortenson
36. Roy Rogers	Leonard Slye
39. Mickey Rooney	Joe Yule, Jr.
40. Jane Russell	Ernestine Geraldine Russell
41. Babe Ruth	George Herman Ruth
42. Red Skelton	Richard Bernard Skelton
43. Gloria Swanson	Josephine Mary Swanson
44. Lana Turner	Julia Jean Turner
45. Rudolph Valentino	Rodolpho Alfonso Raffaelo Pierre Filibert Guglielmi di Valentina d'Antonguolla
46. John Wayne	Marion Morrison

Some stars feel enormously gratified after losing their old name and taking on a spangly new one. "For Marilyn Monroe, it meant the abandonment of a hand-me-down kind of existence," her biographer reported. "The truth was that she soon felt completely at home with *Marilyn*." Others, however, never make their peace with the fabricated label. Roy Harold Scherer, Jr., later known as Roy Fitzgerald, had little regard for either "Rock" or "Hudson," once admitting, "I hated both names."

What to do with the name that has been set aside? Archibald Alexander Leach, famous as Cary Grant, had an answer. As an up-and-coming star, living in Hollywood with friend Randolph Scott, he named their pet terrier "Archie Leach."

Don Johnson achieved eminence as the unshaven, sockless detective in the "Miami Vice" television series. When his career pivoted from that of a journeyman actor to that of a celebrity entertainer, he announced, "You become an actor by being a shadow. I've been the shadow. Now I'll be the light."

The conversion from shadow to light is so momentous that it is certain to involve more than could ever be anticipated. Some of the factual aspects may be foreseen: income will rocket; a person will go from being one among a large cohort of journeymen to being one among a highly exclusive group; where once he or she used to beg for opportunities to work, now opportunities come begging for him. But the full impact of great celebrity upon a person's daily life is nearly unimaginable. Susan Rotolo was Bob Dylan's girlfriend during his early years in New York, and the inspiration for several of his songs. Interviewed later in life, she recalled "an enormous ambition in him, because he had even said he was going to be very big. I took it seriously at the moment, but I had no idea what it meant. *He* didn't know what it meant; he couldn't know then what fame of that magnitude could do to his life."

To successfully accomplish the transformation to stardom, however, a performer must quickly learn how to deal with this new and singular career stage. The details of performance will remain much the same; they brought one into fame and will maintain one there. But now one must handle an enormous amount of unsolicited attention. French writer and critic Edgar Morin, a penetrating observer of the star phenomenon, comments that "the star is the product of a projection-identification of a particular virulence."[3] It is this "particular virulence" that the new star must learn to handle. And it is not easy to do. As Academy Award–winning actor William Hurt confided to his onetime costar Kathleen Turner, "You can have all the acting training in the world, but nobody teaches you how to be a star."

The first thing new stars must do is to withdraw from close public contact. Their status depends upon public response, but they cannot afford to rub up against people in normal ways. Once anonymous players will now be accosted whenever they are in a public place. Such contact is rarely an unalloyed pleasure; it usually falls somewhere between being a nuisance to being genuinely threatening. In 1985 one of Madonna's bodyguards, a man who had worked a few years earlier in the same capacity for Michael Jackson, commented, "I can feel it happening again. Pretty soon the jogging and window-shopping—we're going to have to give that up."

More treacherous than casual public encounters are the moments when a star must confront a throng. The new star has to learn to avoid crowds, or if they are unavoidable, to have arranged for proper security. Asked how she was handling the public recognition in the months after her Olympic triumph, Mary Lou Retton replied gamely, "I haven't gotten sick of it yet," and then went on to say, "In big crowds, though, it is kind of scary because people just crowd around." One of the matters that the newly celebrated Beatles wanted to discuss with Elvis Presley, when they met at Graceland in Memphis, was how to handle the enormous and ferocious crowds of fans at concerts.

Freshly crowned performers must also learn to deal with the mediating agency of the press, and learn as quickly as possible. The art of granting interviews must be fully mastered. According to biographer Albert Goldman, Elvis Presley's first interview was by Memphis disc jockey Dewey Phillips: "'Mr. Phillips,' trembled Elvis, 'I don't know nuthin' 'bout bein' interviewed.' 'Just don't say nuthin' dirty,' snapped Phillips."[4] Avoiding obscenity is good advice, but it is only the beginning of being a successful interviewee. Apprehension may get in the way: eighteen-year old Molly Ringwald uneasily greeted an interrogator, "Do you want to know my dream man, my favorite colors, or what I read on the john?" Mistakes will be made: the young Martina Navratilova admitted, off the record, having had a lesbian relationship, and was astonished to find the account in print. "It was gullible and naive of me to have shared my strongest feelings with a reporter who had other priorities than my security, my happiness. But you live and learn," she reflected.

Transformed players receive so much attention from the public and the press, and can be so flattered by it all, that it is easy for them to become unpleasantly conceited. As Hollywood agent Dolores Robinson commented, "One day nobody knows who you are, and the next day everybody in the world knows who you are. People tell you 'Now don't change,' but you feel yourself changing because you've got to change. It's a rare case of somebody who can really keep it all together." Soon after Joan Crawford ascended into celebrity in 1932 she said, "I want so much to fight off conceit." Whether she was able to or not, she did uphold this as an important goal. Conceit can turn performers into their own worst enemies. When John Travolta became a star some observers believed he grew so self-centered that he was impossible to work with; reportedly he did not correct his egotistical excesses until his career began to suffer.

It is especially important for new stars not to lord it over their co-workers, and to maintain good relationships with the supporting crew. Katharine Hepburn established the habit of providing a picnic lunch for the cast and crew on her movie locations. Kathleen Turner developed an awareness of how a star should treat others on the set: "One word, one gesture means so much, and its importance is so out of whack with what it would mean in a regular relationship that you have to be careful. You learn not to lavish attention on a crew member one day and forget his name the next."

Some performers who learn to deal adeptly with the public and the press, and who are able to keep their egos in adequate check, are ecstatic about their celebrity. Gypsy Rose Lee was thrilled when general popularity came her way. Robin Williams said about his apotheosis, "All of a sudden you are surrounded by a whole group of people that you haven't seen before. Your normal senses say, 'Wait a minute, what is happening?' But your ego says, 'This is great. More, please.'"

Others players, although they manage to endure the transformation to stardom, are left reeling by the impact of enormous acclaim. Benny Goodman could not completely hide his ambivalence from an interviewer: "That this whole business has turned out to be something beyond my rosiest hopes doesn't mean that I'm not happy about it, or in any way displeased. I'm just trying to put across the thought that I'm still so much in the middle of something that is a surprise even to me that it is a little bit hard to stand aside and look at it from the outside." When the Monkees became instantly famous, Mickey Dolenz and his three partners were suddenly known to everyone: "That kind of success is exhausting, mind-boggling. It was a devastating experience." Pierce Brosnan found prominence as the star of the television show "Remington Steele," and for him the sensation was of discomfort: "I feel like I stepped into the lions' den. I feel like there is no breathing space. I am like a mouse running around on a little wheel." In 1986 rock singer Sting observed pointedly, "I went from being a teacher in a mining town to being a famous person. There's nothing worse than everything going well."

For a large number of inductees to Star Village, the experience is accompanied by crippling distress. The burdens of success turn out to be knee-buckling. Often narcotics contribute to a collapse. As a young actor Michael Landon landed a starring role on the hit television program "Bonanza." "I thought I was prepared, but I wasn't," he stated later. Trying to cope, Landon grew addicted to prescription drugs. Richard Dreyfuss, his celebrity confirmed with an Oscar for his performance in *The Goodbye Girl*, succumbed to a devastating cocaine habit: "It took me by surprise, this success. Here I was, this guy who knew he wanted to be a star his whole life, who knew he wanted to win the Academy Award, and suddenly I found myself acting like a small child. I just didn't anticipate the guilt and fear of success. I didn't anticipate the down side of success at all." New York Mets pitching sensation Dwight Gooden had similar problems with drugs and alcohol; "It all came so fast for him," said his general manager Frank Cashen. "He's really just a kid. We robbed him of that."

One's age at the time of induction into Star Village does seem to influence the ease or difficulty of the process. Those who are older and who have spent a longer time as journeymen generally appear to manage the transition better. Charlton Heston commented, "Celebrity is a corrosive condition, and I think I was lucky that it came to me slowly, so I could adapt."

Once past the gateway of Star Village, once having learned

the protocols of their remarkable new occupation, many stars find the satisfactions they had imagined at the start of their ascent to be strangely elusive. Speaking obliquely and yet still revealingly, Clark Gable told one interviewer, "You want to be a movie star. You think you'd like it. Maybe you would and maybe you wouldn't. You might turn out to be not so happy as you think you'd be."

Aspirants may initially set themselves on the path to stardom because, in their rosy view of it, fame promises freedom beyond compare. But in fact the job of the celebrity performer is subject to suffocating impositions and strangling constraints. Asked what it means to become a star, Cary Grant replied, "Does it mean happiness? Yeah, for a couple of days. And then what happens? You begin to find out that your life is not your own anymore, and that you're on show every time you step out on the street." According to sociologist Orrin Klapp, such a reaction is altogether typical, for "one of the most characteristic symptoms of having actually become a celebrity is a certain disillusionment, which sets in—after the first thrill of seeing one's name in headlines—upon discovering the obligations and inconveniences of being known by everyone everywhere."[5]

As Marilyn Monroe concluded, "Being a movie actress was never as much fun as dreaming of being one."

☆
USING STARS

6★
STARS AT WORK

ecause Americans perceive what stars do to be a form of upgraded play, the work life of celebrity entertainers is likely to be imperfectly understood. Many people, thinking stars spend the hours of the day at leisure, imagine them almost like classical deities, supine and indulgent. In fact stars are frequently pictured as recumbent: this one reclining in a chaise lounge, reading a script; that one stretched out on a massage table, getting worked on by the team's trainer; several others are poolside and prone. But in reality the lot of the star is the opposite of this impression.

Fred Astaire *(photograph 22)* commented, "People will come up to me and say, 'Boy, it must have been fun making those old MGM musicals.' Fun? I suppose you could have considered them that—if you like beating your brains and feet out." Knocking oneself out to deliver appreciated performances to the public, time after time, is the fate of those ensconced in the star role. The occupation calls for extraordinary effort and ceaseless toil.

Steve McQueen remarked, "I took up acting because it let me burn off energy. Besides, I wanted to beat the forty-hour-a-week rap. But man, I didn't escape. Now I'm working seventy-two hours a week! Acting's a hard scene for me. Every script I

get is an enemy I have to conquer." In a letter of advice, Tyrone
Power the stage actor apprised his son, movie star-to-be Tyrone
Power III, that "acting is work—hard, hard work."

It was hard work that in 1941 led to Joe DiMaggio's still
unbroken record of hitting safely in fifty-six consecutive games,
and it was hard work that in 1985 permitted Pete Rose to exceed
Ty Cobb's record of 4,191 career hits. The 152 live shows that
Elvis Presley put on in 1974—the majority of them one-night
stands—represented backbreaking effort. Mickey Dolenz said
about his life with the Monkees, "We had to record at night, do
gigs on the weekends, rehearse the show during the week. It was
terribly draining." When Bob Hope in 1984 at age eighty-one
made 250 personal appearances, and John McEnroe the same
year played eleven straight months of tournament tennis, they
were leading the life of the star.

Since the star role first materialized, the work life of its occupants has been characterized by exertion and drudgery. As
Mary Pickford recounted in her autobiography, "I had no friends
outside the studio; and there was this unending marathon of
work." Charlie Chaplin, who wrote that "my consolation was in
work," tried in vain to enjoy a romance with Paulette Goddard,
but "underlying these pleasures was a continual sense of guilt:
What am I doing here? Why aren't I at work?" Although Douglas
Fairbanks, Sr., appeared to glide merrily and effortlessly
through his films, that illusion was painstakingly produced. His
stunts were the result of daily physical training and arduous
rehearsal, which eventually resulted in a sublime execution before the camera. Fairbanks's observation was that "the man
that's out to do something will have to keep in high gear all his
working time."

Like Pickford, Chaplin, and Fairbanks, the majority of stars
who succeeded them have been driven by an intense desire to
perfect the performance that granted them celebrity. There have
been exceptions—Babe Ruth would forgo batting practice, and
John Wayne preferred shooting scenes without a run-through—
but only a few. For most stars the preparation for performing
begins with a general readiness. Professional athletes work out
countless hours to maintain their physical condition. Singers
exercise their voices daily, practicing their delivery and keeping
their vocal cords in shape. Actors take classes to hone their per-

formance or spend time carefully observing others, so that a fuller range of behaviors can become part of their repertoire.

From a base of readiness, the star goes on to prepare assiduously for a specific performance. The quarterback spends the week strategizing about the upcoming game, and rehearsing the strategy on the practice field. The rock band practices its songs for the concert; the comedian works on new material; and the actor will concentrate on a new character and try to become familiar with it. Jane Fonda described her preparation for a film role: "Before I did *The Dollmaker,* I lived in Arkansas and worked for a family there for two weeks. I chopped their wood, and milked their cows, and churned their butter. My hands were totally limp from the hard work. But in the process of doing that I became someone else. It's like you can actually feel yourself leaving a reality, and entering another reality."

Actors must go over their lines again and again, working to get them right. One who epitomized obsessive rehearsing was Montgomery Clift. "I've never seen anyone as meticulous," Burt Lancaster said. Deborah Kerr recalled about her work with Clift and Lancaster on *From Here to Eternity:* "We had only one scene together. I walked behind him and Monty was supposed to say to Burt, 'Who's that?' He spent two days figuring out how to say, 'Who's that?'"

Before going on, the star has to be costumed and made up. While hardly a drain on the performer's energy, this process can be time-consuming—it took three hours to get Pickford's curls right—and nerve-racking. Toward the end of his career Presley would get testy as he was being girdled and outfitted.

In the moments before performance, the enormity of the occasion will give many stars the jitters. Gracie Allen, Marilyn Monroe, and Roy Rogers all became highly anxious. Oscarwinner William Hurt said about performing, "I would be so scared, my mouth would go in to a spasm and start to close." Some, like Red Skelton, became so nervous they vomited. Carly Simon's stage fright was capable of paralyzing her. It may help the entertainer to remember that once he or she goes on, the performance is likely to proceed as planned. As Liberace once said, "Offstage I'm not too sure of myself, but onstage I'm in command." A few lucky stars do not get anxious before their performance begins. One of the calm ones was Joe DiMaggio, who in response to a reporter's question about pregame nerves replied, "It doesn't pay to get excited in this game."

The star and the audience are not the only parties to the performance; there are also the many colleagues who are supposed to be supportive of the star: the production crew, the rest of the cast, the others on the team. Often they are not supportive at all, but rather hostile and sometimes subversive. Their treason may stem from envious and spiteful feelings toward the star. The other members of the basketball team may begrudge the center the attention and salary he receives. The other members of the band may be jealous of the lead singer and fearful that he or she might desert them. Hollywood crews often show condescension toward stars, although they well know that their own jobs and the industry itself depend on celebrities. So in performance the star may be working with a wariness about the less-than-ideal aid of those who are putatively in support.

No matter what stars may feel about the adequacy of their preparation or the contributions of those around them, at a certain moment the performance starts. The production may be as expensive and complex as a military campaign—the making of *Cleopatra*, a Super Bowl, the Michael Jackson Farewell Tour—but the star cannot let it overpower him. He is the draw, and he must loom large in the proceedings.

Now the hard work truly begins. The star must concentrate, with an extraordinary, exhausting mental effort, on the task immediately at hand. Energy must be applied and facility demonstrated. The singer must hit the notes, the slugger must connect, the comedian must establish timing, the actress must emote. Mick Jagger in concert has been described this way: "In the space of a line, he will march, mince, strut, chase, kneel, implore, roll over, and suddenly be airborne like the Nureyev he has sometimes wished he was." Perspiration begins to appear on the star's brow and torso. The performer sweats in exertion.

What a star is expected to do, more than any ordinary player, is to produce wonderfully and completely, on cue. The star has been engaged to deliver, within the framework of the performance, the right act at the right moment. The audience expects that the running back will gain a hundred yards yet again, the comedian have the perfect punch line, the actress cry when it is required. Crying, in fact, is one of the great bugaboos of acting: it is difficult to fabricate, for the glands must secrete and the drops must glisten visibly whether the individual feels like it or not. Many performers dwell on a sad memory to get the tears rolling. Clara Bow recounted, "It was easy for me to cry. All I had to do was think of home," a reference to her tormented childhood. But not all stars can cry on cue. According to Michael Landon, Bette Davis used to jerk out a nose hair so the pain would start her weeping. Lana Turner reported that camphor crystals would be blown through cheesecloth into actresses' eyes to prompt the flow. When she balked at this on the set of *Dr. Jekyll and Mr. Hyde,* the director, in a fury, simply twisted her arm until she bawled.

Performing is a risky business. Unless there is some degree of tension and jeopardy the audience will not watch, and without an audience there are no recurring performances. Sometimes the risks are purely physical ones. Every football star going on the playing field knows that, to satisfy fans' needs for a thrilling game, his well-being is going to be in genuine peril. Lineman Jerry Kramer suffered numerous injuries over his playing career: three brain concussions, a detached retina, two broken ribs, four other broken bones, a hernia, strained ligaments, and pinched nerves. Gloria Swanson told a story about being in an enclosure with a lion while making *Male and Female* for Cecil B. DeMille, and having the beast lunge at her twice: "Oh, I suppose the hair stood up on my spine, but at the time I wanted to get on with it. The next day I was a little shaky from it." Sylvester Stallone calculated that in making his string of action-jammed films, his nose had been broken three times; his hands had been broken twice; he had suffered a concussion and a ruptured stomach; and his various flesh wounds required a total of 160 stitches. Michael Jackson, in an elaborate fiery production number for a Pepsi-Cola commercial, had his hair singed and had to be hospitalized. Victor Morrow died in a helicopter crash during the filming of *Twilight Zone: The Movie.*

Stars thus take genuine risks when exposing themselves in performance. In recent years "exposure" has taken on a literal meaning, since nudity has become acceptable and more stars are asked to display themselves unclothed. Julie Andrews goes topless, Burt Reynolds lounges pantless, and Bo Derek achieves fame stark naked. It is not always easy for performers to unveil themselves to a mass audience; while some are thrilled by the fact that their bodies are considered attractive by the populace, others find public nakedness belittling and humiliating. The singer Fabian posed for *Playgirl* magazine and regretted it profoundly: "I knew it was a mistake the minute I saw the thing sold in a brown paper sleeve. I could barely live with myself." Sharon Stone appeared disrobed opposite Ryan O'Neal in *Irreconcilable Differences* and said afterwards, "It took me three months to get over doing that scene. When I dropped my top, my heart was in my feet."

Exposure of an emotional sort is more the rule, and is potentially more devastating. In the heat of performance stars bring their psychic innards out into public display. When a basketball player sobs over a lost game, it is undeniable that he has poured his all into the contest. Comedians feel they are turning themselves inside out to get us to laugh. Actors frequently lay their vulnerabilities, their deepest selves, out for spectators' view. "Our job is to explore every weird, mixed-message facet of our personality, bring that to our nerve endings, and translate and communicate it, like an arrow, to another target," Jodie Foster told an interviewer about acting. "Being an actor is some kind of neurosis, like being an athlete. Why else would you want to feel pain? It's the need to communicate your innermost feelings to people you don't even know. Why would you want people you don't know to know these things about you?"

Stars work under a particular cloud—the chance that the risks they assume will not be surmounted and that failure will occur. For most people, a failure at work is noticed by few; for a star, failure can bring disgrace in the eyes of millions. The quarterback who last year led his team to triumph is this year, after a few losses, greeted with thunderous boos. Crooner Robert Goulet, stepping up to sing the national anthem before the Muhammad Ali–Sonny Liston heavyweight championship bout in 1965, forgot the words in front of a worldwide audience of tens of millions. When Roger Maris entered a batting slump he received more public notice than when he had been hitting superbly. Marilyn Monroe *(photograph 23)* was haunted by a fear of failure, and to British interviewer W. J. Weatherby in 1960 she confessed, "There were times on *The Misfits,* in those emotional scenes, when I had a feeling I'd fail however hard I'd try, and I didn't want to go to the set in the morning. I was sorry then I wasn't a waitress or a cleaning lady and free of people's great demands. Sometimes it would be a big relief to be no longer famous."[1]

Whenever failing, a star dies a small death. The comedian who works with an unresponsive audience and cannot bring them to laugh is said to "die." Pitcher Jim Bouton reports in *Ball Four* that when a major-leaguer falters and is sent back to the minors, he "dies." When critics spot inadequate performances they are quick to swoop in upon the carrion, adding to the performer's distress. Ali MacGraw related about the critical reception to her acting in a television miniseries: "After *Winds of War* I never thought I'd work again. *Time* magazine did a cover story on the show, and I couldn't have been more shocked to find out that they thought it was terrific—except for a singularly atrocious performance by me. I didn't read any of the rest of the reviews. I only heard they were all awful. Hurt? I was devastated. I felt absolutely worthless."

To stave off such failure and avoid the abject humiliation of flopping before millions of people, a star's only recourse is to work even harder than before, to prepare even more strenuously. A number of stars are recognized by their intimates as perfectionists. According to biographer Geoffrey Wansell, Cary Grant's "compulsive perfectionism made him endlessly question everything on the set, every piece of furniture, every accent, every line of dialogue." Some stars labor so relentlessly that they have no private life at all. Week long, dawn to dusk, they apply themselves to their craft. Raymond Burr, looking back over his career, said that the "Perry Mason" series was "the only thing I regret in my life—I'm sorry I spent nine years of my life tying myself down. I couldn't be married, have a family, even have friends."

A few stars work so intensely in practice and performance that they eventually harm themselves. A singer may wail through session after session until nodules sprout on her vocal cords; a football star may launch himself play after play until his kneebones have splintered beyond repair. According to Marilyn Monroe's biographer, Fred Lawrence Guiles, her drive to perform successfully was destructively ferocious; he writes that "excessive abuse of her innate sensibilities—for Marilyn plunged soul and body into each film—eroded her emotional stability. Within a few years, her work undermined her psychic balance to such an extent that her personality and behavior were noticeably affected."[2]

The pressures to perform successfully impinge even more fiercely upon child stars. As youngsters they have an undeveloped sense of the proper balance between work and the rest of life, and can be easily misused. California lawmakers eventually recognized this danger and instituted codes for the protection of young film performers. Nevertheless, as ex–child star Diana Cary ("Baby Peggy") observed, the studios and parents found it to their financial advantage to keep children at work as much as possible; schooling "was simply an obstacle, to be gotten around with the maximum speed and minimum time."[3] Dick Moore concurred, reporting that only a handful of his fellow child stars received enough education to make them eventually admissible to a college.[4]

Like their seniors, child stars had to cry on demand, and they often found this particularly difficult. "In almost every film kids did there was a crying scene," Moore related. "Crying on cue was a source of both pride and anxiety." When Shirley Temple was very young the production people would simply tell her that she could not have lunch, and she would weep. After this trick no longer worked, one of her directors said, "I'd take her aside and tell her, 'Now Shirley, I want you to think that you'll never see your mother again. Think hard, she's gone, gone for good. She'll never, never, never come back.' I'd go on like that and pretty soon the tears would boil out of her."

Not surprisingly, successful work by child performers is rarely achieved without significant personal costs. Gary Coleman, a young television star, said in 1986, "Unless you're prepared to have only 30 percent of something memorable from your childhood, or nothing at all, you shouldn't be in this business." The pressure to perform well can be overwhelming; after years of superior work Kristy McNichol abruptly withdrew from acting in 1983. Later she explained, "It was just exhaustion, stress, and constant pressure without taking enough time out just to be a kid."

Whether adult or child, the chosen player becomes a star because performances can be relayed to a gargantuan spectatorship through the technologies of mass communication. It is curious, therefore, how much of the work of a star is not mediated, but rather achieved in live performance. (The whole idea of "live" performances, it should be pointed out, is a neologism, since before Edison developed the phonograph and moving pictures, no "nonlive" performances were possible.) The starring athlete plies his or her trade in stadiums before fans numbering in the tens of thousands; only then is the performance conveyed to the millions at home. Rock stars execute their best performances live to crowds of raving enthusiasts, who subsequently buy the recorded songs or videos. Comedians regularly try out their material on live audiences, practicing for the unseen throng of television viewers or moviegoers. Even Hollywood actors feel the occasional need to attempt stints in the theater, to hone their skills in front of people in the quick.

The live performance, seemingly archaic in the era of mass media, is actually crucial, for it is the way leading players maintain rapport with their audience. To a greater or lesser extent, depending on the performer and the entertainment field, stars must resort to this ancient mode of contact in order to sense the audience's pulse. Here is where subtle matters of movement, timing, and execution can be adjusted before responsive humans. Asked how she learned to deliver her "Moonlighting" lines, Cybill Shepherd replied, "I learned about comedy doing dinner theater, because a live audience is your best teacher." Therefore, although stars owe their fame to the broad dynamics of the mass media, they owe their performing facility to the smaller dynamics of the live audience—the one and only touchstone in the vapors of electronic entertainment.

In live performance a star's work becomes even more difficult. When there is a time lag in the delivery of the mediated performance, the opportunity exists for editing and revising the entertainer's effort: a better scene can be substituted, a better musical track can be selected. But there is no such capability to correct live performances; the risks are going to be greater, the threat of failure more harrowing.

In addition, when performing live a star usually loses another of the major advantages of the electronic media: its ability to transmit the performance everywhere, enabling the star to avoid the hardships of travel. Live performances frequently involve touring; instead of the performance being circulated to the nation electronically, the star circulates in person. Thus the star baseball or basketball player spends a large part of his professional life on airplanes, in strange hotels, in distant cities, in a constant state of dislocation; yet the expectation remains that he will perform with as much finesse and power as if he were at home. Musicians on tour are in a relentless, debilitating cycle of unpacking, setting up, packing again, and moving on. When Elvis began to tour again in 1971, Priscilla Presley described what it was like to accompany him: "Jump off the plane, rush to the hotel, unpack as little as possible, since you had to check out the next day, go to the performance, then back to the hotel for a little rest before heading back to the airport."[5]

Bringing a live performance to audiences is exhausting. The average major-leaguer loses four to eight pounds a game; singer James Brown typically loses seven. The strain of it all is indisputable, and may be the reason that Brian Wilson of the Beach Boys suffered a mental breakdown while on tour. Touring can also be mortally hazardous, as when Patsy Cline, Buddy Holly, and Rick Nelson died in plane crashes.

And yet despite the costs and the risks attendant on live performance, stars press on. George Carlin remarked, "A stand-up comic wants to take risks, which are big in terms of immediate failure and in terms of never getting rewards. So what he or she hopes to get from it must be pretty good stuff to risk the down side, because it's real rejection when they don't like you." Stars are driven by the desire to display their talent, to entertain well, and to receive the uplifting surge of appreciation from the audience. As Bruce Springsteen said, "Some nights when I'm up there, I feel like the king of the world. It's the greatest feeling on earth. I get the strength and energy to do it from the crowd."

Entertaining the American public is the beginning but hardly the end of the work of stars. The grinding exertion of the performer's act is only half the challenge. Stars perform in several other domains as well—in one of which they are compensated, and in the others not, at least not directly.

The first type of supplemental performance is scarcely exalted, but the star is paid so well that it silences any reservations. As personalities for hire, stars will be taken on by advertisers, who will put them to work in commercial messages. There the star's job is only partially to entertain; the real task is to get consumers to buy things. If the advertising is going to appear in print, stars need only appear for a photography session and suffer through it, but if television is the medium, then stars must fully perform—perhaps in miniature, but omitting no steps. They must be prepared, costumed, made up, run through, directed, drilled, and steeled for many repetitions. A thirty-second spot may be as elaborate as Michael Jackson's 1985 production number for Pepsi-Cola, but even if it is as plain as George C. Scott's addressing the camera and commanding people to buy Renault automobiles, celebrities' time and energy are requisitioned, not to mention their professional (if hypocritical) probity. Stars who are successful at this sort of activity— Bill Cosby, for example—perform as well in these messages as in any regular production, and vastly augment their income. According to the Screen Actors Guild, its members receive about 60 percent of their income from commercials; this may approximate the overall proportion for those in the star echelon, too.

As well as appearing in mass-media advertising, stars are also hired by advertisers to make so-called personal appearances (like "live audience," another neologism needed for the age of electronic communication, when nonpersonal appearances are possible). On these occasions the star is trotted out for brief viewing in the flesh: a one-time athletic star, having appeared in a beer company's commercials, says a few enthusiastic words to a meeting of distributors; a glamorous actress has something to offer to a convention of perfume industry executives. At other times the affair is less formal and the star is not required to deliver any lines from the podium, but simply to mingle gingerly with those assembled. Stars can be retained at a price for openings or ceremonies. When in 1986 the Sun Valley ski resort celebrated its fiftieth anniversary, it was something other than coincidence that brought George Hamilton, Brooke Shields, Paul Newman, Mary Lou Retton, Janet Leigh, and Jamie Lee Curtis to the affair.

Making money for others in these ways, some stars recognize they can do the same sort of work for themselves and keep the gain. Either independently or in cooperation with established businesses, they will formulate their own product lines and proceed to promote them. Jane Fonda worked to stimulate sales of her workout book to the general public, as well as sales of exercise studio franchises to entrepreneurs. Sylvester Stallone took an interest in the merchandising of Rambo paraphernalia. In 1987 Elizabeth Taylor went on tour to promote her perfume, Elizabeth Taylor's Passion; she was disappointed to find that reporters were less interested in the product than in her budding romance with George Hamilton.

Inadvertently Taylor was giving another sort of "performance": the revelation of her personal life. For in addition to their work as athletes or artists, and as hawkers of goods, celebrity entertainers are also compelled to disclose some of their after-hours existence. Americans are so riveted by stars that public gaze strains to bore on through to whatever happens offstage, offscreen, off-field. The populace wants to know about celebrity players' loves, pregnancies, progeny, purchases, illnesses, pets, and so forth—endlessly. Is there any other role in American life whose occupants are queried about their night clothes? Marilyn Monroe once said she had nothing on in bed except the radio, and the nation twittered ecstatically.

Most stars find this thirst for intimate details to be the most unpleasant aspect of their work, although fans may find it difficult to understand why. After all, stars do not have to exert themselves for this aspect of their performance; it takes no preparation or effort—all they have to do is acquiesce to general curiosity. Could stars' reluctance stem from the fact that they are not directly paid for this sort of exhibition? Leading more mundane existences, we do not hear many calls to bring our own private lives out into public view, and we might even think it flattering that so many others would want to know us so fully.

But this extra exposure is difficult for leading performers to sustain. Just as there is no perfect accord between the persons we are on the job and the persons we are off, so a performer is not the same off duty as when in the star role. After hours players like to step out of the star role and to rest and repair, just as we take leave of our occupations until the workday begins again. Chris Evert said about her onetime date, Burt Reynolds, "I envisioned him as someone who would be totally 'on' all the time, but he wasn't. Among friends, totally natural, he yearned just to ease back on the throttle." No one wants to be on the job every waking moment, especially a job as demanding as a star's. No wonder Henry Fonda, eating breakfast one morning when on location, snapped at a gawking bystander, "Young lady, someday I'm going to come over to your house and watch *you* eat breakfast."

Some stars will categorically resist this sort of disclosure. Yul Brynner objected that "how I brush my teeth, or what goes on in my family, is none of the public's business. If the public's interested in me, let it buy tickets." Nevertheless, most stars acknowledge that something resembling their private self has to be made part of their public performance, and they attempt to make their peace with this extraordinary intrusion. They will try to be buoyant and presentable when they leave the refuge of their homes. As Sammy Davis, Jr., said, "Whenever you step outside, you're on, brother, you're on." Joan Crawford took this responsibility quite seriously: "I owe everyone on that street, including the doorman, when I walk out, to look like Joan Crawford, movie star." While married to Elizabeth Taylor, Richard Burton once commented about the length of time it took her to get dressed: "She'll take about three hours. We're only going around the corner, but she treats everything like a premiere."

How do stars avoid being seared by this intense public fascination with their private lives? Media scholar Joshua Meyrowitz has developed an analytical scheme that may help explain how they withstand.[6] As Meyrowitz sees it, people (stars included) conduct their lives and maintain their emotional balance by shifting back and forth between "onstage" behaviors and "backstage" behaviors. "Onstage" occurs with the performance of a social role such as salesman, mayor, mother, or star; "backstage" is when people momentarily shuck the role and let their hair down. For celebrity performers, some of their backstage behavior, or private life, must form part of their onstage behavior, or public life. The celebrity's only recourse, writes Meyrowitz, is to develop an even more secret "deep backstage" region, where true privacy can occur. The star then permits normal backstage matters to be revealed, and so buys off the audience. Thus stars, while pretending to let prying eyes see some of their private lives, and in fact while making this part of their overall performance, actually manage to preserve adequate privacy.

Problems arise when these small and premeditated disclosures of a star's offstage life turn out to be insufficient to appease public inquisitiveness. Yet more is asked of the star—more than he or she is able or willing to exhibit. Under these conditions where demand exceeds supply, whatever the star attempts to hold private is subject to reckless invasion. Sometimes the star is caught unprepared. Paul McCartney tried to convey the flavor of this to an interviewer: "So I go on holiday and I'm building sand castles with the kids, and I really hate having to hold my stomach in the whole time in case there's a photographer behind a bush. It drives me mad."

"A photographer behind a bush" is not just a figure of speech; it is in fact a common way in which a star's hard-won privacy is violated. Priscilla Presley described kissing her husband while they were sunning themselves at their backyard pool in Los Angeles, and hearing the click and whirl of a camera mechanism from a photographer concealed in the landscape. Stars' dismay over candid photographs can be hard for fans to understand. When Kareem Abdul-Jabbar resisted the efforts of an Italian tourist to take pictures of him in a Phoenix mall, sympathy in the ensuing flak may have gone to the vacationer. In normal lives an unexpected snapshot is unlikely to be consequential, in part because the audience for it is sure to be small. And aren't stars, who constantly expose themselves to cameras in their lines of work, really expecting to have their pictures taken whenever and wherever? It would seem to be part of their job.

But a star sees unregulated picture taking in a different light. As Elizabeth Taylor once explained, a star's image is his or her stock in trade, and it has to be carefully protected. A photograph of a star taken offstage and out of performance is not only a discourtesy; if it is disseminated it can jeopardize the image that the star has worked so hard to create, and which is the essence of his or her work life. Thus stars can react unpleasantly, even hostilely, to attempts to capture them on film when they are not performing. After three photographers followed Paul Newman and Joanne Woodward into the lobby of their

New York City apartment building, one reported, "He just went crazy. He said we were trespassing and cursed and pushed and shoved us. We all ducked when Joanne swung her bag at us."

When Martina Navratilova, following her loss at the 1982 U.S. Open tennis tournament, grabbed the camera of a snooping photographer and exposed his film, we may be mystified at her vehemence, and the judge who fined her $50 may think her remiss, but what she did was perfectly logical from the star's point of view. She was refusing to allow a moment of private grief to become a part of her public performance. When John McEnroe pushed an Australian photographer over a chair, he was exercising the same determination to decide what images would and would not be a part of his public performance. Sean Penn was on location in Macao when a local photographer tried for some unauthorized shots and was tossed around; the photographer groused, "Sean Penn is unlike any other celebrity I have encountered," but in fact the opposition of stars to off-screen, out-of-performance pictures is common. The frequency of stars' resistance prompted critic Rex Reed to suggest facetiously that "the quickest way to become a celebrity is to hit a photographer." The truth is much the opposite: a quick way to fall out of the star role is to lose control over what is photographable performance and what is not.

The great number of reclusive celebrities in the short history of stardom testifies to the hardships involved in making one's private life part of public performance. Of the original triumvirate, Mary Pickford and Charlie Chaplin clearly disliked disclosing anything about their personal lives; only Douglas Fairbanks, Sr., fully mastered the art of appearing open and yet shielding himself at the same time. Greta Garbo carefully protected her privacy all her career, as did Marlene Dietrich, who when well into her eighties told Maximilian Schell, "I have never mixed privacy with my profession." When Schell evinced interest in making a documentary about her, she responded, "No one has, no one ever will, enter my private world." Ted Williams reacted haughtily to efforts by the press and public to know him better, and Montgomery Clift *(photograph 24)* was repelled by the demands that he reveal more of himself.

Clift's recoiling was due both to the common desire of performers to protect their privacy and also to his special situation as an active homosexual. In a period when deviation from perceived norms was tolerated even less than usual, he was vulnerable to humiliating disclosure and ostracism. As his fame increased, so did his terror of exposure. Between films he lived away from Hollywood in New York City, where he felt he could conduct his personal life in relative obscurity.

The star who is perhaps best-known for refusing to allow any of his private life to become part of his public performance is Marlon Brando. "My private life is my business," he told a reporter in 1986, reiterating his position of some thirty years' standing. "I have no right to ask you personal questions. Why, because I'm an actor, have you the right to ask me?" On the rare occasions when Brando is interviewed, it is under strict guidelines: only professional or philosophical questions, and nothing about people, especially friends, children, or wives. He has done so well at concealing his private life that, in spite of his notoriety, it is not known how many times he has been married or how many children he acknowledges.

It is a comment on the hunger of Americans to "know" stars that we take the reclusiveness of those who refuse to reveal themselves to us and convert that very trait into personality data. Whatever Greta Garbo and Marlon Brando were truly like, we have integrated their secretiveness into the images we hold of them. In our mind's eye, Garbo was quiet and deep, Brando's reticence a surface hiding inner turbulence. Garbo may in truth have been a chatterbox and Brando a cipher, but no matter—we've got them this way. Whether they wanted to be known intimately by us or not, we were determined to do so.

Between Star Village and the public cascades a stream of information—or what is made to look like information—about performers and their performances. Americans are told about this upcoming movie and that concluded ballgame, about a star's old habits or new aspirations. Some of this material is placed by publicists working for stars or the stars' employers, and some of it is gathered by journalists working in theory for the spectators. Publicists and the press operate more or less in collusion, and keep the flow steady.

It is easy for some commentators to dismiss this content as worthless drivel. But in spite of the charge of being inconsequential, information about stars must be considered among the most significant content of modern communications—witness the amount of media time and space devoted to it every day. This material helps performers and audiences adjust to each other, finding a relationship that is mutually satisfactory. It assists in the modulation and continuance of the relationship—sometimes by filling in the low spots in a star's career, sometimes by controlling audience fervor. It comprises a large portion of the messages that course through American society, and which foster a sense of cultural unity.

The types of stories about stars have remained fairly constant over the history of stardom, but the vehicles for their dissemination have changed. For many years the principal medium was fan magazines. As soon as movie stars were identified by name and the thirst of the audience for information about them was recognized, these publications began to appear regularly. The first, in 1911, was *Photoplay*, brought out by the appropriately named Cloud Publishing Company. Martin Levin reports about this sort of publication that "the wonderful, nonsensical catalysis of films and ballyhoo hits its apogee in the 1930s and begins to lose altitude rapidly in 1941."[7]

Fan magazines were gradually eclipsed by newspaper gossip columns. In these syndicated columns items planted by publicists, items dug out by the columns' legmen and legwomen, and items spitefully tattled by stars' detractors were all blended into a potpourri of information about stardom. These materials constituted much of what Americans knew about celebrity entertainers.

In the 1940s the two grande dames of star gossip were Louella Parsons and Hedda Hopper. Born Louella Rose Oettinger and Elda Furry, these rivals altered their names much like the performers they covered. At their peak they claimed a combined readership of 75 million, almost half the nation's population. Because they had such sway with the public, they inspired awe throughout the Hollywood community, particularly among stars. Ingrid Bergman, arriving in Hollywood from Europe and seeing everything with fresh eyes, later told an interviewer: "I was very surprised at the power those women had. People were so afraid of them and everyone read their columns—I think it was the first thing they turned to, never mind about the war. It just stunned me they were so important." Hopper liked to gesture dramatically at her mansion in Beverly Hills and say, "That's the house that fear built."

In the interest of maintaining their places in stardom, the leading performers of the 1940s curried favor with Hopper and Parsons. Stars tried to make sure their studio publicists would forward only the tidbits that were consonant with their image and would advance their careers. They telephoned the two women directly with "scoops." They tried in every way possible to ingratiate themselves with the writers; Bergman recounted, "I knew they were against me because I never sent gifts. They couldn't get into their houses on Christmas Eve for all the gifts they were sent!"

Indeed Hopper and Parsons were hostile toward Bergman and Charlie Chaplin and a number of other celebrity performers. If top stars began to waver in their careers, the duo would rush in and try to knock them over. George Eels wrote in *Hedda and Louella* that "the truly first-rate seemed to infuriate them. Charlie Chaplin, Orson Welles, Greta Garbo, Katharine Hepburn, Laurence Olivier, and Vivien Leigh all received harsh treatment."[8] Part of their social function, it appears, was to bring about the downfall of those stars who were too lofty to tend their public image carefully. They pruned the celestial pantheon and thus appeased those elements of the public who liked to see the mighty fall.

They were somewhat better at destroying stars than at making them. The newcomers they mentioned and the featured players they promoted did not suffer from the exposure but were not necessarily elevated either. The columnists' chief positive service was one of star maintenance, of keeping entertainers' names and deeds before the public so they would not succumb to general indifference.

The two frequently got facts scrambled. Parsons once reported that "Conrad Nagel's latest heartbeat is Clare Olmstead. They were a devoted twosome the other eve at the Brown Derby." The next day she had to amend: "Clare is a he and not a glamorous female." Hopper often did not bother to retract her errors; her inclination was to forget mistakes and plunge onward. Perhaps she was correct in her assumption that truthfulness was not the point. Benny Rubin, a comedian, was once attacked by Parsons for drinking excessively and hitting a woman with his violin. When they happened to meet he told her that he did not drink and did not own a violin. Parsons realized she had confused him with someone else and said, "Oh, how can I make it up to you?" He replied, "Just keep printing my name." He was acknowledging the service that the columns provided for stars—keeping their names in print and before the public.

While the heyday of the gossip columnists is past and the mode of distribution for star information has changed, the kinds of stories and the interests of the audience remain constant. Today there are a variety of channels for this communication. Newspapers, in addition to devoting complete sections to the accomplishments of sports stars, have added more wire-service accounts of entertainers. The subscriber to a regional newspaper on October 31, 1984, to pick a day at random, could read that Kristy McNichol did not have a "chemical imbalance"; that baseball pitcher Steve Garvey might be appearing on an ABC series; that Dolly Parton had a new Christmas album out; that Tiny Tim's daughter Tulip was now a teenager; that Victoria Principal was not going to leave her show; that Bette Midler was considering a new movie script; that Morgan Fairchild would not be shot by a nonunion photographer; and that Paul Mc-Cartney said he had found happiness. For many Americans this material is the sum and substance of their daily news; few readers avoid it entirely.

Star information appears in other periodicals, too. Weekly supermarket tabloids like the *Star* and the *National Enquirer* carry a large quota of stories about leading performers. Magazine sales soar when an actor or athlete is pictured on the front cover and the story within spells out every facet of the latest triumph or tragedy. And since 1974 *People* has kept an enormous audience informed of the comings and goings of leading performers. Its original managing editor, Dick Stolley, has said about the magazine's success that "the country was in the need for a celebration of the individual. We caught the wave."

Television also conveys information about stars to the nation. They are discussed on the sports segments of broadcasts, on MTV, on shows like "Entertainment Tonight"; they participate in celebrity golf matches or "roasts" to further their images; they appear on television talk shows, local and national, to sell their latest film or recording; they submit to interviews on the morning news shows or by Barbara Walters.

Attempting to control this information that appears in the print or electronic media is considered to be a critical part of stars' work lives. Bob Hope's career was strengthened by his close supervision of his press releases and judicious selection of media contacts. According to Kitty Kelley, "Little has been printed about Sinatra that wasn't first shaped and refined by his publicists. Over the years writers had to cooperate with his press agents or they didn't get a story."[9] The star rides a tiger of public information; if he or she cannot control the tiger, it can devour him. Errol Flynn's reputation suffered when stories came out about his relationship with the nubile Beverly Aadland. Suddenly he began to look more like a child molester than an enviable sexual athlete.

Stars hold to certain professional goals that aim to govern the flow of information about themselves. These goals may not always be articulated, but they are binding nonetheless. First, the fires of public adoration can die back but they must never be allowed to go out. At appropriate moments the embers need to be stirred with planted items and strategic exposure. Second, whatever kindles public interest must complement the star's image; to violate type is to risk dropping out of stardom. It is all right for Stacy Keach to be caught with cocaine while entering England; he plays tough-guy roles, and this episode adds appropriate scarring to his persona. But it is not all right when the same thing is reported about Judy Carne; she is supposed to be frolicsome and light-hearted. Third, with public attention not extinguished and with image intact, the star must draw the audience to the latest performance. Publicity must be managed so that large numbers of people will once again want to observe the star at work. In this profession, audience size remains the ultimate gauge of success.

To swell the dimensions of the audience, the release of information about a star is frequently tied to upcoming performances. If a miniseries is about to be televised, a movie distributed, an album released, or the play-offs to commence, then the star is urged to submit to a series of interviews and photo sessions. Most stars acquiesce to this responsibility and would agree with Gloria Swanson, who said, "I feel that it's your duty to the studio, or whoever is hiring you, to do as much as you can for the exploitation of a picture." A record may have been set by Liberace, who in one year sat through over 200 interviews.

Yet to be scrutinized and questioned at close range by an interviewer is not easy. On the occasion of her eightieth birthday Katharine Hepburn told a reporter, "Death will be a great relief. No more interviews." Stars are practiced at engaging large audiences, but in one-on-one interview sessions they are expected to act in a more restrained and disclosive manner. They must affect this smaller performance successfully, pretending all the while it is an intimate conversation, yet knowing that whatever they say, however casually, is going to be immediately dispatched to an extensive readership. This contradictory situation, where carefully chosen words are to be aimed at both the one and the many, can only be stressful and draining. In one of his few interviews, Michael Jackson uneasily confessed, "I'm not as comfortable now as I am onstage, 'cause that's where I was raised." Ostensibly passive in interviews, stars must in actuality control the situation, promoting themselves strongly but not beyond the point that all credibility is lost. Charles Higham, who interviewed many Hollywood stars, once noted naively that whenever he moved a conversation away from the performer or the performance, the star would appear to lose interest. He took this as a reflection of stars' egos, but it is just as likely that the stars were discreetly trying to steer the conversation back to the business at hand.

Compounding the difficulty of interviews from the star's point of view is that, since most celebrity entertainers are inaccessible most of the time, the interviewer is likely to take advantage of this rare availability and to delve into the star's personality and private life. Martina Navratilova observed that "reporters gain an interview by claiming to be interested in tennis, but you know they're going to ask about your love life." Or as Marlene Dietrich tersely put it, "They want you to bring out your intestines."

Some leading performers sense they are not going to fare well in interviews and simply refuse to do them, in spite of all the incentives. A surprising number of starring athletes never accede to requests for interviews. Clark Gable rarely gave them. Cary Grant did only a few print interviews, and none on television. Montgomery Clift avoided interviews after his career was in high gear, although his friend Elizabeth Taylor reproved him for it. Decades later, she too became leery of interviews, giving them only when she felt she absolutely had to. "After my first movies," Robert De Niro said, "I gave interviews. Then I thought, 'What's so important about where I went to school, and hobbies? What does any of that have to do with acting?'" Thereafter he refrained.

Stars must also submit to regular photo sessions, often when dressed as in the performance being publicized. The famous quarterback will pose with his shoulderpads and shirt on, the leading actress will have a number of stills taken in her soap opera costume. Being photographed may not be as trying as an interview's verbal sparring, but neither is it effortless. Joan Collins related, "Nobody realizes how exhausting photographic modeling can be. Sitting or standing with a frozen smile or a sultry sulk on one's face for hours and hours under hot uncomfortable lights, wearing ridiculous outfits and trying to look as if this was a joyful or significant experience takes an enormous amount of discipline and concentration."

The effort is warranted, though, because in an age of visual communication what the photographer captures is the essence of what the publicly perceived image will be. Dietrich attentively supervised her sessions, specifying how she was to be posed and lit; she even directed the retouching afterward. Each print needs to be carefully checked before it is released; Marilyn Monroe put much time and effort into the selections, once mentioning that photographers thought they made use of her but the truth was just the opposite. If placement in the media can then be influenced, it is all to the good from the star's point of view. For David Bowie, "It did not matter what people wrote. The right pictures in the right places would make him the greatest star of the century." [10]

If public attention upon a performer is especially intense at a given moment, it may be an economical use of the star's time and energy to participate in a press conference. In meeting a large number of correspondents and cameramen at one time, the star may feel more comfortable than in the bogus intimacy of the interview, and find it easier to perform. If the conference falters, however, and the star is not able to supply the necessary energy and intelligence, then the flub is going to be known universally because of the large number of newsgatherers in attendance. In 1986 Bob Dylan had to appear at a press conference publicizing a film. His behavior sank below his usual reticence, descending to the stuporous. Asked if he were being deliberately evasive, he mumbled, "I don't know."

The press corps that does nothing else but cover stars is sizable, providing further evidence of the importance of this kind of information in American life. About 2,000 correspondents will report from the Super Bowl and try to interview the leading players, while a World Series game will attract about half as many, representing the wire services, magazines, large newspapers, networks, makers of sports news films, and so on. Roughly 1,000 journalists cover the entertainment business with Hollywood as their regular beat—not quite but nearly the same number who are stationed at the seat of national government in Washington, D.C. Their numbers being so large, the competition among newsgatherers for the best stories and pictures is keen. They cannot always be satisfied with a routine interview, photo session, or press conference. Stars therefore are subjected to an extremely avid press, thundering after whatever story is hot at the moment. As Charlie Chaplin *(photograph 25)* stated about being besieged by the press, "Metaphorically, I was being devoured." Those close to the star are also susceptible; in her autobiography Vanna White wrote, "By now, anyone who's known me, no matter how casually, has been harassed by reporters who call them on the phone at all hours of the night and actually turn up on their doorstep!" Dealing with a ferocious press corps is part of a star's work life, and far from the most congenial part.

In 1974, as Hank Aaron was about to hit his record-breaking 715th home run, more than 100 reporters were assigned to keep tabs on him, both on the field and off. "The news media," he later said about his supreme effort, "was the only pressure I felt." Trailing him day and night, badgering him with inane questions, they almost got the best of the testy player: "The hardest part in going through breaking this kind of record is talking to people that don't recognize and understand baseball, and trying to be nice."

Stars often find themselves having to fend off an aggressive press. When Joe DiMaggio arrived at his first spring training in 1936, the publicity buildup had been so intense that he was advised to avoid all contact with the press and to let the hoopla simmer down. Chris Evert says that her husband John Lloyd helped her maintain concentration before a big match by diverting reporters from her. During the production of *Cleopatra*, nine-year-old Michael Wilding kept the press away from Richard Burton and Elizabeth Taylor, his mother, in an unusual but effective way: "It was insane. There were all these reporters and photographers. They tried to climb over the walls of the villa where my mother and Richard Burton were staying, even when we put cut glass on top of the walls. But for a kid it was fun. They let me stand down below and turn the hoses on the reporters."

To control the flow of information about themselves, stars need to have people on their side, working expertly and devotedly on their behalf. In the golden age of the movie studios, each star was assigned a publicist, to be joined by other publicists whenever a film featuring that star was being made. Together they cranked out the press releases that would usher a new film onto the market. But there was more to the work of a star's personal agents than beating the drums for a new performance. Sometimes the task was just the opposite: to dampen interest, or to suppress a particular story angle if it might prove injurious to the star's career. Bette Davis commented, "Studio press agents are your shield, your moat, your fortress against the world."

To this day, the promotion of the performance is only half the job of stars' publicists. To prolong a star's career publicists aim to modulate public response—quickening it during slack periods and as a new performance is about to begin, and squelching it if it threatens to get out of bounds or to fix on an unfavorable account. When Marilyn Monroe hired publicist John Springer, his job was to keep publicity to a minimum. James Garner said, "I hire a PR man just to keep people away from me."

No matter how hard stars and publicists try to control the flow of information, blatant untruths will occasionally end up in the media. Lana Turner, like most stars, was hurt but outwardly stalwart: "I have had to turn my back on outrageous fabrications, some of them sadistically cruel." Bette Davis, ever the trouper, observed in her autobiography that "a celebrity must and does expect and consequently hardens himself to all sort of erroneous coverage. If every time I was misquoted or misunderstood I had worried about it, I wouldn't have had time for a career."

But sometimes the distortions in the press are so flagrant that the star will look to legal remedies. In the 1950s *Confidential* magazine knew few limits in reporting fabricated scandal. When it stated that Maureen O'Hara had enjoyed sexual intercourse with a South American gentleman in the balcony of Grauman's Chinese Theater, she took the magazine to court and won a settlement. Where *Confidential* left off, the *National Enquirer* took up. Carol Burnett sued the publication over a story that reported she had been drunk and disorderly at a restaurant, and won. In 1982 the *Enquirer* published a story on a romance between Tom Selleck and Victoria Principal, although the two had never met. Selleck's libel suit was settled out of court, and the *Enquirer* printed a retraction.

If stars get indignant about lies, they can also get indignant about truths—when the truths are contrary to the image the star wishes to promote. If the press finds out that a star has been married more times than has been admitted or is not the age insisted upon, then feathers will be ruffled. Track star and golfer Babe Zaharias insisted she was born in 1914, until a reporter discovered that 1911 was the correct date. Liberace pretended that he was not a homosexual, and when publications dared to imply otherwise he would huffily maintain this ruse and sue. In two major court cases—one in England and the other in the United States—his bluff worked, and he won. Charlton Heston represented himself as a country boy whose favorite childhood pastime had been hunting rabbits; a reporter sought out his mother, who stated that Charlton had grown up in an affluent Chicago suburb and had "never hunted a rabbit in his life!"

A star's performance and the slivers of private life he or she cares to reveal are bundled together into a kind of projectile; press accounts provide the gunpowder and the wadding, and through the cannon of the mass media the sum is lofted into the body of American life. Then, as if following a law of physics, a mighty reaction can ensue in the form of public response. Dealing with this return flow of vehement popular adoration becomes a major preoccupation in the work life of a star.

It may seem surprising that public response is such a cause of concern. Acclamation is what performers have pursued so strenuously; aren't they getting what they wanted? The problem is not one of kind, but of degree. Some positive response is sure to be appreciated, for it signifies that the target of public regard has been struck. But in a mass society approbation can quickly become overwhelming, even threatening. Perhaps speaking for other stars as well, Tyrone Power *(photograph 26)* referred to his fans collectively as "the monster."

Messages pour in, bags and bags of them. The largest number of telegrams ever delivered to a single individual by Western Union did not go to a head of state, but to Hank Aaron when he finally hit his record-breaking 715th home run. Leo Handel observed that in 1950 stars expected about 3,000 letters a week.[11] In 1927 Clara Bow was on the receiving end of 10,000 weekly letters; 12,000 per week went to Gene Autry in 1939; Roger Maris in his banner year of 1961 averaged 3,000 a week; Sylvester Stallone in 1987 was confronting 6,000 epistles weekly.

In one of the few systematic studies ever undertaken to analyze the content of this outpouring, Leo Rosten in 1941 reported on 1,821 letters to two stars, one male and one female.[12] The writers were almost totally female (89.0 percent of the actor's mail and 86.5 percent of the actress's) and, in nine cases out of ten, under the age of twenty-one. The girls made a number of requests of the two stars, and Rosten listed a sample of them, to convey the flavor of fan mail:

    Cake of soap
    Piece of fur
    Lipstick tissues
    Salt and pepper set
    "Piece of gum you've chewed"
    Three hairs
    Shoe
    Telegram to cousin on birthday
    Cigarette butt
    Button from coat
    Autographed pair of shorts

Collar button
Blade of grass from the star's lawn
Banjo

Other fans were in a giving mood: one offered to say prayers for the star, and another offered to take the place of the star's dog. A prolix miss sent eleven pages of "I love you" written 825 times.

As a generality, letter writers want to enter into some sort of transaction with their idols. Many request something, but many others want to prompt the relationship by offering something. Thus stars can be deluged with unwanted devotional items. In the early 1940s Joe DiMaggio complained, "I've been getting all this fan mail, every day, and there's always a good-luck charm or something in every letter. It's just too much." Betty Grable had most of her gifts returned, but did develop a liking for the monogrammed handkerchiefs, which she kept; she soon had a drawerful. In their study of the public response to pop musicians, Fred and Judy Vermorel learned that many rock stars left instructions to discard all incoming gifts.[13]

A few leading performers actually attempt to answer this voluminous and eager correspondence; Joan Crawford was one who accepted this chore, laboriously dictating responses. Liberace employed a staff paid to reply to every letter. Others, like Vanna White, will open and answer a sample of the mail. But most stars simply ignore it, not having the resources or the inclination to exchange messages with fervid fans. Marshall Smelser wrote about Babe Ruth in 1923: "Fan mail cluttered Ruth's clubhouse locker. He usually threw it on the floor. The trainer opened those letters which seemed to be from businessmen, and the players opened the rest, most of which were from women, often uninhibited ones."[14] Shortly before his death in 1986, Cary Grant told an interviewer, "I must receive two sacks of mail every day. So you can't answer the people. You feel sorry you can't, especially when there are children concerned, but it can't be done." Stars will try to pass the responsibility of fan mail on to their employers, but today most entertainment or sports organizations find that the effort to respond is an inefficient use of their budgets and personnel, except when they are in the buildup phase of a new release and elect to distribute photographs. The Vermorels discovered that mail to rock musicians would be opened, cash or checks removed, and the letters consigned unread to the garbage.

One step better than a return letter, from the fans' point of view, is to encounter a star in person and obtain an autograph. A twentieth-century rage, the autograph provides devotees with an individualized emblem of their treasured idol. Obtaining an autograph means affirming the essential accessibility of the star. When Cpl. Elvis Presley was stationed in Germany, the only sign outside his rented house simply stated: "Autographs between 7:30–8:00 Only." Baseball players, having spent time in the locker room autographing balls, walk onto the field past young admirers who are leaning over the railing with pens and paper, clamoring for their signatures. Roger Maris, a churchgoing Roman Catholic, puzzled, "They even ask for autographs during Mass." Tiny Shirley Temple was taken to visit a department store Santa Claus, and afterward was miffed: "He asked for my autograph and said he saw all my movies." In the view of Cary Grant *(photograph 27)*, "This autograph evil, and I do think it is an evil, has got entirely out of hand." Many stars, like Katharine Hepburn and John Denver, simply make it a rule not to give autographs, since once they halt for one a crowd quickly collects and the signing becomes interminable.

Stars sometimes elicit another response when chanced on by members of the public: being stared at and commented upon as if they were inanimate objects (which to some extent, given their properties as icons, they are). But to be ogled in such an odd way is disquieting. Ingrid Bergman told an interviewer: "When you meet people, for instance, in an elevator, they talk about you as though you weren't there. 'She's much taller than I thought she was.' 'Doesn't she look nice?' And you're standing right next to them." Asked about the liabilities that celebrities endure, Jackie Collins—novelist, sister of Joan Collins, and inveterate Hollywood observer—replied, "I'd say the main drawback is that they can't do anything without being bothered. People watch them and say, 'Oh, he's shorter than he is in the movies,' or 'He's got a funny voice,' or 'He's fat,' or 'He's thin.' People always criticize celebrities in loud voices as if the celebrities weren't aware of them talking. Celebrities become objects, objects that belong to the fans."

For the privilege of staring at a star, fans will follow an entertainer into parties, restaurants, and even bathrooms. After an operation, Joe DiMaggio in his hospital bed came out of the anesthesia to find a man and woman looking beadily at him. They continued to stare while he tried to find his voice, then departed silently. Every day tour buses bring hundreds of Americans past the homes of celebrity performers, on the off-chance they will find a star outside and be able to peer at him or her. Before such buses were restricted in Beverly Hills in 1984, Lucille Ball said about the constant file of bus after bus, "You could smell carbon monoxide, and your eyes would tear." According to Ernest Borgnine, "When we lived in Beverly Hills, the tour buses used to come by packed with people hanging out the windows. I would be out watering the lawn and they would start shouting: 'There's Ernest Borgnine!' And I would shout at them, 'If I was Ernest Borgnine, with all his money, do you think I'd be watering the lawn?' And they would go away so disappointed."

The do-it-yourself admirer can be directed to stars' residences by one of several maps sold widely in the Los Angeles area. In New York a $5 "Celebrity Locator" pinpoints the apartments of some 120 eminent players, from Woody Allen to Pia Zadora. The fan who does not want to undertake a fruitless vigil can purchase from Celebrity Service, Inc., intelligence about whether the star is currently in town or not. Stars' telephone numbers can also be obtained from this firm; perhaps the pursuer will want to call ahead. Or perhaps not—whole families would appear unannounced at Liberace's doorstep or show up poolside. Even garbage from the homes of stars is not safe, as Bob Dylan learned in 1971 when someone removed and scrutinized his.

Sometimes stars have to live with the unremitting presence of fans camped at their front doors. As Clark Gable's popularity waxed in the late 1930s, packs of women hung around outside his Hollywood home, to his dismay. Marilyn Monroe took such surveillance gracefully; she always stopped to exchange pleasantries with a group that come to be known as the Monroe Six— four girls and two boys, approximately eighteen years old, who were stationed outside her residence in New York City. John Lennon tolerated the vigilant young women who stood across from his London mansion in all sorts of weather. But most stars

find such obsession discomforting and try to dissuade fans who
hang around too long. The worship can become unnerving: for
five years singer Joni Mitchell unwillingly suffered the presence
of an ostensibly harmless fanatic who pitched a tent across the
street from her house.

Mere observation, however, is frequently insufficient to satisfy the desires of the public. Stars also have to abide the elemental compulsion of people to touch them; being perceived by
sight apparently has to be confirmed tactilely. After she had won
a tennis tournament in Houston, Chris Evert was thronged by
spectators; "They didn't just want my autograph. They all
wanted to touch me," she recalled with a shudder. In Monroe's
account of this practice, "Everyone is always tugging at you."
Billie Jean King was equally appalled: "I hate it when strangers
touch me, even though I understand it is almost always for
love." Esther Williams's rule, bred of experience, was: "Walk
fast. Don't stop and shake hands. You touch them, they don't
touch you."

A number of fans, propelled by their ardent idolization, will
struggle to meet the stars in person. Every celebrity entertainer
has stories to tell about the efforts of people to make contact
with them. Rock stars are especially susceptible to overtures
from their admirers, since their publicity identifies them as
being in town and their youthful audience is extremely avid.
Rolling Stones fans would crowd all the entrances to the band's
hotels, and some would invariably manage to evade security
and infiltrate the musicians' quarters. In Los Angeles the
Beatles rented a house atop a supposedly impregnable cliff; the
perimeter alarms went off one night when two girls without any
climbing equipment managed to scale the height. Singer Jimmy
Buffett said that concertgoers often attempt to talk their way
backstage: "The common thing is to tell my road managers that
we have a relative in common." Someone once tried a more
headlong approach with Sean Penn, crashing a truck through
the gate of the actor's Los Angeles home.

Writer Bob Greene reported in 1984 on what some letter
writers said they would do to meet the members of the rock
band Motley Crue.[15] In a contest organized by a San Antonio
radio station, those with the best answers to the question,
"What would you do to meet the Crue?" would get to go back-

stage and greet the musicians. A thirteen-year-old girl volunteered, "I'd do it with the Crue till black and blue is all you can see." Another thirteen-year-old wrote about her favorite band member, "First, I'd spread whipped cream all over my body. Then, I'd let Vince Neil lick it all off." A fourteen-year-old boy offered his mother. Greene telephoned all the letter writers, and they confirmed their offers; the boy's mother said yes, she would do what she could to see that her son won the contest. Greene may have been amazed, but the fact remains that many Americans have an intense desire to draw close to their stars.

Romance is often on a fan's mind, and a star's pursuit by a love-struck follower can quickly get out of hand. Madonna reported, "People get these psychotic fixations on you. It's scary. Strangers feel like they know you because you are a public figure. I've had guys I've never seen before come up to me on the street and try to kiss me." Brooke Shields was the object of the affections of one Mark Ronald Bailey, who attempted to break into her New Jersey home; the judge put him on five years' probation. Lavon Muhammad of Los Angeles insisted that Michael Jackson was the father of her twins; she was arrested three times for trespassing on his property (the last occurring as she carried a bottle of champagne across his backyard), and was sentenced to 300 days in jail. While David Letterman was on the West Coast, a mentally ill woman who claimed to be his wife installed herself in his East Coast home.

John L. Caughey, a psychology professor at the University of Maryland, collected information on what he calls "artificial" relationships, which entail a fan yearning after a star of the opposite sex.[16] He examined seventy-two of these episodes, fifty-one initiated by female fans and twenty-one by males. Most such infatuations get no further than letters or telephone calls, Caughey reported, but when the intensity of the obsession increases beyond a certain point, then an element of pathology is introduced. Such was the case, he noted, when a sixteen-year-old girl made contact with Chicago Cubs first baseman Eddie Waitkus and at their first meeting shot him with a pistol. The desire to possess the star had reached its psychotic extreme.

Something similar was going on in the deranged mind of John Hinckley, Jr., the would-be presidential assassin. He did not try to possess his beloved Jodie Foster by shooting her, but took another route to that end. In his dementia, he aimed to kill President Reagan and thus be elevated to the great notoriety and appropriate status whereby he thought he could win her. John Lennon's murder by Mark Chapman is the capital instance of a star's inadvertent eliciting of insane and homicidal behavior. Although television actress Rebecca Schaeffer was not a full-fledged star, when she was killed in 1989 by a deranged fan leading performers everywhere began to wonder about their personal safety. Stars risk attracting psychopaths who are simply following the rays of public attention to their focal points. Lacking normal constraints, these psychotic killers act on their impulses to fuse with the nuclei of American culture.

The dread of being assassinated has thus become another worrisome aspect of stars' singular profession. Playing at Wimbledon, John McEnroe was the subject of a telephoned threat: "Don't let John McEnroe go on court today, or he will be assassinated." The death threats can pour in: Michael J. Fox received 5,000 menacing letters from an unbalanced shipping clerk.

In this murderous ambience, it is not surprising that stars try to protect themselves. When the situation calls for it, they hire bodyguards; depending upon circumstances, Sylvester Stallone has had as many as ten in his employ. Sometimes stars feel the need to carry lethal weapons themselves. When Cybill Shepherd went out for her daily jog not only did a bodyguard follow her, but she tucked a .38 revolver into her sweatsuit. Elvis Presley carried two pearl-handed .45s, plus a two-shot derringer in his boot. His most gnawing fear was that not only would he be killed, but that his assassin would live to boast about it; he made everybody on his payroll pledge that they would immediately retaliate if he were shot, so that no killer could survive the bloody scene.

As if the fear of a deranged murderer were not enough, celebrity performers are also exposed to another kind of threat from the public that can be even more frightening: at one time or another in their careers, most stars experience the virulence of crowds that have gotten out of control. From the day of Florence Lawrence's exposure to the riotous mob in St. Louis, crowd frenzy has been a fearful component of the work lives of stars. As an innocent publicity stunt for World Team Tennis in 1977, Chris Evert played a double match with Billy Carter as her partner. "Everyone was friendly and hospitable until the match ended. Then the crowd swarmed through the security guards and almost trampled me." She was left "humped over, shaking, waiting for additional security." Bobby Thompson recalled what happened after his last-ditch home run gave the New York Giants a National League pennant in 1951: "There was just this fantastic mob scene at home plate, and then it kind of turned into a riot. The next clear thing I remember was people trying to rip pieces of my uniform off. I thought, hey, I could get killed."

Although no star has yet died in this manner, the potential for serious harm under conditions of mob turmoil is altogether real. When the Beatles landed in San Francisco in 1964, airport authorities placed them in a steel enclosure for their own protection, then thought better of it and removed the foursome seconds before a surging crowd trampled and crushed the structure. Christina Crawford told of accompanying her mother and her nursemaid, Miss Brown, to a New York restaurant. When word spread that Joan Crawford was inside, a crowd began to build up on the sidewalk. As the party tried to leave the restaurant the throng became unruly. Mother and daughter managed to get through, but "Miss Brown was not with us. She'd been stabbed in the head with a ballpoint pen and had to be taken to the doctor."[17]

Such star mania has even been known to descend upon the supposedly professional press corps. In 1957 Marilyn Monroe, together with Laurence Olivier, held a press conference in a New York City hotel to announce their upcoming film, *The Prince and the Showgirl*. According to her biographer, "Then almost without warning, the scene at the Plaza had turned into bedlam. For a moment she was trapped. She was backed up against a wall. . . . This was her first major press appearance since her flight from Hollywood, and otherwise intelligent men were reduced that afternoon to frenzied baboons."[18] When she traveled on to London, her husband, the playwright Arthur Miller, experienced with her the crush of the press: "He recalls that it was a little like drowning. There seemed to be no air to breathe, voices became a muffled roar, and life stopped for the several minutes it took them to reach the ramp."

The spotlight of intense public attention, hard enough for stars to withstand, is no arena for amateurs. When Bruce

Springsteen married, his new mother-in-law pleaded with the press, "I knew this would be exciting, but I didn't know it would be this overwhelming." Myra Lewis, who made the mistake at age thirteen of marrying her cousin Jerry Lee Lewis and having the relationship made public, asserted later in life that she did not "ever want to marry anyone famous again." A real estate developer took his yacht, named *My Way Again*, on a 1984 vacation cruise and found himself rumored to be Frank Sinatra. Hundreds of fans jammed the wharf where he had innocently docked. They threw unwanted gifts on board, including sandwiches, salamis, and imported olives. Dick Cavett dropped by to visit. The Associated Press dispatched a wire story that brought out many more gawkers.

In the end the star, although epitomizing playfulness, cannot be rompish at all. He or she is a prisoner of sorts, held hostage by an unrelenting public fixation. Roger Staubach *(photograph 28)* complained that "for years I've been unable to treat my children to things like a baseball game. I resent that part of my notoriety." When John Lennon returned to Liverpool to play a concert, he confided to an old chum that he would love to be able to go out to a pub and have a quiet pint. According to Woody Allen, "My idea of a good time is to take a walk from my house to the office and not for the entire walk have to worry about hearing my name being called from a passing car or being spoken to at all. That would be perfect."

When celebrity performers wish to move about freely, they must often go to great lengths to disguise themselves. Garbo put on dark glasses and a big hat, Monroe wore a scarf and left off her makeup, Hedy Lamarr donned a blonde wig. A writer related about Michael Jackson at the peak of his fame, "While the people were working to make their hair and clothes and movements look more like Michael Jackson's, Michael Jackson sat in a hotel room applying a false moustache and a worn hat to try to look more like them. Like them, he found it easier to go out in the world in disguise."

Celebrity performers survive the exertion and fatigue of performance; they permit their privacy to be poked at; they work at their publicity; they suffer the indignities of being pawed by fans. But at bottom what makes them stars is that they do all this not for a short spell, but for the long haul—year after year, decade after decade. The average career length among the performers in this book's study of 100 stars was twenty-seven years.

The real work of the star is therefore the maintenance of a long-term persona. Stars often perceive this endurance in terms of steadfastness and pacing. Like long-distance runners, they must regulate their work lives, operating in the range that is short of exhaustion but above the point at which they will be bypassed. Professional athletes must try to keep a regular pace that will get them through a long season without burnout, and through the maximum number of playing years. There is no reason, in spite of the crowd's urging, to bring oneself to the breaking point and to end a career prematurely.

Similarly, Hollywood performers must work attentively at preserving and prolonging their hard-won stature. From the scripts made available and the opportunities presented, stars must carefully select the roles that will forward their public images. As well as for their intrinsic merit, roles are chosen to fit into the tempo of a star's career and to lend the most propitious exposure—neither too much nor too little. The star must cautiously play a cat-and-mouse game with public attention, trying to arrange appearances so that the twin perils of overexposure and underexposure are circumnavigated.

There is a decidedly physical side to the business of keeping a star's career running. More so than with most other occupations, stars must keep themselves fit. Whether athlete or actor, the star must watch his or her diet and exercise with regularity. Jane Fonda is hardly the only Hollywood performer to be obsessed with a flattering physique. Since the days of Douglas Fairbanks, Sr., and his home gymnasium, it has been an expectation that stars will be in good physical form. Cybill Shepherd's regimen was this: "I eat five or six small meals a day and concentrate on healthy foods. I work out for an hour three or four times a week, and 10 minutes five days a week. I also bicycle, race walk, and swim." If Sylvester Stallone was compelled to miss his daily exercise session, he felt blameworthy: "I go through withdrawal, I really do, when I can't work out. I think, 'My god, you're just falling apart, you're getting lazy, you're getting into that syndrome. You've made your money and now you're going the way of the dodo bird.'"

When stars do get flabby, as Elvis Presley or Bette Midler tended to, then their body size becomes a matter of public fascination, and expulsion from stardom looms as a possibility. As Elizabeth Taylor added pounds in the early 1980s, she grew more and more defensive: "I don't like questions about my weight because I don't think it's anybody's damn business." But because she was a star it was everybody's business. She became the target of comedians' vitriolic gibes; Joan Rivers could get an audience howling by saying, "I took Elizabeth Taylor to Mc-Donald's and she got stuck in the arch. I had to butter her thighs to get her out. I stood in front of her with a Twinkie and said, 'Come and get it.'" At this point Taylor had to begin dieting and exercising with determination to regain the figure the public demanded of her; the other choice was to remain a target of ridicule and be forced out of Star Village.

Mid-career, many performing artists seek medical help in maintaining their appearance. Clark Gable had to have a mouthful of decaying teeth removed and dental plates fitted; Burt Reynolds needed hair transplants. The plastic surgeon will be visited repeatedly. Face-lifts were had by Mary Pickford, Gary Cooper, Merle Oberon *(photograph 29)*, Rita Hayworth, Joan Crawford (at least two), Lana Turner, Henry Fonda, and Dean Martin. Cher confessed that "the reason I come off being sexy and attractive—I still can't bring myself to say 'pretty'—is because I have had myself rebuilt. I had the hair under my arms taken care of. And I had an operation to firm up my breasts. I'm the female equivalent of a counterfeit $20 bill." Michael Jackson reportedly had several nose jobs, cheekbone implants, a chemical skin peel, lip work, and permanent eyeliner. He admitted to getting a dimple put in his chin, and then having it taken out.

Cosmetic surgery can slow down the ravages of time, but it cannot halt them. The threat of aging out of one's persona constantly shadows performers, particularly women and athletes. There is only one other stratagem, and it is employed by all: to lie about one's age. Jim Bouton stated that baseball players routinely dissemble so that they will not be judged too old by their teams' front offices, and can thus lengthen their major league careers by a year or two. Many departed actresses, when their obituaries are compiled, are discovered to have been living with a discrepancy of several years between their stated ages and the ages indicated by their birth certificates. Dick Moore said that like most child stars, he and his parents falsified his age: "How do you kill the clock? We lied about my age. At eight, we said that I was seven; at nine, we said I was eight; at ten, I pretended to be nine."

By huffing and puffing at exercise, by consulting the plastic surgeon, by fibbing about age, stars are working hard to maintain the public image they have shaped. The difficulty of these efforts over the long haul depends in part on the degree of discrepancy between the image and the true nature of the performer. Rarely, of course, are the two identical. Hollywood entertainers are the most aware of the differences between themselves and the mediated personality; Charlie Chaplin referred to his film character as "the little fellow," and Jean Harlow remarked, "These are two distinct people; the Jean Harlow that's me and the Jean Harlow I see on the screen." Near the close of her career Katharine Hepburn described this sense of otherness to an audience at her alma mater, Bryn Mawr: "There's the image and presence that's been created on the screen, a product of my work and others. But then there's me. I'm very different from the Katharine Hepburn everyone seems to know. She's a legend. A creation of, by, and for the public. But I really don't know her. I'm sort of like the man who cleans the furnace. I just keep her going."

Sometimes the discrepancy is not a strain. John Wayne *(photograph 30)* hated horses but otherwise was ready to go to work. The wonderfully sinister onscreen personality can be good and decent off—witness Boris Karloff. Those who are calm and slow-paced in performance may be inwardly tense, as were Jack Benny and James Stewart.

But the gulf can be much wider. Those who play confident characters may be profoundly insecure. Clark Gable fretted and worried his entire life and was always ill at ease when meeting or socializing with people. A woman who dated him commented, "He was a dream and a darling, and the loneliest, most insecure man in the world. If we'd go to a party, he'd shake like a leaf." According to Katharine Hepburn, the longtime companion of Spencer Tracy *(photograph 31)*, "Living was never easy for Spence. He was deeply troubled—not at all like that totally confident figure the public saw up there on the screen." Performers trapped in a voluptuous image can be privately conservative, even prudish: Theda Bara, seductive in her movie roles, was highly proper in her personal life; Jane Russell the temptress would hardly recognize Jane Russell the devout wife and mother. Doting couples in performance may be incompatible in real life, as were Lucy and Desi, Sonny and Cher, and Ike and Tina Turner. A star with a paternal aura, like Henry Fonda, can turn out to be an uninterested father. And a star who can successfully play a devoted mother, as Joan Crawford did in *Mildred Pierce*, may be sadly deficient as a parent.

Oddly, screen paragons of passion are often unsuccessful at personal romance. Jean Harlow's love life was marred by her naïveté and chronic dissatisfaction, while Lana Turner, who thought sex was extraneous at best, entered into seven feckless marriages. Rudolph Valentino likewise was a failure at his two brief unions. And Cary Grant, who played the debonair screen lover to perfection, was a misfit as a romantic partner; he once reflected, "When I go courting, it's a very sad experience." In divorce court Grant's first wife described him as "sullen, morose, and quarrelsome." To an interviewer Grant allowed, "We are all the opposite of what we appear to be." Virile movie lovers may not even be heterosexual, as Americans were stunned to discover after Rock Hudson died from AIDS.

Vincent Furnier, who became famous as the rock star Alice Cooper, discussed how tiring the assumption of a performance persona can be: "I had to drink two bottles of whiskey a night just to cope with Alice. I say cope, because I felt I had to be Alice all the time, otherwise the audience would lose their love affair with Alice. What I didn't realize was that you can't live an intense character like that all the time—that's what happened to Jim Morrison and Keith Moon." Marilyn Monroe said that "I carry Marilyn Monroe around with me like an albatross."

As difficult as maintaining an established image may be, the work becomes all the more arduous when the audience's need for variation is sensed by the performer. It's time for a new twist, he or she may intuit. As John Travolta remarked, "You surprise people with a new ability, and that will keep up interest." But the performer now has to be exceedingly careful not to overdo anything, or he will violate the bounds of his niche in Star Village. In the words of Jackie Collins, "Being a celebrity is like walking a tightrope. You have to stay balanced the entire time and be very aware of where your next step must go. Otherwise you slip. And it all falls down." When Dolly Parton suddenly lost tens of pounds and sported a much slighter figure, she captured attention but also ran the risk that her shape would be found less endearing by the audience.

In contrast to Hollywood, the pop music world is much more tolerant, even encouraging, of alterations in images. The music industry is highly attuned to the annual wave of young new consumers. Each crop of teenagers is looking for its own particular sound and stars, and so a relatively greater premium will be placed on novelty rather than continuity. Pop performers who endure in the musical star ranks must therefore be prepared to transform themselves. Bob Dylan went from folk singer to rock singer to gospel singer and back to rock singer. A particular master of the fluctuating image, David Bowie has over twenty years adopted many guises: gay, bisexual, black (in sound and style), alien, "Thin White Duke," yuppie.

For the most part the public applauds its stars, whom it after all originally uplifted, and supports their efforts for an extended career. The audience will indicate a preference for certain kinds of details about a star's life, usually those that confirm and prolong the star's image. People wanted to hear folk wisdom and malapropisms from Yogi Berra, because he was the lovable type, just as they were interested in Billy Martin's scrapes, to the exclusion of any other information about him, because he was the abrasive type. In accounts about the Beatles, we were receptive only to the boyish escapades, never the churlish. Americans wanted to hear about Warren Beatty's single lifestyle because he was the available type, and they wanted to know about Paul Newman's married life because he was the desirable but unavailable type.

But at the same time that the audience buoys stars and lengthens their careers, a countervailing force is sometimes also at work. The public is often not adverse to seeing a celebrity entertainer stumble and fall. In most stars' careers there are moments when the rug is pulled out from under them. The comedian is greeted with deadly silence; the aging athlete leaves the playing field to a chorus of boos; the rock singer's fans never show up at the concert. Even Elvis Presley at times bombed in concert. Members of the public are sometimes waiting for a performer to turn up overfed and thick-tongued, or cancerous and wan. A small thrill occurs when a star is exposed as a tax evader or a drug addict. This latent destructive urge within the general public can find its gratification when an idol is rocked.

An airplane keeps itself aloft and flying forward through the relative balance of several elemental forces: thrust, drag, lift, and weight. Analogous forces work to keep a star on a long flight. There is the propulsive thrust of the star's skills in performance and the spark of new attributes; the practiced image that creates the rudder's drag; the enormous lift of public approbation; and the weight of vague public malice. As long as these forces remain in just proportion a star can wing through the firmament for decades.

One of the longest-lasting careers in the entertainment business was that of Bing Crosby. By making use of a technology just emerging in the early 1930s—the microphone and its amplification systems—Crosby was able to deliver a new kind of singing, one not requiring the booming voice of earlier popular baritones. His intimate, mellow tone lent itself to lyrics of highly affectionate content, and a love affair between performer and audience was struck up. The sales of his records far outstripped his closest rivals'.

So appreciative were Americans of this projected aura of affection that Crosby was able to slip easily over into a second career as a movie star. For five consecutive years, from 1944 to 1948 (longer than any other star before or since), Crosby was the top-ranked box office attraction in the United States. He starred in such films as *Going My Way* (1944), *Bells of St. Mary's* (1945), *Road to Utopia* (1946), *Road to Rio* (1947), and *The Emperor Waltz* (1948). Continuing to perform through the 1950s and 1960s, Bing ran up a total of almost 100 movies. Throughout his career he kept himself in good shape. Early on he conquered a penchant for alcohol and thereafter drank only moderately. He exercised regularly and played golf every day he could. He was on a golf course when he suffered a heart attack and died in 1977 at age seventy-four.

Crosby's lasting popularity was due to the personableness of his performance. The songs he sang and the way he sang them warmed and calmed the American people during periods of acute national distress—the Great Depression and World War II. The good-hearted movie roles he played enhanced this kindly image for years. His performances on stage and screen were reinforced by glowing press accounts of his personal life, for Crosby was always depicted as a loving family man. Bette Davis could be as affected by this emotionality as anyone else; in her autobiography she recounted a time when she was operating the Hollywood Canteen for GIs: "One Christmas Eve there was a knock at the kitchen door of the Canteen. I opened it and there stood Bing Crosby and his three very young sons. He grinned at me and said, 'I thought maybe we could help out tonight.' They sang Christmas carols for the next hour. There wasn't a dry eye in the Canteen. Bing's sons represented everything the GIs were fighting for—a country without war in the future for little boys like these."

Once the country had come through the war and families were forming at an unprecedented rate, Bing, his wife Dixie, and their four sons were seen as the model of a successful home life *(photograph 32)*. So well did Crosby do at this that after Dixie died in 1952, he played the devoted husband and father all over again with his second wife, Kathryn Grant.

All his professional career Crosby worried about his image and tended it carefully. He conscientiously read his fan mail and responded to it. It was fitting that he operated prudently, because apparently his public persona was widely at variance with his private temperament and behavior. For instance, in spite of the published accounts of his devotion to his wives, he was known throughout the entertainment industry as a unrepentant womanizer.

In truth, this man who personified affection to millions of people for decades was an unpleasantly emotionless person. One acquaintance revealed, "I don't think Bing had any real friends—cronies, yes, but not real friends. He was cold. Cold." Bob Hope, who knew Crosby for forty-five years and was paired with him in numerous films, could never call him a personal friend. Crosby's coolness extended to the members of his family, according to biographers Donald Shepard and Robert F. Slatzer.[19] He was unfeeling toward his first wife and absented himself as she was dying of cancer. He was distant toward their sons and occasionally vicious. His second wife fared no better;

in his will she was effectively barred, after twenty years of married life, from receiving any direct inheritance.

Yet because Crosby did attentively manage his image, choosing with care the songs he would record and the roles he would accept, and watching over his publicity, his strong relationship with the public was never breached. Performing so well, he was richly rewarded and became one of the wealthiest men in the United States, a millionaire many times over. By his diligence and through the concurrence of the audience, he had endured in the star role for a remarkably long time.

There is a tendency to see the work life of stars as a hubbub of action—the frenzy of performance, the fencing with the press, the constant application and resourcefulness that sustain a lengthy career. But focusing exclusively on these activities may conceal one of the more disagreeable features of the star's occupation: the sodden periods of enforced idleness. Richard Schickel wrote about stars: "Thus, people whose natures cry out for gregariousness, for play, for the center of attention, are left with endless empty hours, days, weeks, months to fill, yet have less natural capacity to occupy that time profitably than anyone else."[20] These lulls are trying and can be disabling.

Stretches of inactivity, when the energy of the performer is switched totally from go to stop, are also involved in performances. The singer waits in the wings, costumed and with heart racing, for the moment to go on. Until the defensive squad comes off the field, the quarterback sits on the bench, at first resting and then anxious to get back in the game. The baseball star impatiently squanders long minutes in the dugout, waiting to bat or to retake the diamond. Viewers see the star's performance in a television show or film as continuous, with one scene swiftly following another, but the actual production is ruled by a maddening number of starts and stops. The actor, primed to perform, has to stand by for tedious minutes and hours while the lighting crew and the sound people fiddle with their equipment, the director restages, the camera crew rehearses a difficult maneuver, the extras are called for or dispatched. Typically, a star spends four minutes out of every five on the set not performing, but waiting to perform. The intervals, the moments when the performance is held in check, can only be frustrating.

Dolly Parton, as a novice actress on the set of *Nine to Five*, found the protracted waiting to be agonizing beyond conception.

After performances are over there are longer lulls with even more devastating effects. The movie production is finished, the tour is done, the playing season has concluded, and the next major project is not scheduled until the following year. Stars can suddenly find themselves with a great deal of time on their hands. If the next engagement is not booked already, then they are—worst of all possible words—"available." Carlene Carter, the daughter of June Carter and stepdaughter of Johnny Cash, and the wife of rock singer Nick Lowe, says her mother advised her, "You've got to remember that when you're out on the road, everyone is telling you you're fantastic. Then you have to go home and you've got to be normal again. It's really hard to adjust, and you usually get the blues real bad." The doldrums set in.

For movie stars, as the spells of inactivity stretch on for months they can seem interminable and oppressive. Anthropologist Hortense Powdermaker remarked about the Hollywood figures she studied that "an actor is only half alive when he is not performing, and, unlike the painter or writer, he cannot work alone but must have a job in order to function. He will suffer privations for years in order to have this opportunity."[21] Montgomery Clift's biographer reported that he, like many actors, completely lost his sense of confidence, purpose, and identity when he was not working. John Wayne's wife stated, "There were days when he literally didn't know how to fill the empty hours. Duke could be a monster when he was bored, quick to anger and very demanding."

Other stars can turn to self-destructive behavior if they fail to cope with the dead spaces between performances. The use of narcotics can become particularly tempting. The wife of Rolling Stones musician Ronnie Woods observed that "a lot of musicians get into drugs when they've got nothing else to do with their time. So that's why I keep Ronnie busy all the time." In Bob Woodward's analysis of John Belushi's drug-induced decline, "Free time was the killer."

The inaction can continue until the star begins to wonder whether his or her career is over. For most working Americans retirement can be anticipated and reconciled to, but the star, unless retiring voluntarily, never has the benefit of foreknowledge. During slack periods it cannot be known with certainty whether the career is in a slump or is finished. The doubt gnaws at the celebrity entertainer; few accept such a time with equanimity. Henry Fonda remarked, "If I have something down the line—six months or a year away—then I can handle myself. But if it is a period when I have no offers, I think, 'Well, that's it, Fonda. Nobody will ever ask you to work again.'"

The work life of a star thus possesses an erratic quality whose severe abruptness is difficult to imagine. The irregularity of the occupation may at first be tolerable or even stimulating, but it quickly wears thin. Most Americans would find this sort of inconstancy to be trying, particularly as they age and value steadiness, and stars are no different. The uneven pulse of their careers is accompanied by a sense of frustration and powerlessness. We perceive stars as legendary, powerful figures, but they often experience their occupation with a resignation about the insufficient control they exert over their professional lives. They feel prey to unseen forces.

The final fundamental characteristic of the star job is that celebrity entertainers must establish their own price for the work they do. Because they excel at attracting enormous throngs of onlookers, they are exceptionally valuable. But precisely how valuable? Stars are so rare and their work so extraordinary that there are few guidelines for their earnings. Compensation must be negotiated and then negotiated again for the next booking or contract. This haggling, a trial for all involved, occupies a greater proportion of the work life of stars than it does for virtually any other occupation, since in most lines of work the amount of compensation is more or less standardized. Reaching an acceptable fee is such a preoccupation that it is no wonder the first chapter of Jim Bouton's *Ball Four* is not about pitching at all, but about his salary history and negotiations. In trying to reach agreement, the star's ultimate weapon is to withdraw services—a strain in its own right. Joe DiMaggio held out in 1937 for a salary of $15,000 and then came back saying, "This holdout business is tougher than playing. All I want to do is get back to work."

The compensation is bound to be so large that the need to

manage the flow of dollars wisely becomes pressing. Money
matters can start to consume more and more of a star's time
and attention. Daniel J. Travanti said, "If you have success as an
actor, you're forced to become a business person. That can be
very frightening." The person whose entire orientation in life
was to perfect skills at performance is now compelled to think
in the completely different language of dollars and cents. Like
many stars, Elvis Presley detested the business side of his career
and tried to ignore it. If a performer cannot rise to this financial
challenge then he or she has to hire people who represent themselves as experts at it, and concern himself with overseeing
them. Stars have no special talents at fiscal supervision; for
years Tyrone Power was cheated by his business manager. Those
who do manage their own fortunes effectively can find themselves being drawn away from the activities that elevated them
in the first place. The wife of rock star and movie actor David
Bowie remarked that he is "a very astute businessman. You have
to be that now, though. I don't think he gets the pleasure out of
entertaining as much as he used to because now it's an enormous business responsibility."

Newly wealthy stars may need to become schooled in law
as well as in business. It is probable that they will be involved
in a string of lawsuits during their careers; others will sue them,
and they will sue others. In one month, June 1988, Paul Newman had both courtroom experiences: he was sued by a delica-
tessen owner who claimed a share of the profits from Paul Newman's Salad Dressing, and Newman sued the firm that held the
rights to *The Sting* because he was receiving no proceeds from
its videocassette sales. The sums involved in such suits can be
enormous: in 1970 the Rolling Stones sued ex-manager Allen
Klein for $29 million in damages. People frequently begrudge
the success of stars' works, cry plagiarism, and bring suit.
George Harrison was found guilty of stealing a tune, while Mick
Jagger was acquitted of a similar challenge. A Peruvian mystic
and writer on the occult leveled this-worldly charges against
Shirley MacLaine, claiming she had lifted portions of her book
Out on a Limb from his work.

In a litigious age, the conspicuousness and wealth of stars
invite lawsuits of all sorts. Ex-lovers will sue: Lee Marvin was
taken to court in the first "palimony" suit, to be followed by

Billie Jean King, sued by her lesbian lover, and Liberace, sued by his male companion. Neighbors will sue: a man who claimed to have been nipped by the dog of Charles Bronson and Jill Ireland said he wanted $25,000 in compensation. Perfect strangers will sue: a guard at the Hotel Pierre in New York, asserting he had been hit by a piece of glass thrown by Ryan O'Neal, demanded $3 million.

Stars are sure to enter into contractual relationships with those who employ them, and there is the rub. To secure equitable value, a contract is usually highly prescriptive about what a star must do and must not do. Christopher Reeves's contract stipulated that he could do nothing to discredit Superman (whom the actor referred to as "Supie"). Stars are players, and many of them have a rebellious streak to their temperament; the stipulations which they acceded to at the moment of signing may come to be sensed as overly restrictive. Performers may begin to feel "owned" and cantankerous. They have to go to the sound studio and make the recording when told to, and they may resent it. They may be compelled to go out on tour whether they are up to it or not. Among actors the sense of being owned was even more prevalent during the studio era, when stars were signed to seven-year contracts that told them when to breathe in and when to breathe out. Ruled by these agreements, stars could be ordered to any movie set and "loaned" from their studio to any other. A few resisted; having become a top-ranked star at Warner Brothers, Bette Davis, with an extraordinary application of daring and resolve, managed to cast off her contractual shackles. Today the license to dispatch a star wherever the contract holder desires is still a feature of several professional sports, whose players can be traded without any say-so.

Overall, the work life of a star is subject to excruciating pressures that can be difficult for an outsider to appreciate. If we stop to reflect on it, we might sense that the path upward to stardom is bound to be torturous, entailing constant rejection, incessant maneuvering, and a capricious audience. We may also recognize that eventually there will be a decline in the need for a star's services, and that this can hardly be a pleasant period for the entertainer. But for the span in between the difficult rise and the difficult fall, it may appear to us that the star's tenure is paradisiacal. Even Leo Rosten, an otherwise shrewd observer of the complexities of stardom, was guilty of this misperception when he enthused, "But in Hollywood the work is a form of play, and the people love their work, and they are paid handsomely for having fun. They are paid for doing things which other people would like to do without being paid."[22] But the work life of celebrity performers is hemmed in by crushing forces and racked with torments.

It is worth summarizing these pressures and conflicts:

• The worry that a performance will prove inadequate is everlastingly present for most stars, who move from one potential failure to another. Will the leading batter be able to keep up his average? Will the crowds turn out for the rock star's next concert? Will the new film bring in acceptable receipts at the box office? Consciousness of imperfect performances can energize stars (Vivien Leigh said, "I am never satisfied with what I do; each performance provides another glimpse or insight") but it can also make them anxious and fearful. Throughout his long career James Stewart was always afraid his acting was not good enough. Despite all his accomplishments Eddie Murphy worried, "I wonder if I'm good-looking, if I'm talented, if I can sing. I wonder how funny people really think I am, or if it's a fluke."

• Life as a celebrity performer has an unpleasant, disconcerting rhythm to it. Modulation is lacking. There are the fiery moments when one is "on" and the lengthier intervals of languid waiting. By being switched so decisively and abruptly from on to off and back on, the star's sensation often is of being crudely manipulated.

• The star image that the performer and the public have settled upon can be difficult to maintain. The caretaking of the image—"like the man who cleans the furnace," as Katharine Hepburn put it—calls for unceasing vigilance and application.

• Stars frequently find it difficult to strike a balance between promoting themselves to the public and holding themselves back in the interest of emotional preservation. Young stars especially find the proper equilibrium to be elusive. Hollywood agent Bernie Brillstein told this story about his client John Belushi: the two men were riding in a limousine up Sunset Boulevard, while Belushi was complaining heatedly about his lack of privacy. Suddenly the comedian spotted a knot of people outside a nightclub; Belushi's reaction was to roll down the window and wave wildly to catch their attention. Some stars find it hard not to misstep. Marilyn Monroe said ruefully, "I sometimes feel as if I'm too exposed. I've given myself away, the whole of me, every part, and there's nothing left that's private, just me alone."

• The tide of public response can be overwhelming, threatening to drown the celebrity performer. Although the player has worked for popular acknowledgment, the volume of the surge that is loosened is beyond his or her regulation. The star feels powerless, tossed about by thunderous forces. Rudolph Valentino lamented, "A man should control his life. Mine is controlling me. I don't like it." This massive popularity becomes restrictive, sentencing the star to a sort of house arrest.

• Thus, success as a performer is not liberating, it is confining. Stardom does not grant license, it takes it away.

Such is the conflict at the center of the celebrity performer's work life. Stars are presented as sterling exemplars of the individual, radiating autonomy. But while appearing omnipotent, they actually have very little discretion. Not only are they captives of public ardor, they are also captives of their own image. Paul Newman's daughter observed, "I don't know whether it's partly lack of courage, but I think it's valid when he says, 'The general public will not accept me in this part, and if I do this, it will hurt the film.' Well, if *he* can't decide to do whatever the hell he wants to do, then who can? I remember that as being a really frightening moment, that with all that great fame and success, someone's still got you by the tail."

And though little acknowledged or discussed, the fact is that a celebrity performer is usually hired by others and must do their bidding. Few stars are self-employed. Studios, recording companies, entertainment organizations, team managements, impresarios—they contract for the services of stars and specify what stars must do. And stars do it.

Small wonder, therefore, that at their most sardonic and self-deprecating, stars will refer to themselves as commodities, to be marketed to the public just like other commodities. Charles Bronson stated, "I'm only a product like a cake of soap. To be sold as well as possible." This is a reductive perception, stripping away the aura of personality and its significance in American culture, but there is an essential accuracy to it.

Despite all these heightened pressures and conflicts, some stars do manage to fare well. They keep their performance up to a high standard, they are not bothered by the gaps between their images and themselves, they make good use of the lulls, and they successfully manage their public contact. At age ten Shirley Temple was asked by a reporter, "Shirley, don't you ever get tired of people pushing and shoving you and asking you questions and begging for your autograph?" She answered brightly, "No, I don't mind at all. It's part of the job."

But most stars find their work life to be a great strain. Shortly before his death, as he looked back over his lengthy career, Cary Grant said grimly, "It's not an easy profession, despite what most people think."

7.★
WHAT STARS DO FOR THE PUBLIC

tars work hard for their audience. But what precisely are the services they provide? Americans cede them precious money and time, lavishing attention upon them, but what do they give people in return? What is involved in the transaction between celebrity entertainer and audience, the most extensive, formidable relationship of modern times?

It is curious that stars themselves have little sense of the breadth or depth of the services they provide. Puzzlement about the extensive public regard for them pops up frequently in their reflections. James Garner innocently asked, "Why should anyone be interested in our opinions about anything? Why do they put us on pedestals? We're just playing cowboys and Indians— that's all we're doing. We haven't discovered the cure for cancer. None of us." Marlon Brando was thinking along the same lines when he sourly asked a reporter, "Why should anybody care what any movie star has to say or what he does in his private life? A movie star is nothing important." Billie Jean King confessed that she "always felt a little guilty that I was receiving attention that went well beyond what *any* tennis player properly deserved." Spencer Tracy insisted that "acting is not an important job in the scheme of things. Plumbing is." Perhaps their disbelief about their status stems from how subtle and profound their services actually are. The carpenter knows exactly what he does to earn his wages, and the lawyer knows exactly what she does to collect her fees, but the star's services are so pervasive and so abstruse as to be beyond normal comprehension.

First and foremost, stars affect the emotional state of the audience. Following exposure to a leading performer, a person may experience sensations of inner strength, warmth, resolution, or relief. Somehow the entertainer has purged individuals of negative feelings like sorrow, doubt, anxiety, and animosity—feelings that permeate ordinary life.

So at the outset it is obvious that stars pertain somehow to the realm of feelings. They have little connection with the world of work, where employees apply determination and rationality to earn their livings, and a great deal to do with the world of emotions. Hollywood films, although the products of an extremely profit-conscious industry, seldom have business life or work as their central themes; instead they dramatize feelings. One of the few studies to shed light on this dimension was conducted by social scientist James Lull in 1980.[1] He asked 200 high school women for their favorite television actresses, and the reasons for their choices. What struck Lull was that, although the vast majority of the respondents anticipated a professional life for themselves, only 5 percent checked "a successful career" as a reason for admiring a television performer. The populace turns to stars not for what they reveal about work, but for what they reveal about the other side of living.

Dream research confirms that celebrity performers enter deeply into the emotions of the audience. As Americans slumber, celebrities pop up in their fantasies. A recent book by psychologist Dee Burton documents people's nighttime dreams about Woody Allen. Burton placed ads in newspapers and quickly found 112 people who could recall their dream encounters with the comedian. Word of her efforts spread rapidly, and soon she had more dreamers than she could handle. Calls came in from around the world. Of the 144 dreams she transcribed, 80 are reported in her book, *I Dream of Woody.* Male dreamers were likely to experience Allen as someone to pal around with and share a few laughs with, while female dreamers frequently saw him as a highly romantic figure. For all, the dream Allen lodged in their minds was as vivid as the characters he has played in his films.

One reviewer of *I Dream of Woody* asked condescendingly about the dreamers, "Why aren't these people dreaming about their mothers and fathers, or God, or if they have to use some real-life figure, Mother Teresa?" The answer is that the entertainment star plays a mightier role in the psyches of Americans.

Emotional contact is made between the performer and the viewer, and emotional content is shared. While people are normally reticent about opening themselves up to others and exposing their innermost selves, they open themselves up to stars with dispatch. There are apparently two different ways that the aperture to the mind is dilated and contact of this sort is achieved. The first is that the spectator *identifies* with the player and, by an act of the imagination such as only humans are capable of, is temporarily able to take on the role and to act as the performer acts. The audience member "becomes" Jane Fonda or O. J. Simpson, and empathetically shares the star's experience. This psychological process of identification may explain why men prefer male stars and women tend to favor stars of their gender. In reviewing the limited published research on movie audiences, Leo Handel noted that "the reasons for the moviegoers' preference for players of their own sex can usually be traced to 'self-identification.'"[2]

The second mode of star contact is equally captivating but in essence the opposite. Here the spectator does not identify with the star and assume the star's persona, but imaginatively *interacts* with the performer. The male fan of Marilyn Monroe did not become her, but in his mind's eye became her lover or protector. The woman who adores Robert Redford is unlikely to identify with him; she may, however, have other designs. Someone may imagine himself not to be John McEnroe, but his bloodthirsty opponent.

Identification or interaction occurs when a spectator observes a star in performance. In this setting stars apply their magical poultices to troubled emotions—a service Americans turn to repeatedly as they endure the pressures of twentieth-century life. It is not a service easily rendered, and on those occasions when the performance is delivered before a live audience, such as a sports event or concert, stars exert themselves to the point of exhaustion.

The emotional content of stars' work is particularly clear in the case of leading musical performers. Music is addressed unambiguously at the subrational mind, so there is no confusing the appeal of this sort of performance. Singers and musicians find favor because of their ability to influence feelings. The rhythms and harmonies in music replace the dissonances in people's minds, the melodies transport listeners, and the audience follows the lead singer or player into a better emotional locale.

There is no exclusive emotion that starring musicians deal in, although some feelings are more regularly addressed than others. One of these is romance. People engaged by a Barbra Streisand album can find themselves involved in the ups and downs of love. Frank Sinatra kindled similar feelings; bandleader Tommy Dorsey commented about his young singer in the 1940s that "he was a skinny kid with big ears. And yet what he did to women was something awful." One of the reasons Elvis Presley had such a hold on the American public is that when he crooned a ballad many of his listeners felt loved. Affectionate feelings were the trademark of the Beatles' impact on a worldwide audience; cleanup crews following their concerts used to report that a large number of young women had been so transported to ecstasy that their bladders had loosened.

In contrast to the Beatles stood the Rolling Stones—almost as popular, but dealing in very different emotions. Assertiveness and belligerence were significant elements of their performances. For teenagers passing through the throes of maturation, of adjusting to the realities of the adult world they were about to enter, this strident music helped articulate their apprehensions and resentments. As Timothy White comments in *Rock Stars*, "The rock concert is a tribal rite in which an option-addicted culture is allowed to blow off its enormous stores of nervous energy."[3] Such was the response of one fan in Fred and Judy Vermorel's study of rock audiences: "I just stood on a chair and I can remember I just went hysterical. I can remember thinking: this is stupid. But I couldn't stop screaming and pulling my hair. The girl next to me just stared at me. I had butterflies in my stomach and my mouth kept going white all around and I'd wipe it off. And I'd think: What on earth's this? I was actually sort of foaming at the mouth."[4]

Not only music stars, but all leading performers administer to emotions and modify them. It is because of this service that the nation grows devoted to stars. If individuals do not have enough of a particular feeling, such as affection, then stars can skillfully conjure the inclination and vicariously satisfy it. Or, on the other hand, if people have an excess of another feeling— particularly one that social sanctions compel be held in check, like rage—then stars can help to discharge it harmlessly under the controlled conditions of a performance.

One way that some stars coax harbored feelings out of people is by leading them to laugh. Since the beginnings of American popular entertainment comedians have been starring performers. Comedy remains the mainstay of broadcasting, as it has been since the days of network radio, and is a significant element in the movie business and the club concert circuits. The American public retains an undiminishing need for the services of comics.

The premises of a joke are likely to touch on matters troubling and unresolved in the minds of the audience. A representative one, identified by Gregory Peck as the latest Ron-and-Nancy joke, was passed along to an interviewer in 1987: Nancy, "Ron, did you fart?" Ron, "Er—no. Should I have?" For those who enjoy such a joke, analysis would disclose such age-old sub-themes as uneasiness with authority figures, husband-and-wife relations, personal weakness, and flatulence. Much of the content of jokes pertains to hostile impulses that cannot be vented in normal human discourse. Often a laughingstock is set up—a Ted Baxter or Louie DiPalma—and viewers are invited to poke fun. They deride those who are less powerful, more powerful, or simply different. Real life does not provide ample opportunities for this sort of discharge, since the social costs of such animosity would be ruinous, but in the context of a performance a comedian can safely bring it out of an audience.

It is one thing to talk about laughing, and it is another to actually make it happen. Harry Langdon, a starring comedian in vaudeville and silent movies, once reflected that "the oddest thing about this whole funny business is that the public really

wants to laugh, but it's the hardest thing to make them do it."
So much skill and subtlety are involved in getting an audience
to laugh that those few artists who can accomplish it regularly
belong in the fold of true geniuses. Charlie Chaplin was one.
Audiences at first laughed at the Little Tramp, the outcast with
mismatched clothes. They were invited to ridicule Charlie for
his gaffes and inadvertencies. But because of the character's
spunk, the audience came to appreciate his charm, honesty, and
strength of character. Chaplin's magic was that he could move
an audience from merely interacting with the Little Tramp and
ridiculing him to identifying with the figure and being him.
Viewers could bumble along with Chaplin, make fools of themselves, and not be undone. The ability to laugh at oneself, to
absolve oneself, and to go forth—these were the pleasures the
audience took away from its time with the Little Tramp.

Many comedians make themselves the butt of their jokes
and bring the audience's derision down upon themselves—Joan
Rivers or Rodney Dangerfield, for example—but not all can
achieve the added step of getting people to identify with them,
as Chaplin did. Many observers believe that Chaplin's mantle
has been inherited by Woody Allen. Allen plays a character who
appears at first to be a bona fide loser: short, insecure, clumsy
at love, possessor of a dense Brooklyn accent and thick glasses.
But as the plot evolves the character becomes more congenial,
and soon members of the audience find themselves identifying
with Allen. Humorous mishaps become not devastating humil-
iations but rather proofs of character. Identifying with Allen,
filmgoers come to perceive themselves as winners after all,
laughing their shortcomings away. The small person inside
everyone can triumph.

One of the two classic theater masks was comic, the other
tragic. Stars elicit not only laughter, but tears as well. Humans
are universally susceptible to grief whenever important relationships are severed. But because Americans are not expected
to grieve publicly or at length over their separations and be-
reavements, much of this mournfulness is kept bottled up.
Through the tragic tales they act out, stars can help people to
cry and relieve this pent-up impulse.

The movies are today's premier medium for tearjerkers,

1. Bette Davis at the start of her career: "Wave after wave of love flooded the stage." (Photofest)

Mae West: Everyone knew her. (Photofest)

3. Charlie Chaplin, Mary Pickford, and Douglas Fairbanks, Sr., about 1919: America's prototypical movie stars. (Museum of Modern Art/Film Stills Archive)

Katharine Hepburn in 1935: "I ...t wanted to be famous." (Photo-...st)

5. Rita Hayworth: Her hairline was raised. (Photofest)

6. Elvis Presley in Hollywood: "The camera caressed him." (Photofest)

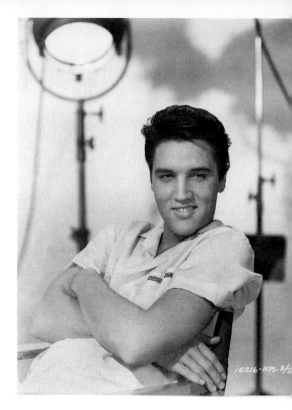

7. Jayne Mansfield: She had always wanted to be a star. (Photofest)

8. Janis Joplin: A late bloomer. (Photofest)

Jim Morrison: A college gradu-e. (Photofest)

10. Lana Turner: Was she discovered this way? (Photofest)

11. Joe DiMaggio: Interest in him has not abated. (Photofest)

12. Errol Flynn: "The public has always expected me to be a playboy." (Museum of Modern Art/Film Stills Archive)

14. David Niven: The urbane type. (Photofest)

13. Clark Gable: Fans liked his earthy roles. (Photofest)

15. Marlon Brando: The antihero type. (Photofest)

16. Shirley Temple: Fifty-six ringlets was the answer. (Photofest)

18. Clara Bow: Her fan mail certified her as a star. (Museum of Modern Art/Film Stills Archive)

17. John Barrymore: Born into Star Village. (Museum of Modern Art/Film Stills Archive)

19. Betty Grable's pin-up photo: 5 million copies were distributed. (Museum of Modern Art/Film Stills Archive)

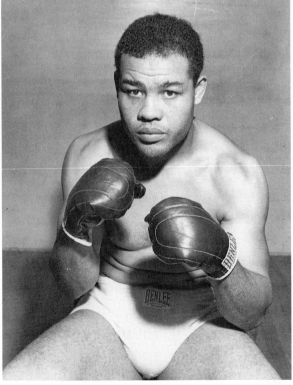

1. Joe Louis: He was born Joe arrow. (Photofest)

20. Joan Crawford as a starlet: Whatever happened to Lucille Le-Sueur? (Museum of Modern Art/Film Stills Archive)

22. Fred Astaire: "Beating your brains and feet out." (Photofest)

23. Marilyn Monroe: "I didn't want to go to the set in the morning." (Photofest)

24. Montgomery Clift: He had something to hide. (Photofest)

25. Charlie Chaplin and the press: "Metaphorically, I was being devoured." (Museum of Modern Art/Film Stills Archive)

26. Tyrone Power: He referred to his fans collectively as "the monster." (Photofest)

28. Roger Staubach: He resented the liabilities of celebrity. (Photofest)

27. Cary Grant: "This autograph evil has got entirely out of hand."
(Photofest)

29. Merle Oberon: After a face-lift? (Photofest)

1. Spencer Tracy: "Living was ever easy for Spence." (Photo-st)

30. John Wayne: The cowboy image vs. the actor who needed to study his lines. (Museum of Modern Art/Film Stills Archive)

32. Bing Crosby at home: His image, twice over, was that of a family man. (Photofest)

33. Mary Pickford rescued by Douglas Fairbanks, Sr.: They were mobbed in London on their 1920 honeymoon. (Mary Pickford Foundation)

35. Rock Hudson: Campaigning for a good cause. (Museum of Modern Art/Film Stills Archive)

34. Marilyn Monroe and Joe DiMaggio: Their 1954 marriage took fans by surprise. (Photofest)

36. Rudolph Valentino as the Sheik: "The constant attention and invasion of his privacy—it just killed him." (Photofest)

37. Ava Gardner and Mickey Rooney: She was the first of his nine wives. (Photofest)

38. John Belushi: "I'm just so lonely." (Photofest)

39. Henry Fonda: "I've been married five times, and I'm goddamn ashamed of it." (Photofest)

40. Peter Sellers: No purple on his sets. (Photofest)

41. Liberace: An insomniac. (Museum of Modern Art/Film Stills Archive)

42. Louis Armstrong: Marijuana was his drug of choice. (Photofest)

43. Roy Rogers: A voluntary departure. (Photofest)

44. Roger Maris: "It would've been a hell of a lot more fun if I had never hit those sixty-one home runs." (Photofest)

45. Billie Jean King: She committed a double fault. (Photofest)

46. Mickey Mantle: "It's tough to realize when you're through." (Photofest)

47. Jackie Robinson: A restaurant executive in his second career. (Photofest)

48. Doris Day: In retirement, a caretaker of stray animals. (Photofest)

49. Bill Haley: He was snappis in retirement. (Photofest)

50. Babe Ruth: When his career was over, he felt "hopeless, desperate, desolate." (Photofest)

. Groucho Marx: He was
rsed at home. (Museum of Mod-
Art/Film Stills Archive)

52. Carole Lombard: She died in service to her country. (Museum of Modern Art/Film Stills Archive)

53. John Lennon: "I can't believ‹ he's dead." (Photofest)

54. Glenn Miller: He vanished mysteriously over the English channel. (Photofest)

. Will Rogers: "No man has en so universally appreciated d loved." (Photofest)

56. *Life* magazine covers of Marilyn Monroe: The immortals are few in number. (Photofest)

57. Judy Garland and her baby, Liza Minnelli: Generations of stars. (Museum of Modern Art/Film Stills Archive)

having taken this function over from nineteenth-century melodramas. Many actresses have found their strongest parts in
roles that caused theatergoers to get out their handkerchiefs
and tissues: Bette Davis in *Dark Victory*, Jane Wyman in *Magnif-
icent Obsession*, Deborah Kerr in *An Affair to Remember*, Susan
Hayward in *I Want to Live*, Olivia de Havilland in *Gone with the
Wind*, Lana Turner in *Imitation of Life*, Merle Oberon in *Wuth-
ering Heights*, Jennifer Jones in *Farewell to Arms*, Barbara Stan-
wyck in *Stella Dallas*. The tearjerker genre has continued un-
abated through the years, encompassing *Love Story*, *Midnight
Cowboy*, *Ordinary People*, *Terms of Endearment*, and *Out of Africa*.

Other emotional services delivered by stars in performance
are equally profound but result in more interior responses. Entertainers provide a warmth of human contact—in surrogate
form, and in varying degrees of intensity—that is often lacking
in their audience's real lives. In a 1985 survey of 40,000 adults
by *Psychology Today* magazine, more than 50 percent said they
sometimes or often feel lonely.[5] In an era of isolated lives, stars
can temporarily fill in these gaps; an illusion of friendship can
be cultivated by vicariously interacting with Mr. Rogers or Lily
Tomlin or Johnny Carson. If the star is featured as the member
of a group, viewers can identify with the player and experience
a flush of interpersonal feelings as he or she deals with the others. Twisting the dial until they find their favorite performer,
people participate psychologically in the Cosby family, the A-
Team, the Cheers crew, the Hill Street precinct. Americans enter
these fictional groups and momentarily feel themselves caught
up in a net of sustaining human relations.

Vicarious group membership is one of the chief pleasures of
watching athletic contests. Fans are likely to identify with a
starring player and to experience the sensations of working intensely with others to achieve a common goal. Their own lives
may be filled with inadequate and conflictful relationships, but
for the game's duration they can imaginatively interact with
others, harmoniously and purposefully, against a common opponent. Spectators sense and recreate feelings of pure sociability as team members support each other in the interest of a mutual triumph.

Perhaps the commonest "relationship" that stars offer is romance. Love affairs are a staple of entertainment because satisfying ones are so elusive and so much desired in the real world. As the twentieth century has worn on, the individual's search for sustaining love has become ever more arduous. Into the breach have stepped stars, who through their performances have become the providers of purified romance. A spectator can identify with the star and love as they love, or can fantasize being loved by the leading performer. When the performance is over, the viewer is left with a lingering balm of affection.

In the cause of surrogate relations, stars do more than offer up romantic attachments. Responding to the appetites of the audience, they can also provide sexual excitement by proxy. A French poll reported that making love with a movie star was a fantasy for about 50 percent of each sex; similar proportions may occur in the American population. Female "bombshells" have a long and lascivious history in stardom, from Eva Tanguay on the vaudeville stage to Madonna on MTV. Male stars used to be more discreetly suggestive but have become less so since the days of Elvis Presley.

Along the way from the suggestive to the anatomical, the actress who most popularly defined mainstream American sexuality was Marilyn Monroe. The successor to Mae West, Jean Harlow, and Betty Grable, she performed the job of sex symbol so magnificently that no one since has equaled her. Her platinum hair, sculpted figure, breathless voice, and enticing walk made her the ultimate object of desire for the male audience of the time. She wiggled firmly into the fantasies of Americans through her performances in such movies as *Gentlemen Prefer Blondes, How to Marry a Millionaire, There's No Business Like Show Business, The Seven-Year Itch*, and *Some Like It Hot*.

Stars also help to satisfy other, more destructive urges. Actors maim and kill on the audience's behalf and so help to exorcise hostile impulses. Their success at this service explains at least partly why violence has become such a large and intractable component of American entertainment. Every human being builds up stores of irritation and animosity that have to be discharged somehow. But since an overt display of aggression is usually damaging to the social fabric of daily life, there are inadequate opportunities to release this vitriol. It is conceivable that, as the American labor force has become more white-collar and office-bound, with less call for physical exertion, levels of withheld antagonism have increased. By aggressing onscreen or onstage, stars perform the important psychological service of helping to vent anger. Moviegoers vicariously play the soldier who in the name of patriotism guns down the enemy, or the detective who in the name of justice careens a police car through town, or the football player who in the name of sport smashes through the opposing line. In the aftermath people feel relaxed because they have successfully shed some hostile feelings, and have done it without risk, remorse, or recrimination.

One of the celebrity performers who have specialized in aggression has been Clint Eastwood. Throughout his highly successful career Eastwood has generally played two stereotyped tough guys: the Western gunslinger or the renegade crime fighter. From his first roles as a slit-eyed gunfighter in Italian-made Westerns to his later character of detective Dirty Harry Callahan, Eastwood has exuded hostility. "Make my day," he snarls at the quaking bad guy who tempts him to blast away. So popular have Eastwood's characters been with the American public that theater owners have ranked him among the top ten box-office attractions for more years than any other living star. Although in real life Eastwood is a calm and cautious businessman, independently producing his own films, his performances as a vicious gunman have won him an enormous following among those who need to aggress empathetically.

Stars thus aid in the management of those sexual and violent impulses that cannot go unleashed in middle-class society. Chaos and terror would ensue if everyone were permitted to fornicate or aggress to their heart's content, but through a star's performance a modicum of gratification can be vicariously obtained.

There is a more pleasant side to the psychological services stars provide: they succeed for us. In most films leading performers are likely to play the role of someone who wins in the end. This is not always true—Humphrey Bogart may get shot, Dustin Hoffman may die on the bus, Marlon Brando may succumb—but it is the case more often than not. According to Albert McLean in *American Vaudeville as Ritual*, winning and achievement were the underlying lessons of vaudeville for the then newly urbanized audiences; ticket buyers saw enthusiastic performers in feats of legerdemain or in uplifting vignettes and went away with notions of being successful themselves.[6] In other countries the social imperatives may be for the individual to fit in well and to fulfill an ascribed role perfectly, but in the United States ambition is stimulated and achievement rewarded. When performers play members of the affluent class, like Fred Astaire in *The Gay Divorcee* or Larry Hagman in "Dallas," they are enabling the audience to mentally step into that role too, and to briefly indulge a desire for achievement and status. Spectators are taken on an imaginative flight to the kingdom of rampant success.

Sports stars symbolize success even more straightforwardly, since winning and its opposite are the very stuff of athletic contests. The games are structured to incorporate opposition, conflict, striving, and a decisive conclusion. The fan identifies with the starring players and follows them to victory. If they are not victorious and continue to lose, then the fan is likely to look for other players to support. Crowds follow winning performers and not others, as every team owner who watches his gate receipts knows. To experience success from sports stars, more than half of all American adults will watch at least one broadcast game over the course of a week. They are looking for an antidote to their own personal failings and a stimulus for their pursuit of success.

Identifying or imaginatively interacting with stars in performance, people take leave momentarily from the constancy and obligations of their daily lives. Time with stars affords a small psychic vacation; just to escape from the daily grind for a while is experienced by most as a refreshing change of pace.

To sum up, the fundamental reason the public is engaged by celebrity entertainers is that they help to articulate and regulate emotions. Repressed aggression is sublimated through the rock star's concert, the movie detective's actions, the comedian's jokes, or the athlete's powerful charge. Excess sexual energy finds its fantasy object in an attractive performer. Needs for companionship are also answered, and suffering and self-pity are discharged. Fears of failure and the drive for success are addressed by star performances.

And when the performance is over we feel intact, resolute, endorsed. We have been entertained.

We admit stars into the *sancta sanctora* of our minds to work on our emotions. We permit them access to ourselves in ways we permit no others. Perhaps because we allow them such license with our innermost selves, Americans come to revere them. Such admiration easily leads to emulation.

A historical analysis (see chapter 2) indicates that the star role was crystallized in the 1910s when an urbanizing and unsure populace found itself in desperate need of exemplars of the self. Stars came to be models of the person within, and were duly labeled "personalities." Stars today continue to exemplify personality attributes for certain sectors of the population. Those with the greatest need for personality models, the young, are often the most avid admirers of celebrity performers. Boys are the most rabid sports fans, delighting in seeing their heroes take on the opposition. The largest consumers of popular music are teenagers and young adults, who buy the bulk of the recordings and concert tickets and intently watch the music channels for their favorite performers. The film audience is tilted radically toward the young; while the median age of the American population is over thirty, the median age of the moviegoing audience is under twenty.

The importance of entertainment idols in the lives of the young was underscored by a survey of teenagers conducted in 1986 for *The World Almanac*. Of the top ten admired public figures most often mentioned by U.S. adolescents, nine were performers and one an ex-performer (Ronald Reagan). No other politicians, and no business leaders or creative artists, made the list. That year these leading heroes for the nation's youth were:

1. Bill Cosby	6. Chuck Norris
2. Sylvester Stallone	7. Clint Eastwood
3. Eddie Murphy	8. Rob Lowe
4. Ronald Reagan	9. Arnold Schwarzenegger
5. Molly Ringwald	10. Don Johnson

Whether young or not-so-young, members of the audience ascertain a star's personality via two sets of revelations. Viewers study the star's work a number of times and from these exposures deduce a particular self. Continuities in the performances are sought, in the belief that they will describe the performer's essence. For this purpose the entertainer had better be more or less constant, or the exercise will be defeated. "I firmly believe that the public must know 75 percent of what to expect from an actor," Bette Davis once remarked. The other 25 percent may be the art of the immediate performance, but the 75 percent is the raw material of the ongoing relationship between star and audience.

Second, the public absorbs fragmentary accounts of stars' private lives as these crop up in the press. Then people align these items with their first-hand impressions obtained from the performances, and soon they become convinced that they know stars' true personalities. That is, in fact, what they fundamentally care to know. Should they chance on someone who has actually had contact with a star, the first question is likely to be, "What's he really like?" What is Hank Aaron, Dolly Parton, Joe Montana, or Chevy Chase "really" like? Americans need to know.

At these foci of public curiosity appear a wide range of character traits. The audience perceives stars as personifying kindness and meanness, sweetness and aggressiveness, shyness and conviviality, endurance and vulnerability, and on and on. A whole garden of personality traits is thus available for contemplation and possible selection.

In particular, celebrity performers model gender roles for the modern world. Stars parade several ideals of masculinity and femininity. Viewers can scrutinize prototypes of the assertive male, the genteel, the cunning, the attractive, the comic. Similarly various versions can be seen of the independent woman, the maternal one, the seductive type, the witty.

Americans are in great need of such prototypes of masculinity and femininity because gender definitions have been in flux throughout the twentieth century. What served earlier generations no longer constitute comfortable standards; the staunch patriarch and the indefatigable housewife are less in evidence. Stars not only model the replacement types that have been increasingly realized—the sensitive male, the bold female—but they have ventured further into the androgynous outer reaches of sexual identity, serving as brave explorers into once-

proscribed deportment. When Marlene Dietrich wore male attire in her private life, when Katharine Hepburn sported pants
and blouses with broad shoulders, the conventions of what it
meant to act or look like a woman were being tested. When Jack
Benny made use of feminine mannerisms, when Cary Grant and
Jack Lemmon and Peter Sellers impersonated women on screen,
a cross-gender incursion was going on. Male music stars have
often stretched the definitions of masculinity the farthest: audiences may have sensed something subversive about Liberace
or Little Richard or Elton John without knowing quite what it
was. Michael Jackson transports his fans beyond the common
demarcations of gender roles into a territory where things are
neither this nor that. Such androgynous displays have helped
society feel its way through this century's swerves. Even if the
most daring exemplars were not widely imitated, the models
put forth by stars have given the public ample alternatives to
ponder.

Even more obviously, stars have become models for standards of physical appearance and fashion. While not all stars
are handsome or beautiful, many are, and they make real the
abstractions of physical appeal. This is an important service,
since degree of attractiveness has become a key gradient in
twentieth-century social order as other traditional measuring
sticks such as family standing or ethnic origin have lost meaning. Before the turn of the century, standards for attractiveness
were dim and of limited applicability, but today they are applied subtly but forcibly to an ever greater proportion of the
population. More and more people try to adjust their appearance in the light of those norms; even the elderly feel compelled
to look attractive. The audience wants those in the limelight to
model good looks, so that these standards will be personified.

The indexes of attractiveness change over time, and this
fluctuation and the unexpectedness it introduces cause people
to be ever more attentive to stars. Males stars are ectomorph
one decade—Fred Astaire, Jimmy Stewart, Henry Fonda, Frank
Sinatra—and mesomorph the next. Bosoms are important for a
while, then not; legs have to be perfect now but were not then.
New appearance models rotate in among the roster of stars, and
old ones take a back seat.

"A hairdresser could write a history of the movies starting

with Mary Pickford's curls," noted Edgar Morin.[7] Beginning with those ringlets—whose loss caused a genuine clamor—and coming forward in time, this history is more revealing than Morin suggests, for it documents change not only in the movies but also in the social effects of movie stars. Women studied Jean Harlow's platinum tresses, Rita Hayworth's waves, Veronica Lake's peek-a-boo style, Marilyn Monroe's blonde hairdo, Farrah Fawcett's curls, and Tina Turner's wigs, and then went home and changed their own appearance.

The extraordinary growth of the U.S. beauty industry since 1920 has been due generally to the need of women in the rapidly expanding middle class to appear stylish to the world at large, but has also been due specifically to the particular styles exemplified by movie stars. Before World War I makeup was solely an upper-class practice, but afterward, spurred by the examples of screen actresses, it diffused throughout society. The expanding cosmetics industry and the proliferating beauty parlors reinforced the ideals of physical attractiveness that were established in Hollywood. Pancake makeup, supposedly named for the panchromatic shades required in color filming, became a household item far removed from its origins in the movie industry.

Back when clothing modes tended to be either stiffly formal or vocationally practical, Douglas Fairbanks, Sr., pioneered a fresh wardrobe of sports clothes for newly leisured urbanites. Clara Bow led many to headbands, and Shirley Temple inspired a run on polka-dot dresses. Turbans came into fashion after Lana Turner began wearing them, and strapless gowns after Rita Hayworth appeared in one as Gilda. Diane Keaton instigated the layered look in the 1970s, and Madonna epitomized the trash chic of the 1980s. Such fads cause considerable repercussions within the apparel industry, since sales for a star-sponsored style are bound to be large. When Michael Jackson started up a demand for sequined gloves, some manufacturer somewhere was delighted, and when Don Johnson went sockless on "Miami Vice," other manufacturers elsewhere winced.

Modeling one sort of apparel and not others, leading people to purchase this outfit but not that one, stars are offering guidance in American society's fundamental enterprise of consumption. Never has such a large proportion of a population had such wealth at its disposal. The twentieth century has seen the spectacular development of a vast social strata that, although labeled middle class and often seen as unremarkable, is actually in historical perspective a strikingly new phenomenon of extraordinarily prosperous people who are able to obtain such items as freestanding houses and automobiles as if they were birthrights. The rapid rise of this consumer culture has created a need for prototypical consumers who can model appropriate purchasing decisions.

Since the 1910s this need to see how consumption ought to work—what to purchase and what it is supposed to do for the buyer—has underlain popular fascination with stars. This curiosity explains in large part why Americans demand to observe stars not just in performance but in their private lives as well. The public needs them to show how to spend money. And, thanks to press and television coverage, the stars do so. Beyond observing stars' choices in cosmetics, clothing, and jewelry, the public can take note of their selections in personal services such as hair stylists and physical trainers. It watches them purchase homes, fill them with furniture and art, and then buy second homes in Acapulco or Vail. It watches them buy cars by the tens, then perhaps a string of horses and a ranch for the horses. It watches them travel. All this incessant observation provides lessons in consumption that are crucial to the operations of U.S. society and its economy.

First Hollywood and then Beverly Hills have been viewed as demonstration sites for the high art of consumption. Visiting Americans are loaded onto buses and conveyed past the residences of stars as if they were sacred shrines. Stars think that these tourists have come great distances in search of them, and indeed for the pilgrim spotting a star would be a wonderful plus. But what the visitor most counts on seeing are the stars' possessions: the houses, the landscapes, the cars in the driveway, the service people who might be around. These are the sacred trappings of consumption, American style.

If Star Village had an earthly location, it would have to be in the suburbs of Los Angeles. Here many leading actors and actresses maintain their homes; athletes relocate here when their playing days are over; starring musicians stay in the vicinity when they are not on tour. As described in chapter 4, the pantheon of stars is considered by Americans to constitute a sort of hypercommunity: stars are expected to know each other and to consort with each other.

However, just as the true nature of a performer imperfectly matches a star's image, so the realities of Los Angeles do not fully correspond to people's notions of Star Village. Many stars do not live in proximity to each other, and for those who do maintain homes in Southern California, there is a minimum of genuine communal spirit. Some camaraderie does exist, but it is far more the exception than the rule. As Charlie Chaplin commented, "No, stars among stars give little light—or warmth." Nearer the end of the century, George Hamilton told an interviewer that "Hollywood is not a real community, as far as I've found. I've knocked on a lot of doors here, and nobody's *ever* home—especially when you need them. This is a unique town, unlike anywhere else. I come here to go into the trenches. I don't come here to bond. There's no bonding here. Forget that."

When anthropologist Hortense Powdermaker studied the Hollywood community in the 1940s, she commented on the extravagantly overfamiliar tone of interpersonal relations. It was "darling" this and "sweetheart" that, with constant touching and kissing. But, she explained, it was all a ruse, "a sugar-coating for a deep impersonality."[8] The displays of friendliness were only a pretense to conceal a fundamental unfriendliness.

This lack of meaningful sociability among stars stems from reasonable causes. Stars intuit, and rightly so, that only so many performers can remain highly popular with the American public. One star's success does objectively imperil the longevity of another. With his or her own survival on the line, each star must privately desire the other's failure. In such an environment of envy and hostility, it is highly unlikely that genuine friendships will be spawned or a sense of community arise. According to critic Richard Schickel, whenever stars are compelled to gather in one place, as for a ceremonial event, the affair resembles "a business convention, an occasion of the wary gregariousness, the strained (not to say false) bonhomie of people who, having been thrust together for a time, strive to maintain civility, despite the fact that they spend the rest of the year competing for shares of the same market."[9] Star Village exists nowhere on this planet, either as a geographical locale or as a spiritual community.

And yet public belief in Star Village remains unshakable. Recognizing this, the press singles out those rare moments when stars do consort together, and relays to readers photographs of several celebrity performers in one frame, flashing smiles and interlacing limbs. Americans seek out this confirming evidence, and paparazzi and photo editors rush to oblige.

Star Village is an imaginary, surrogate community, filling a void in twentieth-century citizens' scheme of belonging, and compensating for the tight communal experience that has been left behind. The celestial hamlet lends a sense of placement to those who feel uprooted. Social scientists Donald Horton and Richard Wohl coined the term "para-social" to apply to Americans' friendly feelings toward mediated performers, and noted that "this function of the para-social then can properly be called compensatory, inasmuch as it provides the socially and psychologically isolated with a chance to enjoy the elixir of sociability." [10]

Americans take stars as demonstrators of both how to be and how to belong. Considered singly, the star reifies the very concept of the individual, a concept that has become meaningful only as prescriptive social institutions have receded. The star—whose origins are not elite, whose prominence is not due to status within a traditional institution, whose existence is heartily and widely appreciated—shows how to be a modern person of integrity. Then, almost paradoxically, stars in the plural are believed to describe a community, and in a century in which the net of participation has frayed, to exemplify companionableness. They provide a sensation of belonging. Can there be any denying the importance of these two services? In fact, for the maintenance of a culture, can there be anything more crucial?

A flash point in the public response to celebrity performers is reached whenever two stars marry. Popular delirium can ascend to giddy heights. In the events leading up to and following the wedding, the public pursues stars with a passion many times magnified. Not only is the nation galvanized, but a worldwide audience can be also.

If the reaction to the marriage of Mary Pickford and Douglas Fairbanks, Sr., in 1920 was not the first of such frenzied episodes, it was the greatest to that point and set a standard of sorts for those that have followed. On their honeymoon, the two were kept prisoners in their New York and London hotels by fascinated and rejoicing throngs. On their second day in London the newlyweds were to be guests of honor at the annual and fashionable Theatrical Garden Party. As they arrived at the affair in an open automobile, well-attired women turned manic and tried to snatch Pickford from the vehicle. Fairbanks shielded her, and once the car had stopped, lifted her to his shoulder and forced his way through the mob; photographs of the moment show her face frozen in panic *(photograph 33)*. When he set her down, the crowd regrouped and forced them apart, pushing her into a bush and him into the side of a tent where prize-winning preserves were being displayed. The structure collapsed, and Fairbanks, dignity lost, was compelled to flounder through a gooey disarray.

At the 1948 marriage of Tyrone Power to Linda Christian in Rome, the whole city seemed to go berserk. In Christian's words, "Tyrone's arrival at the church created a near hysteria, and as my car arrived I heard the insistent roar of 'Ty-ro-ne—Magnifico!' Even the motorcycle police escort made no impression on the wall of humanity. The car could only inch its way forward." After the ceremony, as the two were driven across the Eternal City to receive a papal blessing, delirious motorists trailed in madcap pursuit, creating a rash of traffic accidents.

When Marilyn Monroe and Joe DiMaggio married on January 14, 1954, it was on short notice, almost impetuously *(photograph 34)*. Yet the corridor outside the judge's chambers at the San Francisco City Hall quickly filled with well-wishers. A window was opened for ventilation, but the roar from the gathering crowd in the plaza below caused it to be closed. Afterward the couple fled the melee and went into seclusion. The nation first reacted to the headlines as if stunned; the marriage became a topic of discussion everywhere. At the end of January the two reappeared, to fulfill a previously made obligation to tour baseball facilities in Japan. When their plane stopped to refuel in

Hawaii, a mob at the airport ran amok as they disembarked, putting the stars' lives in peril. People tried to pull strands of hair from Monroe's scalp. Finding an equally large throng at the Tokyo airport, they escaped from the plane through the luggage hatch. A howling crowd surrounded their hotel for days. While DiMaggio dutifully carried out his baseball commitments, Monroe went on to entertain American troops in Korea. Soldiers rioted at her shows, threatening to storm the stage. At least one GI was trampled in the tumult and hospitalized.

Shortly after Elizabeth Taylor and Richard Burton were married in 1964, they flew to Boston, where he was scheduled to appear in *Hamlet*. At the airport crowds broke through the barricades and dashed along the runway after the incoming plane. When the couple emerged people grabbed them, jerking them about; Taylor's back was wrenched. The two managed to get to a car and were chauffeured to their hotel, where another mob was waiting in the street. The lobby provided no sanctuary; in the crush they were separated and Taylor was yanked about again, her face shoved into a wall. Her tearful comment to reporters later was: "I have encountered mobs all over the world, but nothing to this extent."

The press corps, agents for the nation's obsession with star weddings, can be just as unruly as the general public. Lana Turner's first marriage was to bandleader Artie Shaw, and when they returned to Los Angeles from their elopement the press was lying in wait. Her new husband, she related, "double-locked both front and back doors, closed and locked all the windows, pulled down the blinds and closed the drapes as though fending off a siege. A siege was what it turned out to be. We heard banging and then the crash of breaking glass from one of the windows." When rock star Madonna wed actor Sean Penn in 1985, there were 100 photographers stalking outside and eight media-hired helicopters hovering overhead. The press assault can be so fierce that it turns deadly; just before Monroe and Arthur Miller were married, a reporter in a car speeding after theirs was killed in an accidental rollover.

Why does the marriage of two stars elicit such fixation and passion? The answer is that these ceremonies represent the conflux of several vital matters in American culture, matters so momentous that when combined into one event, they can catalyze a fury. The various ways in which stars serve as models for the populace are here brought to a head.

The underlying emotional issues are those of love and marriage. For twentieth-century Americans these are vexing issues indeed. Not that love and marriage were minor problems in previous centuries, but modern times have lent them a special prominence. Before the evolution of urbanized and industrialized society, the conduct of romance was highly regulated by explicit sanctions and moral injunctions. Choices in romantic partners were guided if not dictated. Young men and women were certain to hear a great deal from their elders about who was "suitable" and who was not. But in modern times people operate largely without such strictures or directions. When a high premium is placed upon the individual, then each person must find his or her own way. The range of possible behaviors widens, and the field of potential partners expands. Under these conditions the need to receive instruction in romance redoubles. The result is that love has become the prevailing theme for much of contemporary entertainment—no list of top music hits is complete without love songs; almost every film has a "love interest"; no television series ignores relations between the sexes; and performers are sometimes perceived as love incarnate.

Through the celebrity press the public watches stars dally, date, and marry, noting who does what with whom. Reports on star liaisons constitute a large portion of the information collected and relayed to readers every day. The nation studies these romances for new patterns. If older women stars are getting together with younger men, Americans want to know. The age of Mary Tyler Moore's new husband is not only her business, onlookers make it their business as well. Whenever older male entertainers take a fancy to a teenage lass, that is a desideratum too. Beverly Aadland, fifteen years old when Errol Flynn took up with her, later commented, "Younger girls and older men fall in love every day. Nobody says anything about it, and it certainly doesn't get into the papers—unless one of the two parties happens to be a star."

People scrutinize the breakups of stars' alliances as well. In 1950 Frank Sinatra was panting after Ava Gardner, and when he left home his wife Nancy told the press, "If he wasn't a famous singer, known all over the world, we could have a quarrel just like any other normal married couple and no one would think anything of it." Since he was a star, however, his love life was of great interest, and was thoroughly instructive.

In the pitching seas of modern love and marriage, a wedding involving two stars is perceived as a saving occurrence. In such a ceremony all the romantic uncertainties plaguing these times can seem momentarily resolved: two paragons have found each other, and the institution of marriage is reaffirmed. For this affirmation Americans could not be more thankful; appreciation turns fervid.

The union of two stars also reifies something else. When like marries like, it confirms for the public the existence of a celebrity community: Star Village, within whose precincts man finds woman and woman finds man, seems to be validated in these ceremonies. Further confirmation comes if press reports mention other Star Villagers in attendance at the nuptials. And since *both* the principals are "known" beforehand, the audience's ties to the heavenly hamlet seem further strengthened.

When a star marries another star, the fans of the bride or groom will be captivated by this significant event in the life of a person they have come to care very much about. They will study their idol's appearance and demeanor as revealed in photographs of the event. They will reflect on their star's choice for a spouse, and speculate on the chances for happiness. It is all taken by fans as another lesson in how to be a successful individual.

A star's marriage subsequently becomes an important item in the star's story, as known and recited by adherents. Part of the reason a fan becomes attached to a particular star is that the performer's story line is intriguing. The star's marriages and divorces are added to other biographical details, and a narrative is constructed. Fans often date what happens to them relative to what has happened to the star; they feel as if their lives and the star's have been woven together over the years. Spectators ponder how a star's story line will turn out. What is going to happen to Jack Nicholson, to Elizabeth Taylor? Will he ever marry Anjelica Huston? Will Taylor find yet another husband?

In sum, stars model loving and they model marrying. They model unions with others, and they model the individual's successful passage through the stations of life. All this comes together in a crescendo when two stars wed.

There is so much that celebrity entertainers do for the public. The performance of a star can turn bad feelings into good ones. The personality of a star, as it is inferred to be, offers a model for the personalities of others, a guide to the best inner qualities as well as to the most attractive surfaces. Stars as a group are taken to constitute a longed-for substitute community. Events in stars' lives become benchmarks in the lives of many citizens.

And still there is more. The fame stars have won lends them power. It is not power in the ancient sense, by which a few can legitimately exert authoritarian control over others, but rather power in a modern sense, by which a few have license to influence on a vast scale. Americans turn to stars for the guidance they can provide; Jane Fonda shows how to exercise, Jill St. John tells how to cook, Christie Brinkley demonstrates how to apply makeup, Vincent Price instructs about art.

Ceding stars such power, the public cedes them magical properties. In extreme cases, stars can even heal the sick. This phenomenon often involves sports stars, and it works better with impressionable youths than with their elders. In at least three instances Babe Ruth was credited with bringing children back to good health. The most widely reported of these involved a New Jersey boy named Johnny Sylvester who underwent a serious operation in 1926. His recuperation was difficult, and the boy's father begged Ruth to visit the hospital. At bedside Ruth autographed a baseball and promised the boy he would hit a home run for him at that day's game. Ruth did hit a long ball that afternoon, and the boy did get better in due course.

From that time forward, newspaper photographs and broadcast footage have shown sports stars visiting children's wards, where they try to improve the spirits of the ill. Baseball star Steve Garvey reported on a 1971 visit to a young cancer patient in a Los Angeles hospital that "the doctors said he had an 18 percent chance of living." The boy seemed to respond to Garvey's ministrations, and several years later was able to attend an annual night for crippled children at Dodger Stadium.

"Ricky that night gave me a medal with an inscription that said, 'To Steve Garvey, thank you for giving me the will to live.'"

Stars are also depicted visiting drug clinics and halfway houses; the patients invariably fix their eyes on the performer, seeming to wish for redemption. For the majority of fans, however, the healing service of stars is more often a matter of a performer's therapeutic example. When Elizabeth Taylor goes to a clinic and dries out, the addicted take notice. When Ann Jillian has a double mastectomy and continues her career, women study her example.

The power granted to stars is more broadly suggested by the fact that they can get people to do things they would not do otherwise. Simply through their exhortations stars can alter the behavior of some. They cannot do this widely or always, since the tolerances for this instruction are limited. But they can manage it on occasion because of the credit they have built up with the public. There is a small amount of risk for the star, since this store of goodwill can be expended; some observers believe that Jerry Lewis has exhausted his supply through his Labor Day weekend telethons for muscular dystrophy. But when Americans have no real cause to resist, a star can persuade them of something.

The easiest task along these lines is for stars to get people to do something already acknowledged as moral or good. During both world wars stars raised money for the cash-starved federal government through their sale of bonds. Chaplin, Fairbanks, and Pickford went on the road while World War I was raging and raised some $3 million—an enormous sum at the time. Singer Kate Smith, in one of the most remarkable persuasive efforts of the century, sold $600 million worth during World War II.

Stars can lead people to contribute to charitable causes *(photograph 35)*. For many years Danny Kaye encouraged Americans to ante up for the United Nations Children's Fund. When Yul Brynner implores people from beyond the grave to stop smoking and contribute to the American Cancer Society, many follow his suggestion. Irish rock singer Bob Geldof organized rock stars for Band Aid and Live Aid performances that raised millions for African famine relief and won him a nomination for a Nobel Peace Prize. As he puts it, "The trick was to sell famine relief like a hit record, and it worked."

It is not a great leap from extracting money for good causes to extracting money for products. Because Americans already consider stars to be the acmes of consumerism, it is easy for stars to influence purchasing decisions. The vast majority of Americans are active consumers, completing dozens of purchases every week. These selections are made from among the thousands of brands competing within the U.S. marketplace. Advice and direction are needed, if not always sought. Although everyone knows stars are royally compensated for touting items for sale, both familiarity with the performer and a need to know about products lead viewers to cock an ear when a celebrity endorsement begins.

Some stars go all the way and lend their names to products. Since the early film days, when child star Madge Evans had her name sold to the Madge Evans Hat Company of New York, performers have been willing to bind themselves to goods. Babe Ruth Cigars proved highly remunerative for the Babe. The danger is that if either the star or the product sinks in public esteem, so will the other. But apparently this is a risk performers and manufacturers are willing to take, and so we have had Reggie Bars and Cheryl Tiegs Clothes.

More often, a star will endorse a product only for a contractual period. Rodney Dangerfield briefly pointed Americans toward Lite beer. Martha Raye and Rocky Grazziano were solid if temporary supporters of Polident dental cleanser. In response to these endorsements, some advertisers will find their own star to pit against the opposition's. James Garner enjoys a cozy relationship with his Mazda, yet can he withstand when George C. Scott commands people to buy Renault? Cliff Robertson had kind things to say about AT&T, but Burt Lancaster, *au contraire*, wanted consumers to go with rival MCI. E. F. Hutton had Bill Cosby on their side, while Smith-Barney trotted out John Houseman. And so it goes, on and on, performer after performer undertaking the great American ritual of introducing products to consumers.

Starring athletes have proven to be especially successful representatives of products. It has been estimated that in prime-time television one commercial in twelve will feature a sports figure promoting a product. Michael "Air" Jordan attracted so many to Nike shoes that he was credited with reviving the company. It apparently does not make any difference whether the product is sports-related or not. Take panty hose; few would have thought that Joe Namath could have sent a hose manufacturer's sales skyward, but he did. Eveready battery sales were pumped up by Mary Lou Retton. Although some athletes are not successful at this—Mark Spitz, Billie Jean King, and Hank Aaron among them—a surprising number are. Athletes have earned a place in the hearts of Americans by the earnestness and purity of their efforts. Their fame may not be greater than entertainers from other realms, but it is coupled with a lack of artifice that disposes consumers to trust them and to give the products they represent a chance. If Don Meredith says Lipton Tea is the best, why not find out?

Stars have particular utility for products that are new entrants in the marketplace. Celebrity endorsers are familiar figures, and if they say a product or service has value, then people are drawn that much closer to finding out for themselves. Sun Country Classic Wine Cooler was an unknown until Ringo Starr touted it.

Some celebrity entertainers refuse to play this important twentieth-century role of mass merchandiser. Katharine Hepburn, Carol Burnett, Marlon Brando, Robert Redford, and various others have resisted the continual entreaties of businesses, no doubt believing that hawking goods is a tawdry exercise that would reduce their stature. Their disinterest does not decrease their value to advertisers. Those who set prices on celebrity services believe that such scruples only whet public interest: if one of these reluctant stars were to share some commercial words of wisdom, viewers would be especially heedful.

For some people, buying products associated with stars can serve as an emotional link between devotee and idol. If a star's fans are especially zealous, as a worshipful act they will want to purchase items bearing the star's name or likeness. Beginning in the mid-1950s, Col. Tom Parker arranged to have between fifty and one hundred Elvis products always available for fans—lipstick, phonographs, jeans, fountain pens, and so forth. In the mid–1960s Beatle products were everywhere; the first was a Beatle wig that admirers could use to impersonate their heroes.

Arch-fan Pamela Des Barres wrote that her "entire room was covered with Beatle paraphernalia. I wrote with a Beatle pen, slept on a Beatle pillowcase, and breathed with Beatle lungs."[11]

Celebrity performers enjoy such good standing with the public that the possibility for misrepresentation and deception exists. When this occurs, it is usually not of great consequence: Joe DiMaggio, spokesman for Mr. Coffee, actually prefers to drink tea; Cybill Shepherd promotes the beef industry in public, but in private avoids red meat. But at times the deception is not so harmless. Insurance being sold to the elderly through television commercials featuring such personalities as Art Linkletter, Ed McMahon, Tennessee Ernie Ford, and Lorne Greene turned out to be highly defective. Dick Van Dyke told potential buyers that the policy he was promoting would provide "protection for your loved ones" by shielding savings, while in truth the policy's benefit was only $500. If the fraud is undeniable and the public's confidence has been breached, no amount of accumulated credibility can stop citizens from being vengeful. In 1986 George Hamilton and Lloyd Bridges were taken to court by disgruntled entrepreneurs who believed the performers had duped them into making losing investments. But such breakdowns are rare. Americans trust stars to give guidance, and in the interests of their own longevity if for no other reason, stars are unlikely to violate that trust (although they may test it a bit for purposes of commercial puffery).

Stars' example may also inspire fans in religious matters. Some followed Pat Boone into a fundamental Christianity, and others followed Muhammad Ali to the Muslims. Stars can also guide voters among political perspectives, exhorting them to join a political party or vote for a particular candidate. Frank Sinatra brought voters to Hubert Humphrey, while Sammy Davis, Jr., did the same for Richard Nixon.

Marlon Brando groused, "Once you become a star actor, people start asking you questions about politics, astronomy, archaeology, and birth control." Stars' opinions are indeed matters of interest; knowing them and reacting to them helps people in the process of forming their own opinions. It is not just stars' words but their entire images that can help Americans negotiate the universe of abstractions. Stars come to symbolize ideas in the minds of the public. Jim Morrison proclaimed in 1972 that "if Spiro Agnew stands for law and order, all right, say I stand for sex. Chaos. Movement without meaning. Cop baiting. Fifty-two-week paid vacations with double over-time every year." Morrison was delighted with his symbolic role, but other stars can find such assignments disquieting. Asked how he felt about being a symbol of rebellion, Mick Jagger responded, "I don't think my knowledge is enough to start pontificating on the subject. I didn't ever set myself up as a leader in society. It's society that's pushed me into that position."

Like it or not, a star will be put to symbolic purposes by the population. It may even be difficult for Americans to contemplate important issues without a star in mind who personifies that issue. Richard Schickel writes, "It is not too much to say that we have, in about a half-century's time, reached a point where most issues, whether political, intellectual, or moral in nature, do not have real status—that is, literally, the status of the real—until they have been taken up, dramatized, in the celebrity world."[12] If people are to make sense out of women's rights, it may help to think of Marlo Thomas. Saving the environment must be a good idea if Robert Redford is identified with it. Old age gets redefined with the help of George Burns. It is hard to comprehend the significance of a disease like AIDS without the case of Rock Hudson, or a disorder like anorexia nervosa without Karen Carpenter's story. One of the reasons that nuclear issues may be difficult for Americans to grasp is that, with the occasional exception of Jane Fonda, no star is linked with them.

In 1979 political scientist Wayne Ault conducted the only quantitative study to date into the personification of issues by performing celebrities. By telephone he surveyed 500 randomly selected adults, asking them what political issues they associated with six stars: John Wayne, Robert Redford, Joan Baez, Jane Fonda, Dick Gregory, and Marlon Brando.[13] The "correct" association of stars with issues ranged from a high of 99 percent for Wayne to a low of 94 percent for Redford. Clearly the vast majority of Americans know their stars and what they stand for. A full 80 percent of the respondents in the survey said they had talked to others about what celebrities say or do concerning public issues. As sources of information on public issues, celebrities were considered by a majority of the 500 adults to be fair, reliable, and prestigious. Fully one third admitted that they had become "more concerned or interested in a public issue" because of the celebrities' political statements or activities.

Richard Schickel, recognizing this influence of performing celebrities upon the thinking of Americans, laments it. In his perspective we are much the poorer for the fact that stars have come to play such a large role in our thoughts. It is conceivable that our conceptual universe has shrunk when images of stars and what they symbolize occupy our minds. But on the other hand, the image of a star can be communicated so far and so fast through a population, and with such agreement on what it represents, that abstract ideas may have better circulation today than ever before. When 99 percent of us recognize John Wayne and what he stands for, or Jane Fonda and what she stands for, then for better or for worse a democratic ideal is being realized.

Stars do so much for the public, at so many corners of people's lives, that appreciation can turn worshipful and ties to the star strengthen to the point of emotional fusion. A David Bowie fan once commented that "the star expresses something up there that's very real to you, and so you mistake that thing for yourself. And you get caught up in his life." The union becomes sanctified. A Barry Manilow fan, a forty-two-year-old woman, offered about his meaning in her life: "I suppose it's the same kind of thing people get out of religion. I can't really explain it more than that. But they obviously get something from God to help them through their lives. And Barry is—maybe I shouldn't say it, but it's the way I feel—he's the same sort of thing. He helps me through my life."

Avidity for stars, and for the salvation they seem to bring, leads fans to cherish tokens of them. This desire goes beyond the merchandise sold everywhere and beyond the ready autograph to hard-won and intimate fetishes. The butts of cigarettes that Greta Garbo had puffed on were jewels to her devotees. Elvis's neckerchiefs, pungent with his perspiration, were objects of fierce contention among front-row enthusiasts. When Washington Redskins quarterback Joe Theismann fractured his leg in 1985, the ambulance paramedics who transported him to the hospital appropriated his jersey as a memento. Possessing such

talismans, people hope to possess some of the magical properties of the star. Among the more remarkable efforts to gain personal mementos of stars was the work in the 1970s of the Plaster
Casters, a group of young women who perfected a method for
making casts of erect penises, applying their craft to numerous
rock idols until they had a museum of chalky white phalluses.

Social order is created, and social membership granted,
when the partisans of stars gather together into cults. At these
moments the loose atoms of twentieth-century society join together and rediscover the missing sense of community. A young
woman described attending a Barry Manilow concert as follows: "Complete strangers catch hold of your hands. And you
are all united, united as one. And to think that one man can do
that to so many people. I mean, he must be special to be able to
do that, to create the atmosphere and this special feeling. He
can't just be ordinary, can he?" In the periods between performances, the sensation of belonging can be continued through
participation in fan clubs. Contributions are made, newsletters
circulated, and correspondence conducted. The Manilow con-
certgoer ended her letter to another fan: "All my Barryhugs &
Manilove and of course Mountains of Manilust!" When such fellow worshipers find each other they find companionship, a
scarce commodity in mass society.

Sharing star information and gossip is common everywhere, since for a disparate U.S. populace stars are among the
few things held in common. Everyone had an opinion on the
marriage of Mike Tyson and Robin Givens. Richard Nixon, touring a tornado-ravaged Ohio town in 1974, did what he always
did when compelled to fraternize—he talked about sports stars.
Hank Aaron's 715th home run, hit just before, provided the president with ample conversational fodder.

The starring American performer is a modern icon, an image upheld and scrutinized by all, an image that, being shared,
imparts commonality to the nation. The star becomes one of
those essential things that hold us together, a component in the
precious gel of culture.

8.★
COMPENSATIONS

ccording to conventional wisdom, stars are compensated beyond all reason—grossly. A prevailing disgust with stars' salaries crops up in letters to the editor and in calls to radio talk shows. If a star is young and has not performed up to expectations, popular resentment over the millions of dollars squandered will run high.

Such responses are not confined to the general public. Commentators on the star phenomenon have raised the level of indignation to great heights. Critic Richard Schickel asserts that the salaries of Hollywood celebrities "bear no conceivable relationship to the actual value of the actor's services."[1] Stars themselves are not immune to this sort of sentiment, and in fact it is a frequent if *sotto voce* observation from them. James Garner remarked, "Let's face it, actors are paid more than they're worth. Producers are idiots for paying what we ask." Ringo Starr, mystified by the riches coming his way, queried, "What's a scruff like me doing with all this lot?"

Whether or not the compensation is excessive, it clearly is enormous. David Bowie, receiving a cash advance for a rock concert in Memphis, amused himself by spreading the dollars several inches thick on the floor of his hotel room, wall to wall, and then wading through them. "The money today is stagger-ing," commented Martina Navratilova, who was swept up into the high-income brackets when stardom was extended to tele-vised tennis players. But the money has always been staggering for those in the star role. In 1915 the newly renowned Charlie Chaplin signed with the Essanay production company for the then unheard-of salary of $1,250 a week plus a $10,000 one-time bonus; one year later his contract with Mutual Film Corpora-tion called for $10,000 weekly following a $150,000 signing bo-nus. At a time when the average salaried American was drawing $1,142 annually, it is little wonder his bonanza attracted great public notice. Mary Pickford's account of her salary history after 1916 was this: "In the next few years my salary staged several spectacular leaps, going from $1,000 to $2,000, then from $2,000 to $4,000, and finally to what was then and, I believe, remained for some time the ceiling of motion-picture salaries, $10,000 a week."

In 1930 Babe Ruth negotiated for and received from the Yankee organization a yearly salary of $80,000, which was at that time an outsized sum for an athlete. President Herbert Hoover was earning $75,000, and Ruth was asked by reporters if he thought it right that a ballplayer should make more than the nation's chief executive. In an insouciant reply that reflected his newly evolved stature, Ruth is said to have answered, "Why not? I had a better year than he did."

As the years have gone by, starring athletes have become ever more highly compensated. The *average* compensation for professional athletes in 1987 was over $200,000 for National Football League players, $300,000 for major-league baseball players, and $400,000 for National Basketball Association ath-letes. It is hardly surprising that more than 100 sports stars that year had earnings above $1 million, according to a survey by *Sport* magazine. Moses Malone was paid $2,145,000 to be the center of the Washington Bullets; outfielder Jim Rice made $2,412,500 for his season with the Boston Red Sox; and $1,400,000 went to Jim Kelly, quarterback of the Buffalo Bills. The highest-paid athlete of all was boxer Michael Spinks, who earned $4 million for a mere two fights.

Even players yet unproven in professional sports are able to reap giant rewards because they show promise of becoming stars. Vinny Testaverde, long before he had ever stepped on the Tampa Bay Buccaneers football field and quarterbacked the team, agreed to a six-year pact worth $8 million. Defensive lineman Brian Bosworth signed his first professional contract with the Seattle Seahawks for ten years and $11 million; it included a $2.5 million bonus, with $500,000 in cash promptly delivered to the twenty-two-year-old. Patrick Ewing was enticed to the New York Knickerbockers with a seven-year contract valued at $12 million. The numbers have become so large that, for most Americans, they lose relevance to the known world.

Compensation is no less grand in other entertainment fields. A successful album for a recording artist can return millions of dollars to the performer. Tina Turner received $4 million for her *Private Dancer* album, while Bruce Springsteen made $8 million from *Born in the USA*. Remarkable as these figures are, they do not constitute all-time records. Lionel Richie earned $15 million for *Can't Slow Down*, and Prince made $17.1 million with *Purple Rain*. But they still fell far short of the $70 million that Michael Jackson garnered from the sales of *Thriller.*

Movies continue to reward their stars exorbitantly. Marlon Brando said caustically, "I'm only doing it for the money," but what money it was: $3.5 million for *Apocalypse Now* and another $3.5 million for a cameo appearance in *Superman.* If a producer wanted Paul Newman to be in a film in the late 1980s, it would set him back $4 million. In 1987 that was what Dolly Parton wanted, too, after making only four movies. Eddie Murphy was paid about $5 million per movie, and so was Clint Eastwood. In the $6 million bracket were Dustin Hoffman, Warren Beatty, and Robert Redford. In 1987 Sylvester Stallone was reported to be demanding $12 million per film.

Television stars were hardly slouches by comparison, although rather than earning their money through a one-time production, they had to work for it in a steadier fashion, episode after episode and season after season. Don Johnson, headliner in "Miami Vice," made $30,000 per show in 1985; when summed with other stints, his take from acting that year totaled $1 million. A year later Cybill Shepherd earned $40,000 for each "Moonlighting" episode; Joan Collins received $47,000 per "Dynasty" show; and with every "Dallas" episode Victoria Principal netted $50,000. For her role on "Falcon Crest" Jane Wyman made $1.6 million a year (while her ex-husband, Ronald Reagan, was earning $200,000 as the nation's president). Tom Selleck was so important to the success of "Magnum P. I." that he was paid an extraordinary $4.8 million per season, year after year.

Remarkable as these salaries may be, celebrity entertainers will usually go on to make much more money by commercially exploiting their fame. Through personal appearances, advertising endorsements, and the sale of merchandise associated with their name or image, stars can double or triple their stream of wealth. Shirley Temple dolls brought the actress a sizable part of her substantial fortune. In 1964 the Beatles' coffers were beginning to overflow with the royalties from their array of products. David Bowie found in the 1970s and 1980s that, while his box-office receipts and recording sales were remarkable enough, the heftiest profits were to be had from the auxiliary merchandise—program books, T-shirts, sweatshirts, scarves, badges, and posters. Top athletes can expect to make three times their salaries from payments by advertisers; the leading sports endorser in 1987 was veteran golfer Arnold Palmer, who brought home 8 million extra dollars. That year the highest-paid person in the United States, bar none, was Bill Cosby, who earned a total of $57 million once his income from commercial accounts and book sales was added to his television salary. The following year he was surpassed by Michael Jackson's $60 million in personal income from a world tour, sales of his album *Bad* and his autobiography *Moonwalk,* Pepsi endorsements, and other sources.

Is it possible that reports on the total compensation of stars are sometimes inflated? There may be some reason to believe so. Publicists might be tempted to jack up the figures, possibly to impress the public—although Americans are surely so numbed by stars' dollars that a zero more or less is not going to make much difference—but more likely to improve a star's stature vis-à-vis other stars, and to create bargaining power for upcoming negotiations with employers. At certain rare moments, however, as in judicial proceedings, stars are compelled to reveal their actual earnings; oddly, what is disclosed is often an even higher figure than had previously been reported by the press.

Two 1987 court cases revealed the true current earnings of a pair of stars. Joan Collins had been married to her fourth husband, Peter Holm, for just over a year when he sued for divorce. It was revealed that during their thirteen-month union she had received a total of $5.2 million, with $1.5 million coming from her role as Alexis Colby on "Dynasty." In a second lawsuit Eddie Murphy was sued by an ex-manager for breach of contract. Evidence presented at the trial documented that the comic actor had earned $58 million over six years solely from performing. When his income from all other sources was added, the six-year total reached $120 million. Murphy's average annual compensation, therefore, had been about $20 million. Asked his reaction to the disclosure of these earnings, Murphy conceded, "It feels like you're pulling your pants down in front of everyone."

As if the money were not enough, stars also are showered with gifts. Objects of greater and lesser value are pressed upon them. Some of this largesse comes from appreciative sponsors or businesspeople whose products the star has endorsed. Some of it comes from grateful team owners or production company executives. Elizabeth Taylor is used to receiving a small but expensive present every day of a shooting schedule. When she made *Poker Alice* in 1987 she was given $10,000 worth of trinkets over twenty-five days by the producers. A company employee reported that "mainly we bought earrings, cigarette lighters, and bracelets."

If such gifts do not come freely, stars can simply ask for them. Their standing with those in a position to give is usually so high that the giver is often delighted to donate and to enjoy a transaction with a star, no matter how one-sided. An acquaintance of Babe Zaharias related what occurred when the athlete spotted a Rolex watch in a store window: "She said she'd always wanted one, and the next thing I know, we're in the Rolex office. She said to the receptionist, 'I'm Babe Zaharias, and I want to see the boss.' Babe was invited into his office. They gave her a gold Rolex. They gave me a gold Rolex. They gave her another gold Rolex for George [Zaharias, her husband]."

For those performers who endure in the star role, a gigantic personal fortune will amass almost unavoidably. When he died in 1977 Bing Crosby's estate was valued at $150 million. Bob

Hope has been estimated to be worth over $200 million. Paul McCartney's wealth has passed the $500 million mark.

Collectively stars are the most highly compensated people in the modern world. *Forbes* magazine, which annually releases a list of the forty highest-paid individuals, has pointed out that most of them are performers and noted, "No longer are steel mills, auto factories or oil wells the principal sources of great wealth. In the post-industrial society, the once-despised entertainment industry has usurped that role."

Let's now examine a heretical position regarding this wealth. Is it possible that instead of being overcompensated, stars are if anything *under*paid? That what they receive is well below their actual value? Consider this: as a general rule, those who employ stars do not lose money on them. The team owners and the Hollywood producers come out ahead. Their investments in star salaries pay out. While exceptions do exist—Brian Bosworth was slow to earn his way with the Seattle Seahawks; Sylvester Stallone and Dolly Parton could not save *Rhinestone; Ishtar* died at the box office despite the presence of Dustin Hoffman and Warren Beatty—they are infrequent. Most stars succeed as drawing cards and stimulate profits for those who have backed their performances. From this perspective stars cannot be considered overpaid. Douglas Fairbanks, Sr.'s version of this fiscal reality, as he explained it to his incredulous brother in 1916, was this: "Actually I'm working for nothing. I'm only making about $500,000 a year. My pictures have been netting the studio more than a million a year each and when you multiply that by a dozen pictures, you can see I really am, comparatively, working for nothing."

Moviemakers continue to depend upon the allure of stars to earn back their production expenses. A few films do well at the box office without celebrated actors, but the norm remains the movie that features those performers who spark popular interest. In the most extensive economic analysis of the entertainment industry to date, Harold Vogel explained why, in theory, producers rely on stars: "It may be less risky to pay a star $1.5 million than to pay an unknown $100,000; the presence of the star may easily increase the value of the property by several times that $1.5 million salary through increased sales in the theatrical and other markets, whereas the unknown may contribute nothing from the standpoint of return on investment."[2] Writing in 1986 about how the film business actually operates, Mark Litwak observed that "pictures are marketed on [stars'] looks and names. Their strong public followings make studios eager to obtain their services."[3] Recognizing the commercial advantage of using celebrity actors, producers compete for them and bid up their prices, but not beyond the threshold at which stars as a group no longer generate appropriate profits.

The presence of a starring athlete will greatly elevate game attendance and gate receipts, but more than local interest will be quickened. The national press will begin to cover the star player, and widespread recognition will result. Broad fame increases the chances that the team will be selected for network broadcasts and thus secure additional revenues. By eliciting both local and national notice star players will repay team owners many times over. They also generate wealth for the broadcasting medium itself which, by transmitting star performances, can assemble large audiences and then sell them at a high tariff to advertisers.

In addition, the services rendered by stars are so momentous as to be virtually priceless. To review the catalog, it is no small matter that stars have the ability to entertain us and to divert us from our travails. When one person can regale one quarter of a billion people, that person is manifestly playing a significant role in national life. Perhaps inadvertently on their part, stars serve as personality models and by doing so help to socialize the population. They provide a facsimile of a community, in an era when real communities no longer command allegiance. Stars lead us into the valley of consumption, specifically by indicating products for our consideration and broadly by their depicted lifestyles. Stars are in fact in the vanguard everywhere, facing the unknown as we trail along in their wake. As the many of us follow the few of them, we are changed from an amorphous throng to a patterned people. Stars lend order to modern times. Can we pay them enough for all of this?

Finally, somewhere in the calculation of whether stars are overcompensated or undercompensated must enter the matter of the psychological costs suffered by leading entertainers as a result of unyielding public scrutiny. This drawback of celebrity can be the most difficult for normal citizens to appreciate, since most people live with a perceived shortage of regard and since fame is what performers have nominally worked for. But from the star's point of view, the pitiless engrossment of a massive public can be genuinely debilitating. As Mary Pickford commented plaintively, "One of the greatest penalties those of us who live our lives in full view of the public must pay is the loss of that most cherished birthright of man's privacy." Lillian Gish reflected about her colleague, Rudolph Valentino *(photograph 36):* "He couldn't take it, all the constant attention and invasion of his privacy. It just killed him." If a star is not careful and self-protective, the attention can become a sort of irradiation. "You can meet someone on an airplane, and it's very nice; the next thing you know, that person's a reporter," explained Sylvester Stallone. "Sometimes you have to be almost an isolationist."

In part, then, the compensation of celebrity entertainers ought to be understood as fair payment for the searing gaze we level at them. Clara Bow complained about the public, "When they stare at me, I get the creeps." Sixty years later, nothing had changed; Harrison Ford said, "I'm very uncomfortable when people stare at me." We stare at stars as we are permitted to stare at no others, and amends should be made.

All things considered, stars work cheap. While the marketplace ultimately and definitively establishes a price for their services, it is not facetious to suggest that there may not be enough wealth in existence to pay them what they are really worth. The remarkable riches that accrue to stars provide a vivid signal of their primacy in American culture. Stars are paid more than all others because they do more than all others for the maintenance of our way of life.

Stars' only binding obligation for this incredible wealth is the payment of their taxes. With the help of managers and advisers, most celebrity performers do manage to discharge this responsibility suitably. Elvis Presley, fearing miscalculation, simply had all his paperwork sent to the Internal Revenue Service, and the agency computed the tax due. Occasionally a star, perhaps through greed or the malfeasance of his or her agents, will come up short. Joe Louis was rocked more by tax claims than he ever was in the boxing ring. At one point Mickey Rooney was $100,000 behind in his payments. Janis Ian, famous for her song

"Society's Child," sold $4 million worth of records in 1975; upon her retirement and return to normal existence, still a teenager, she was presented with a $400,000 bill from the IRS.

Should stars slip up on their taxes, they may be able to dodge the consequences because they are who they are. Paul Newman charmed his way through a 1984 IRS audit. "To be an actor, you have to be a child," he reportedly told the auditors. "I'm making a lot of money as an actor, so I must be a very good child. But you can't have it both ways. If I kept good records, I wouldn't be a good child. And then I wouldn't be in the tax bracket I'm in now."

Once having paid their taxes and covered their business expenses, stars are then free to do whatever they wish with the rest of their money—this is the fun part. Some of it they will set aside, some of it they will give to good causes, but much of it they will spend extravagantly upon themselves. Rolling in, the money rolls out. "When I was with him, he lived like King Farouk and spent all the time," stated a former employee of Frank Sinatra. "He never wanted anyone to think that he was not successful because he didn't have money, so he spent like crazy." Liberace was a champion shopper, and in every city on his tours would relentlessly visit a string of antique shops, galleries, curio shops, jewelers, and furriers. David Bowie and his wife Angela learned to consume with a passion; "When it came to spending they were uncontrollable," biographer Henry Edwards wrote.

Stars will buy houses. Douglas Fairbanks, Sr., and Mary Pickford purchased "Pickfair" in Beverly Hills and set the standard for elaborate, expensive homes. Six decades later basketball star Kareem Abdul-Jabbar owned a house in Los Angeles worth $4.3 million. Not so many miles away sat the estate of Barbra Streisand, valued at $10 million. Frequently stars will buy homes for their parents, too. In 1946 Sinatra paid $22,000 for a large house in Hoboken, New Jersey, for his mother and father. Red Skelton, Mickey Mantle, and Jackie Gleason bought homes for their mothers. One of the first things the Beatles did with their money was to purchase new houses for the parents or guardians who had raised them. Having bought new homes for themselves and their families, stars will frequently obtain second and third houses. Robert Wagner maintained an apartment in Los Angeles, a ranch in San Fernando Valley where he kept

Arabian stallions, and a ski house in Gstaad, Switzerland. At any given time Liberace liked to have about four households operating. Actress Kim Basinger bought an entire Georgia town for $20 million in 1989.

Stars will buy cars—expensive ones and lots of them. The Beatles, some of whom did not drive, each bought several of the most costly automobiles available. Presley bought a fleet for himself, and in a moment of generosity bought more for those around him. For Christmas gifts in 1970, a biographer reports, "Elvis had purchased *ten* Mercedes sedans, which he planned to give away like three-speed bikes. This tab added up to $85,000!" In her autobiography Martina Navratilova described her stable of automobiles: "At one point I owned a Toyota Supra, a Pontiac J, a 733 BMW, a silver Mercedes, a Porsche 928, a 1965 Rolls-Royce Silver Cloud, and a white 1976 Rolls-Royce Corniche convertible, which was valued at $100,000 new."

If cars are not enough, there are planes. John Travolta at one point owned three: a Lockheed Jetstar 731, a Constellation, and a Cessna Citation. Joe Esposito, Presley's former road manager, related that "Elvis would do things like buy a jet in Memphis to be able to fly down to Fort Worth to inspect another jet. That was the way it was. That was the life we led." The singer even acquired a large Convair 880 jet, which he named after his daughter, Lisa Marie; fuel alone cost $400,000 annually.

Stars treat themselves to all sorts of finery. From the beginning Frank Sinatra loved to buy clothes—tens of ties, shirts, and suits at a time. Even as a young adult Elizabeth Taylor spared no expense on her wardrobe. When she went on her first honeymoon, with Nick Hilton, she took twenty-two trunks of clothing, one of them holding nothing but her hats; years later, on tour to promote her perfume Passion, she required twenty-three trunks. Richard Burton was happy to spend $1 million to buy her a diamond of sixty-nine carats. Lana Turner loved to purchase shoes in quantity: "At one time I had a special room, with shelves from floor to ceiling, filled with shoes." Liberace was reported to spend over $2 million yearly on clothes.

The important thing is that stars discharge their wealth so as to please themselves. They can build up collections: Vincent Price bought art; Mick Jagger collected antique silver; Reggie Jackson had a stable of over 100 vintage automobiles; Michael

Jackson purchased oddities, at one time bidding on the remains of England's "Elephant Man." They can indulge in hobbies: Presley abruptly developed a passion for horseback riding and bought a farm and stables outside Memphis. They can do a little bit of everything: actor John Forsythe, in his sixties, collected impressionist and modern masterpieces, cruised in his thirty-foot sailboat, exercised in his own specially built gym, and owned sixteen race horses, saying, "I would gladly give up an Academy Award to win the Kentucky Derby." Or they can simply toss the money aside: Betty Grable, along with her bandleader husband Harry James, managed to gamble away most of her fortune.

Sylvester Stallone has commented that "money does not bring peace of mind. Actually, money brings about problems. Everything is magnified a hundred thousand times." Still, through self-indulgent spending celebrity entertainers will come as close as possible to the ideal of liberation that may have first incited their quest for stardom. Chris Evert, in one of the moments when she was not feeling a prisoner of her role, remarked, "The money has given me freedom. If I want to go to Greece, I go to Greece. It's been a wonderful life." Gregory Peck could reflect, "We do whatever we want whenever we want to do it. I suppose that's the ultimate freedom."

It is not material wealth alone that settles upon the celebrity performer. No less significant is the approbation in symbolic form: the tributes and honors that have no intrinsic monetary value but are still of immense consequence. While all Americans have potential access to wealth, these particular awards can be achieved only by a select few, and so they become markers of ultimate value in our society. They signify how much we prize our stars. No other occupation is the object of such widespread and unvarying public compulsion to hallow and venerate.

The importance of these accolades is signaled by the elaborate ceremonies that transpire whenever they are bestowed. These are no ordinary occasions; as if for a tribal rite, the costumes and accoutrements mark them as exceptional. Men will be formally dressed in tuxedos, women in splendid gowns. Jewelry will sparkle, furs will be displayed. Those celebrated and those celebrating will arrive in luxury automobiles and take assigned seats. The entire affair will be carefully orchestrated. Presentations will be made at a dais. Eyes will be fixed on the winners, and applause will ring out at appropriate moments. An observer from another culture, an anthropologist from another world, would recognize immediately, even if not a single word were understood, that some sort of high ritual was under way.

The number of spectators is far greater than the sumptuously dressed participants in the hall. Thanks to modern media the audience extends far and wide. If the event is broadcast live a large proportion of the nation will be in attendance, watching as those feted are announced. Should television cameras not be there, accounts of the ceremony will be carried by the wire services, together with photographs, and the next morning newspaper readers will learn of the year's winners.

In the world of sports, some coveted awards will go to upcoming stars. Annually the young collegian considered to be the best football player will receive the Heisman Trophy with much fanfare from the New York Athletic Club. Elsewhere the sturdiest lineman will be presented the Lombardi Award. Among established basketball and baseball players, one in each sport will be tapped as that year's Most Valuable Player. To the pitcher who has been most proficient goes the Cy Young Award.

The performing arts have evolved particularly elaborate rituals for celebrating star players. These awards ceremonies have become part of the national calendar of festivals. Grammys go to lauded recording stars in March, Tonys to esteemed actors and actresses in June, Emmys to television performers of choice in September. But the biggest and best of these events remains the one that began first—the Oscars.

The annual Academy Awards represent the celebratory passion at its most ample. The telecast will usually attract the largest American audience of the year, with the single exception of the Super Bowl (another performer-centered event). According to a small but representative survey of Oscar viewers by communications researcher Michael R. Real, the main reasons people watch are "to find out the winners" and "to see the celebrities."[4] A majority of his respondents concurred with the statement, "I usually have my personal favorites picked out before

the awards show." The public clearly has an emotional investment in the ceremony.

Not only Americans attend the Oscars; the global audience
is the largest for any media event originating in the United
States. With the inclusion of China, which receives a tape-
delayed telecast, the total viewership may reach one billion human beings. To ensure that news about the awards is dispatched
in volume to the fascinated world, over 1,000 accredited print
and broadcast reporters will be furiously at work.

The ceremony is a complicated event, so several days of rehearsal come beforehand. Seventeen cameras will have to be co-
ordinated for the telecast, as well as a large orchestra, scores of
dancers, a variety of special effects, and the comings and goings
of presenters plus the dozens of other celebrities featured. On
Oscar night the members of the Academy of Motion Picture Arts
and Sciences will pack the theater. Their attire could hardly be
more costly; Cher reportedly hit a peak in 1985 with a $12,000
creation. When the year's best performers are announced, the
winning actor and actress will deliver another small performance, accepting the statuette with obvious feeling and diverting some—but not too much—of the praise to helpful others.

The Academy Award presentations loom so large in the
present that it may not be easy to remember they have a somewhat checkered history. It was not until 1929 that the first ban-
quet was held—a modest affair for industry insiders alone. Film
executive Louis B. Mayer, who had contributed money to the
formation of the Academy, instructed those who were trying to
think of a way to honor performers' excellence, "Now mind you,
we're not talking about anything grand." Until the mid–1930s
the Academy and Oscars remained very much under the control
of Hollywood moguls who were less interested in acknowledging acting skills than in rewarding those who had served them
well and penalizing others who had been recalcitrant or who
had dared to appear in independent productions. Even after re-
forms were instituted, the Oscars were still heavily influenced
by internal industry politics and bloc voting from the studios.
The result was that the acting awards were distributed on an
inconsistent basis: some minor talents won Oscars (Luise Rai-
ner, little recalled now and little admired then, won twice) and

some major talents never did, among them Richard Burton, Montgomery Clift, Greta Garbo, and Cary Grant.

Although no money is awarded, there is a distinctly financial aspect to the Oscars. Films that receive awards get a second chance at the box office and are sure to reap millions more; if a star has contracted for a percentage of the profits, he or she will be handsomely rewarded. When *One Flew Over the Cuckoo's Nest* received four Oscars, its total receipts rose by $50 million and Jack Nicholson's take soared proportionally. But perhaps more important to the individual performer, an Oscar for best actor or best actress will mean that the star's asking price is going to shoot upward.

Neither the uneven history nor the venal side of the Academy Awards diminishes the public's appreciation of the ceremony. Nor does it even matter that the choices are not those of the public—not directly, anyway. It is the 4,700 members of the Academy who do the voting—or more precisely in the case of stars, the 1,200 members of the actors' branch. Nevertheless, the worldwide audience somehow feels itself to be an integral part of the ritual, celebrators at the celebration. From them streams admiration and regard for the anointed performers.

Beyond saluting the year's best, awards programs also recognize long and successful star careers. In some ceremonial and public fashion, in ways that apply to no other occupation, the most durable performers will be immortalized. Record-breaking athletes will be elected to their sport's Hall of Fame, to which fans make pilgrimages no less devotedly than religious adherents. Baseball, football, and basketball have their sacred groves wherein the memories of outstanding players are preserved. The famous Hollywood performer will have a brass star bearing his or her name riveted to the sidewalk of the Walk of Fame. On the first Saturday of every month, in an act of obeisance, devotees will carefully clean and polish the emblems. To this two-mile stretch of Hollywood Boulevard are drawn an estimated 15 million admirers every year.

Cathy Smith, companion of several celebrity entertainers, observed that "the stars—at least the genuine ones—are tuned into the mass psyche in a way ordinary people aren't. In their work—whether it is acting or singing or playing guitar—they can reach out to what is inside people. That makes them special. But it doesn't necessarily make them better human beings. Some of them turn out to be exactly what you would expect: spoiled, irresponsible, and self-indulgent."[5] Narcissistic and imperious behavior can emanate from stars. As a rule, the world tolerates such displays. Having reverence for stars, the public defers to them. Eddie Murphy concluded, "I think people are reacting to something else when they see me. . . . Like I took some of my watches in to get them fixed. The repairman reached out to shake my hand, and he was shaking and his hand was all sweaty."

As well as being ceded riches and honors, then, a star is also granted the right to behave in a superior fashion. Part of the payoff for being a star is to enjoy the privileges of the rank by exerting one's will over others. The idea of always having your own way is the infant's primal dream of omnipotence; for the star it has some chance of coming true. Stars are permitted dominance, and nonstars submit to it.

A star's power can be revealed in countless ways. Whims will be cheerfully indulged. If Elvis Presley wanted a midnight tour of the Memphis morgue, the unprepared attendant would be happy to oblige; "his fame was his passkey," remarked his wife about that particular episode. If the rock group Van Halen wants pounds of M&Ms with all the brown ones removed, someone will pick through mounds of candies for them. Sylvester Stallone, in Israel to make *Rambo III*, insisted upon pink towels, and the hotel manager rushed to indulge him, although not without grousing to a reporter, "He is very spoiled."

Celebrity entertainers are not expected to be on time for anything. Others will wait for the star, never the other way around. Lana Turner was chronically late, and so was Elizabeth Taylor. Marilyn Monroe would arrive hours after she was due, once admitting, "It's surprising I get there at all." John Barrymore, Ernie Kovacs, and David Bowie were all perpetually tardy. Even nice guy Robert Redford cannot arrive anywhere on time.

When stars do make their appearance, it is incumbent upon those present to note their disposition and adjust accordingly. Priscilla Presley related, "As soon as he appeared, the room would become silent until he revealed his mood. No one, including myself, dared joke around unless he laughed and then we all laughed." A member of Frank Sinatra's retinue made a similar observation about his boss's waking up: "It would take him two hours to wind up and nobody talked until he was ready. Nobody would even go into the room until they knew what kind of mood he was in that day."

Sometimes a star will exercise power over others in the smallest and meanest of ways. Marilyn Monroe, in a confessional mood, told an interviewer that she sometimes snapped at people just to see them cringe. Having become a star through his role in "Moonlighting," ex-waiter Bruce Willis grew overbearing toward waiters. "He's such a pain," complained a waiter in a Hollywood restaurant about Willis, and the cashier said about the star's deportment, "Right after he leaves, everyone says, 'I'll never wait on him again.'"

Stars grow to expect that everyone will accede to their power, that no hindrances will be placed in their way. Much of the time this is the case: police will be fawning and obliging, stores will permit a star to shop privately after hours, private planes can be chartered simply by mentioning the star's name. But occasionally established procedures cannot be bent to accommodate a star, and sparks fly. It may be that an airline is unwilling to bump passengers so that a star without a reservation can fly.

The power of the star is strikingly revealed by the ready availability of sexual partners. Something in human nature leads people to submit themselves sexually to those in power, and stars have been the conspicuous beneficiaries of this trait. The number of those who offer themselves to a performer may be an approximate measure of his or her fame. "Once a man reached a certain level in the movie business, he was expected to screw everything that moved," observed Lyn Tornabene in her biography of Clark Gable; Gable cheerfully met the expectations.[6] In *Ball Four*, pitcher Jim Bouton wrote matter-of-factly about the camp followers who pursue baseball stars, calling them Baseball Annies. Attractive young women would sit in the stands wearing skirts but no underpants, flashing their chosen player a view of their private parts. The wife of a baseball player told researcher Beverly Crute about her initiation into the wandering ways of the players: "One day, when I first got married and several wives were having a motherly talk with me, I was kind of asking questions about how they could stand watching their husbands go out? Two of them kept saying, this is the way it is."[7]

Starring musicians also hold a great attraction for female fans, who during a concert will throw room keys and panties onstage. "Most women, married or single, made themselves readily available to Frank wherever he went," dryly noted biographer Kitty Kelley about Sinatra. When the Beatles arrived in the United States to begin their triumphant 1964 tour, throngs of girls pursued the foursome, laying siege to their hotels; two teenagers had themselves wrapped as parcels and delivered to their suite. Such guile was hardly required; the Beatles, young and randy, welcomed willing young women and considered it their mission to copulate with as many as possible. Their only precept was never to repeat—a rule that, given the numbers of eager suppliants, they violated only occasionally. Bianca Jagger told an interviewer about rock stars, "Of all the worlds, this is really the most male-oriented world that I have encountered in my life. The competition between women is the most frightening thing." Regarding Bianca's ex-husband Mick, a chronicler of the Rolling Stones noted that "the fastidious sneer to be seen on Jagger's face in almost any female company hinted at how easily sex presented itself to him, and how little he esteemed the girls who offered their bodies, in any position, for however brief a proprietal grip on his arm."[8]

Sauce for the gander is sauce for the goose, too. Women performers can benefit as much from the sexual availability of star worshippers as their male colleagues, except that they are supposed to be more secretive about it. This was Clara Bow's problem in 1931, when her trusted secretary spilled the details about the star's sexual antics. Undermined by the revelations, Bow suffered a nervous breakdown several months later. But such consequences have been rare; most women stars have been able to manage extensive but discreet love lives. There is no end of applicants, as Chris Evert explained: "When a guy comes up and asks for an autograph, the look in his eyes shows that he has you on a pedestal. If a woman player might want him in bed, she could have him. Being famous can be a turn-on, even if someone doesn't look beautiful."

The power of stars to collect as many romantic partners as they care to extends beyond casual contacts, and beyond more or less enduring relationships, to spouses. The Judeo-Christian tradition disallows having a number of wives or husbands at one time, so stars create serial harems, dropping and adding marriage partners according to their emotional needs or stage in life. A total of seven or eight marriages is not unheard of. Elizabeth Taylor has had seven or eight husbands, depending on whether Richard Burton is counted twice. Mickey Rooney *(photograph 37)* was married nine times, and Jerry Lee Lewis seven.

The power of a star is such that others will be drawn to it as if magnetized, hoping to share in the recognition and protection they feel it affords. Sycophants and hangers-on will try to fit in under the canopy of celebrity. Susan Rotolo, Bob Dylan's first true love, recalled, "I began to see everyone as wanting my friendship and companionship just to get close to Bob," and she was correct in all likelihood. Marilyn Monroe observed about those who sought to bond themselves to her, "I like to be accepted for my own sake, but a lot of people don't care who you are. All they're interested in is your fame—while you've still got it."

The social power of the celebrity entertainer is so great that, in trying to articulate this twentieth-century phenomenon, stars are often forced to use analogies to traditional religious figures. Phil Esposito led the Boston Bruins hockey team to a Stanley Cup victory, and afterward he reported, "And suddenly I felt like the Pope. There was this mob below us, and I started blessing them." John Lennon ventured, "We're more popular than Jesus now"—an intemperate remark that he was forced to recant, but probably an accurate one.

Wealth, honors, power—the celebrity performer would seem to have it all. What could possibly be missing from the star's cornucopia of benefits?

What is often lacking is something so common in the lives of most people that it is difficult to believe stars do not possess it: simple, honest companionship. A large number of stars experience a constant, foreboding sense of being friendless. They lack the true cornerstone of human existence—the pleasurable, stabilizing company of the like-minded. They have achieved the pinnacle of modern life, only to find it solitary and dissatisfying. "That's when I sat on my bed and realized that I could be Number 1 in the world, have material and personal achievements, and still be unhappy," said Chris Evert. "Something was missing. I felt empty, unfulfilled."

Throughout the century loneliness has been a theme in stars' accounts of their lives. At the peak of his fame the pensive Charlie Chaplin reported, "I had always thought I would like the public's attention, and here it was—paradoxically isolating me with a depressing sense of loneliness." Many decades later it was reported about John Belushi *(photograph 38)* that his frequent complaint to others was "I'm just so lonely." Gary Coleman, the young star of "Diff'rent Strokes," said, "I've hardly got anybody I can call a friend." Judy Garland spoke for many when she remarked, "If I'm a legend, then why am I so lonely?"

How can it be that stars are so often lonesome? It would seem to defy all common sense. By definition they are the most popular people in the United States. Yet it is the case that as a group stars have greater difficulties in establishing friendships than most other people. They are generally unable to form close personal contact with either those who are their empyrean equals or those who are not.

The fact that Star Village is nonexistent, is rather a fantasy of the public's, means that celebrity performers are destined to experience little congeniality among their fellows. There have been a few exceptions: the Charlie Chaplin who felt so alone was a close friend of Douglas Fairbanks, Sr., and to lesser extent Mary Pickford. A number of leading Hollywood actors, including Montgomery Clift, George Hamilton, and Michael Jackson, have felt comradely with Elizabeth Taylor, and she with them. Jack Benny and George Burns were longtime pals. In the 1960s and 1970s many rock stars, young and nearly overwhelmed by towering fame, drew some succor from each other. Philip Norman, in his history of the Beatles, commented that "the Beatles, with Bob Dylan, the Byrds, the Beach Boys, became the nucleus of an exclusive, mutually supportive 'superstar' species, not rivals but confederates, fellow-sufferers, even, from unabating success."[9] But such episodes are rare indeed.

For the most part stars are sentenced to being opponents and do not, cannot, befriend each other. Cyd Charisse remarked about life at a traditional studio, "There was never much of a camaraderie among the women stars at MGM. I imagine that was because of envies real or imagined." Admitting strained relationships with both Arnold Schwarzenegger and Eddie Murphy, Sylvester Stallone said, "There tends to be a little bit of friction. But I think that holds true with anyone that's in a competitive business."

Friendships might seem to be more probable among starring athletes than starring actors. When the emphasis is upon team play the opportunities for forging close alliances would seem to be greater. But the realities in the world of sport are little different from those of Hollywood. A player's performance can only be gauged relative to the performance of others, and even teammates are to some extent competitors. Top stars from different teams, beyond being official opponents, are jousting among themselves for the lion's share of the public's attention; mutual support cannot be expected.

Caution between stars can turn to thoroughgoing animosity. Chaplin and W. C. Fields evolved into archenemies, as did Bette Davis and Joan Crawford. Antagonism is also likely to spring up between a star and his successor: Babe Ruth disliked Lou Gehrig and Joe DiMaggio; DiMaggio was no friend of Mickey Mantle. Bing Crosby said he was disgusted by Elvis Presley, and so did Frank Sinatra, who snarled that Presley's "kind of music is deplorable, a rancid-smelling aphrodisiac." Presley in turn despised the Beatles.

Nor are stars likely to form friendships with their lessers. The status differences between stars and nonstars could hardly be greater; it is unlikely the two would have much in common, or share in any of the similar experiences that draw two individuals together. The star is destined to be estranged from ordinary people. Chaplin's well-known observation was, "It seemed that everyone knew me, but I knew no one." This sense of alienation was echoed sixty years later by Brooke Shields when she reflected on being unable to make close friends with her Princeton University classmates: "It was difficult for me because I didn't know anyone, and everyone knew me."

So while stars are at least as needful as most human beings

for amiable social contact, and in all likelihood are more so, given both their exhibitionist lives and the wear and tear of their occupation, they are unlikely to make friends either among their equals or with their lessers. How is this dilemma resolved? Frequently stars assemble their own small groups of hired friends—a retinue. Lana Turner wrote about this step in her career: "I was forming my own little entourage: Del [the makeup man]; my hairdresser, Helen Young; and my stand-in, Alyce May. More than anything else, having them always with me represented stardom. And the truth is I needed them."

Marilyn Monroe had her entourage and Joe DiMaggio had his; when the two married, their respective groups, unwilling to merge, would eye each other like opposing teams. Frank Sinatra, who reportedly could not stand to be alone, always had in close attendance his valet, several bodyguards, and numerous hangers-on. The star with perhaps the largest entourage was Elvis Presley; dozens of buddies and relatives stood by, ready to assist the King. "Working for Elvis was a twenty-four-hours-a-day job, and the boys were at his beck and call constantly. They played when he played and slept when he slept," reported his wife. Some were permanently stationed at Graceland in Memphis, while others traveled with him to his Las Vegas or Los Angeles engagements. He paid them minimally but from time to time would bestow expensive gifts upon them.

Monroe complained, "Sometimes I think the only people who stay with me and really listen are people I hire. Why can't I have friends who want nothing from me?" But the members of stars' hired retinue may well be an improvement over normal friends because they will not require the give-and-take of conventional relationships. Their compensation comes in the form of a payroll check, so they are prepared to do nothing but be solicitous. The star, having given so much to the public, can now be solely on the receiving end. In the fold of a retinue the star can find surcease and peaceful companionship.

Or at least by all rights ought to. Bob Dylan's entourage built up quickly, and by 1965 he was traveling with a dozen people. Girlfriend Susan Rotolo observed, "He had bodyguards and managers. Just as Dylan got more and more famous, things got more and more oppressive, and more and more people around him—bloodsuckers. I was more aware of ambition and infighting than I had been before."

Bernie Brillstein, a well-known Hollywood agent and producer who has observed many stars, once commented, "The trouble with money and power and success is that you buy a house in the hills and you have sycophants telling you what you want to hear, or bringing you the drugs you want to get. You can have anything you want to get. You can have anything you want—studios, managers, agents, women, men—whatever. What you need around is a voice to argue with you."

Having tasted the fruits of stardom—the wealth, the honors, the power, the obsequious attention of hirelings—a surprising number of celebrity performers then do something odd: they execute an about-face and retreat to the normalities of everyday American life. They do not forgo their professional obligations, but they resolve to live as average an existence as they can manage during the hours when they are not working. Being a star full-time, initially exhilarating, eventually becomes weariful. The realization dawns that they will survive best if they periodically step off the merry-go-round.

Sometimes this retreat is prompted by nothing more remarkable than aging. Young stars, brimming with energy, feel no need to moderate the intensities that accompany celebrity. Their acceptance of stardom is enthusiastic, and the opportunities for excitement are endless. But like most human beings, many stars as they age begin to seek out a less frantic mode of existence, one with spells of more ordinary concerns. Upon turning forty, singer Jimmy Buffett observed, "I have outlived all my vices. Getting older means you clean up your act. I try to stay away from that kind of lifestyle that could have killed me in the past."

Whatever the reasons, many stars come to reaffirm the normalities of middle-class existence, seeking the relationships and routines that can keep a person on even keel. Such a move, seemingly so unremarkable, may prove difficult for the star to achieve: Gable's biographer wrote that "actually, it is hard to comprehend celebrity the likes of Clark Gable's, hard to imagine how far he must travel, or how calculating he must be to get a sense of normality or ordinariness."[10] But when the star persona

can be set aside and the individual can become at least temporarily a conventional person and family member, then a com-
forting stability and purpose can be discovered. Bette Midler,
who began her career as a singer in gay bathhouses, settled
nicely into domestic life with her husband and child. Discussing
how he compensated for the demands of his occupation, Chevy
Chase said, "In my personal life what counts are the simple
things: having a close family."

Like married people everywhere, stars turn to their spouses
for support and sustenance. Before her husband's unfortunate
death, Joan Rivers told an interviewer what he meant to her: "I
have in Edgar somebody who is really, really on my side. Also
he's given me the normalcy that is in the rest of the country. It's
like Erma Bombeck. All the funny ladies really have to be an-
chored in some kind of middle-class reality. And middle class is
still marriage, supermarkets, and the Maytag isn't working."
Paul Newman has spoken gratefully of the love and support he
has drawn from his wife of many years, Joanne Woodward. Con-
centrating on their wives or husbands, these stars can resist the
temptations that come with their occupation. James Garner,
married to the same woman for three decades, said, "I've
worked with a lot of great-looking actresses, and I make it my
business not to dislike any of them. I also make it my business
not to fall in love with them either."

While the romantic escapades of stars make the news and
give the public the impression of a sexual free-for-all in the celebrity ranks, some stars manage to stay married to the same
person for decades, and find genuine strength and sustenance in
those relationships. Included in this group are not only the likes
of Rivers, Newman, and Garner, but others who might seem less
likely. "Wild" Robert Mitchum was married over five decades to
Dorothy Spence. "Evil" Larry Hagman was married over thirty
years to Maj Hagman.

Marriages of stars to only one person are much more common than might be expected. In this book's study of 100 stars,
thirty-four of the performers had contracted just one marriage;
stars married only once included James Cagney, Gary Cooper,
and Babe Zaharias.

Often those who marry more than once express regrets toward the end of their lives about exercising what would seem to

be a star's prerogative. They weigh the gains and losses and find that in the marital sweepstakes they have come out behind. Henry Fonda *(photograph 39)* said, "I've been married five times, and I'm goddamn ashamed of it." Cary Grant regretted his failures in marriage, and so did Bette Davis. Just like most people, stars are likely to hold up the steady relationship as an ideal, even if an unrealized one; Marilyn Monroe speculated, "I wish I could achieve a settled relationship like that. Someone always to come home to, someone always interested in what you're doing—and helping you over the tough spots, helping each other."

As well as resorting to a regular home life, many stars conclude that mainstream recreational pursuits serve them better than anything more exotic. Myrna Loy loved gardening, as does Paul McCartney. For pitcher Tom Seaver, doing crossword puzzles was a relaxing diversion. Carole Lombard's great pleasure was to play tennis. Bing Crosby found golfing to be the most satisfying antidote to the pressure of his career. As well as playing golf, singer Willie Nelson also took up jogging to help him deal with the stresses and strains of touring. Madonna also jogs regularly, whether or not she is on tour. Martina Navratilova finds skiing to be effective recreation.

In the long haul, it is often the humblest things that serve stars better than any of the other conspicuous compensations available to them. Family, hobbies, and exercise—these attributes of middle-class life turn out to be the best medicine for the excruciating burdens of the star role. If all goes well the star may end up like Gregory Peck, who could say at the end of a long and productive career, "I have my work and my wife and my kids and my friends. And I think, 'You're a lucky man, Gregory Peck, a damn lucky man.'"

For other stars the normalities of life provide insufficient anchorage. The small certainties of marriage and family cannot compensate for the large uncertainties of their occupation. They remain unsure why they were picked to become stars, and they wonder how long they are going to endure. Clark Gable fretted constantly about whether his success would continue. As David Bowie said, "Fame—what you get is no tomorrow." The vagaries and insecurities of the star role plague many of its occupants.

In response, a number will try to reach beyond the immediate to something steadier and more enduring, hoping to find balance and repose in the spiritual realm.

Some will turn to the conventional religions that lie close at hand. Bing Crosby was a lifelong Roman Catholic and steered himself more or less by the dictates of his creed. Lana Turner turned deeply religious in the 1980s, commenting, "When you accept God, you're never alone." First an ardent Zionist, Bob Dylan converted and became for a while a born-again Christian.

Some reach further afield, seeking equanimity in oriental traditions such as Buddhism and Indian mysticism. Taking a year off from his acting career, Richard Gere, a practicing Buddhist, advanced the cause of the Dalai Lama of Tibet. In 1968 the Beatles retreated to the Ganges to meditate with the Maharishi Mahesh Yogi; all was heavenly until they learned that the Maharishi's interest in fellow meditator Mia Farrow was other than spiritual.

The astrology in oriental religions and occidental cults has attracted numerous celebrity entertainers. Many Hollywood actors regularly consult with an astrologer to plan and prepare for their days. Montgomery Clift professed a strong belief in astrology and would not make a move without referring to his charts. Marlene Dietrich and Liberace felt the same way. Sylvester Stallone confessed that he was "very influenced by the predictions of psychics, especially a good astrologer."

Superstitions are endemic in the acting world—the Academy of Motion Picture Arts and Sciences skipped from the twelfth to the fourteenth edition of its *Players Directory*—and they are even more pronounced in the tier of stars. Bette Davis insisted that rain brought her good fortune, and Carol Burnett concurred: "I love it to rain when I start a new project; it always brings me good luck." Leading performers have been the captives of remarkable superstitions as they try to calm the tempestuous seas in which they feel themselves bobbing. Peter Sellers *(photograph 40)* would not permit anyone to wear purple on his movie sets, and once had someone fired who had chanced to; purple, in Sellers's cosmology, was the color of death.

Athletic stars, trying to maintain consistently superior performance when everything militates against it, are notoriously superstitious. Baseball players believe that crossed bats are bad luck and will kill a hitting streak. The wife of one player related, "He is superstitious, like he always believes when he pitches he has to have steak and green beans, and now we've added mashed potatoes. One night I added mashed potatoes for a change, and he ate the mashed potatoes that night and he won. So ever since then, we've been having steak, green beans, and mashed potatoes."[11] Even athletes of the steadiest sort defer to a few superstitions: Joe DiMaggio always stepped on second base when he took the field, and Chris Evert had "lucky" dresses that she wore when tournament play became highly challenging.

Some stars go beyond all this, seeking comfort and order in the study of the occult. Jackie Gleason did. Elvis Presley became increasingly intrigued with occult matters as his fame grew. Why, he asked his spiritual adviser, was he the one chosen to influence so many millions of human beings? Perhaps he hoped to find the answer in the library of 250 books on mysticism and the occult that he had lugged along wherever he traveled.

Among stars fascinated by the mystical it is common to believe that one has been born before and has led previous lives. Such a conviction would clearly lend a sense of steadfastness in the face of career vicissitudes. The star least bashful about her previous lives has been Shirley MacLaine, who in every public forum has described her earlier incarnations; her books such as *Dancing in the Light,* which features her in such existences as a princess and a Roman soldier, have topped the best-seller lists. When several stars lay claim on one past existence, congestion can result: Ann Miller said she had been Queen Hatshepsut of Egypt (c. 1500 B.C.), but so did Tina Turner. "Well, my dear," challenged Miller, "we're going to have to fight this one out."

For a number of troubled stars, nothing compensates, nothing at all. Not the money, nor the honors, nor the power, nor the hand-picked retinue, nor the passing attempts at domestic bliss, nor the detours into spiritualism. The fever in the mind never subsides.

Such stars may be unnerved by a fundamental conflict between their view of themselves and the world's view. They will be praised to the skies, but they may harbor the conviction that such universal acclaim is preposterous and unwarranted. As

Marlon Brando put it, "Acting is a bum's life, in that it leads to perfect self-indulgence. You get paid for doing nothing, and it all adds up to nothing."

Stars are frequently trapped between a desire to display themselves and a desire to retreat into the oblivion of privacy. On the one hand they crave attention and cannot live without it. On the other, the attention is excoriating and they cannot live *with* it. The same conflict exists in a larger, career-long framework, too: stars need to maintain their popularity and fear its end, but the pressures of fame may eventually wear them down. Twisted by these contradictory and seemingly irresolvable needs, stars can be perpetually dissatisfied. They will need to take breaks, but will feel uncomfortable and fearful when out of the spotlight. The star, who by all rights should be the most content of creatures, becomes the most disconsolate.

A symptom of this disturbed state is the insomnia prevalent among celebrity performers. Many stars are too wound up, too fraught, to find peace of mind in the bosom of slumber. They will suffer this debilitating disorder chronically. Clara Bow, Humphrey Bogart, Judy Garland, Montgomery Clift, Babe Zaharias, Lenny Bruce, Wilt Chamberlain, Jim Morrison, John Belushi, Ernie Kovacs, Bill Haley, Mickey Mantle, Red Skelton, Bette Davis, Liberace *(photograph 41)*—they were all usually unable to doze off. Cary Grant, sleepless, bedeviled, would telephone his friends and acquaintances at all hours of the night, searching for a calming voice.

The best known and perhaps most plaintive case of insomnia was Marilyn Monroe's. All her life the inability to sleep hectored her, often rendering her unfit for professional commitments. "You must forgive me if I'm not good company," she volunteered to one interviewer. "I've been having trouble sleeping. It makes me grumpy." The desperate actress had little recourse than to dope herself with sleeping pills. "It can become a habit," she admitted to the same interviewer, "but if you can't sleep, what are you supposed to do? You feel so lifeless next morning. Nobody's really ever been able to tell me why I sleep so badly, but I know once I begin thinking, it's goodbye sleep." Her tolerance for the pills gradually increased until, heavily laden with barbiturates at the age of thirty-seven, she finally found the rest that had so eluded her.

Unable to calm down, tormented by the demands upon them and their own conflicting feelings, many stars resort to drugs. Cathy Smith, on the basis of almost twenty years spent in the pursuit of a variety of stars, concluded, "From what I've seen, most people in the entertainment world are or have been involved with drugs. Drugs are everywhere, they're accepted, and they're a means of coping with the pressures and uncertainties of show business."[12] Her friend John Belushi once remarked that "you get caught up in this business and the drugs are inevitable."

Some of the chosen drugs have verged on the exotic. Wallace Reid, an early star for Paramount Pictures, became a morphine addict and expired in a padded cell in 1923. For a number of years Cary Grant was a regular user of LSD. Stardom has seen its share of heroin addiction, too, from Barbara La Marr, who overdosed in 1926, through to rock star Boy George. Louis Armstrong *(photograph 42)* was a steady smoker of marijuana; Eddie Fisher spent twenty years as a methamphetamine addict; Liza Minnelli entered the Betty Ford Center to be treated for her dependency on Valium.

Throughout the century, however, the two drugs most commonly abused by stars have been alcohol and cocaine. Alcoholism is more prevalent among stars than among the general public. In this book's study of 100 stars, episodes of alcohol abuse figured in the lives of thirty-nine performers; of these, fifteen were identified as chronic alcoholics. W. C. Fields, John Barrymore, Mary Pickford, Errol Flynn, Richard Burton, Jackie Gleason, Janis Joplin, Buster Keaton, and others had lifelong drinking problems. Clark Gable was perfectly willing to show up on the set at the appointed hour, but he had it written into his contracts that he was to stop at five o'clock no matter what—allegedly so that he would not be late for the cocktail hour. Robert Mitchum drank gin by the pitcherful. According to George C. Scott, "The more successful I got, the worse the drinking became."

Reporting on Hollywood in 1985, Mark Litwak wrote, "While alcohol remains the most abused drug in the industry, cocaine has quickly seized second place."[13] It may be more accurate to say that recent media attention has made cocaine's ranking more visible; it has probably always occupied second place. Cocaine was common in the movie colony by 1916, when Douglas Fairbanks, Sr., starred as detective Coke Ennyday in *The Mystery of the Leaping Fish*. Decades later, when Tallulah Bankhead was asked about the addictive properties of cocaine, she responded, "Cocaine habit-forming? It certainly is not. I've been using it for years." After winning his Oscar, Richard Drey-fuss went on a six-year cocaine binge. Names associated with cocaine use in the 1980s included Judy Carne, Louise Lassiter, Jodie Foster, Robert De Niro, Robin Williams, Carrie Fisher, and Carly Simon. Richard Pryor set himself on fire while freebasing cocaine, and David Crosby went to jail in Texas for possession of the drug. Arrested at a London airport in 1984 with 1.3 ounces of cocaine, Stacy Keach told the judge before he was sentenced to prison that the drug was "a means of trying to alleviate ex-haustion."

Cocaine use has proliferated in the worlds of music and sports as well. A biographer of David Bowie reports that "co-caine provided him with necessary energy to keep going." The three major professional sports have each suffered numerous revelations of widespread drug abuse. It was asserted that the Boston Patriots lost the 1985 Super Bowl because of cocaine use prevalent among the team members. When New York Giants lineman Lawrence Taylor wrote about his cocaine habit, it was hardly an isolated incidence. Heralded as a new basketball star, Len Bias died of a cocaine overdose before he ever played a pro-fessional game. The same year the Houston Rockets lost three starting players following drug tests. Through the 1980s base-ball was rocked with one cocaine scandal after another. Pitcher Vida Blue admitted cocaine use; Dale Berra was linked to the drug; Steve Howe was suspended three times for drug prob-lems; Dwight Gooden underwent treatment for cocaine depen-dency, and so did teammate Keith Hernandez. Involvement with cocaine was not limited to current players. Joe Pepitone was arrested on drug charges and Denny McLaine, the last thirty-game winner, was sentenced to twenty-three years in jail for drug trafficking.

Whether alcohol or cocaine, a star's use of drugs will usu-ally conform to a general pattern: initially the star will experi-ence some relief. It will, during this stage, help him or her come to terms with the role of the celebrity performer. But at a certain point, perhaps after years of habitual use, the drug will begin to have the opposite effect and create greater harm than good. Instead of being therapeutic, the drug will increase the torque upon a star's life. It will fuel whatever negative impulses the star may have until self-destructiveness flourishes. During John Belushi's last days his ever-increasing dosage of narcotics could not erase the pressures he felt, and only served to put him into a steeper tailspin.

The story of Elvis Presley epitomizes the star's desperate search for compensatory relief. His life destabilized by the forces of an enormous fame, Presley tried first one thing and then another to bring it back into balance. The boundless money, the approbation of not just a national but a global audience, the insulating group of cronies and relatives, the large home staffed with loyal employees, marriage and fatherhood, his spiritual explorations—nothing proved effective for long. His insomnia grew increasingly profound as the years passed. Every night he would take three or four different kinds of sleeping pills, trying to find the combination that would ease him into slumber. When he finally did get to sleep, it would be fitfully; he was a frequent sleepwalker and was plagued by nightmares. The use of one set of drugs to narcotize was complemented by another set to rouse him. With the collusion of his doctors he combed the *Physician's Desk Reference* manual in the search for different mind-altering pharmaceuticals.

Elvis's need to find relief from the star role became more acute as he aged. When Priscilla Presley was married to him, he would often remain in a drugged sleep for fourteen hours a day and then require another two or three hours to fully wake. As she later explained, "Elvis had a lot on his mind, and if something didn't go right, a sleeping pill was the only thing he had that would let him relax. It didn't seem bad to him; he didn't realize what it would lead to. I'm not defending drugs; I'm only saying that at that time that's all this man had to relieve his stress." After the marriage ended, he would with increasing frequency stay for two or three days at a time in his darkened, chilled, tomblike bedroom, ingesting a sequence of soporifics. In retrospect, the eventual outcome of this degenerative effort to compensate for the torment of stardom seems all too predictable.

☆
DISCARDING STARS

9.★
DECLINE

he celebritariat," stated writer Nelson Aldrich about the American public, "is a vast collection of consumers, more or less discerning, who buy, use, and ultimately discard human commodities known as celebrities."[1] Yet of those included in this book's study of 100 stars, forty-seven were not discarded. The likes of Carole Lombard, Richard Burton, and Jackie Gleason remained in the star role to the end of their lives.

For a simple majority of fifty-three, however, the moment arrived for each when it was clear that the player and the occupation had parted company. These ex-stars no longer performed in any significant way, and the public was no longer galvanized by a compulsion to observe them. In a rueful tone Charlie Chaplin noted, "It is a mistake to dally long in the public's adulation; like a soufflé if left standing, it bogs down." The clamor subsides and the stars depart—occasionally voluntarily, as with Greta Garbo, Cary Grant, Roy Rogers *(photograph 43)*, and Ted Williams, but most often not. They have been released from Star Village.

The mode of termination can conceivably be brutal. One thoughtful observer, Richard Schickel, has suggested that "there is some unspoken, unconscious need for a punishing last act in the career drama of the celebrated. It restores our sense of order, our sense that good luck is not lasting, that in the end the rewards of bourgeois virtue and hard work are more permanent."[2] Stars commonly fear that such a sacrificial end awaits them. As Joan Rivers commented, "The public is very fickle. People love to build you up, and then they love to destroy you."

In truth, a great deal of negative feeling does gravitate toward stars. They can be a lightning rod for the unfocused discontents lurking in American culture. In one of the few studies of fan behavior, Fred and Judy Vermorel reported on what most struck them about popular response to leading singers and bands: "To begin with we were astonished by the degree of hostility and aggression, spoken and unspoken, shown by fans toward stars."[3]

During performances the resentments of unhappy fans will take the form of boos. Boos invariably come when stars could most use encouragement and support, but they will muster a resolute exterior and hope that dismay with their performance will not become a recurring feature of their appearances. For athletic stars, being booed from the stands is a regular part of the work life. Babe Ruth, suspended at the start of the 1922 season, rejoined the Yankees but was slow getting back his old form; when the crowds booed, he mischievously tipped his hat. One time, however, the catcalls got the best of him and he leapt into the stands, bat in hand, after a heckler. During the 1987 football season, Cincinnati Bengals quarterback Boomer Esiason, tough on the playing field but vulnerable to fans' jeers, complained, "They've booed me and I've thrown for 400 yards twice. I don't know what else I can do. I've taken the approach now that if I'm not wanted out here, I sure as hell don't want to be here." Leading musicians will also be booed from time to time. Asked if it ever happened to him, Bob Dylan replied, "Oh, there's booing—you can't tell where the booing's going to come up. Can't tell at all. It comes up in the weirdest, strangest places and when it comes it's quite a thing it itself. I figure there's a little 'boo' in all of us."

Starring actors and actresses are not often actually booed in performance. In the theater a negative reaction results in temperate applause, and film audiences rarely respond out loud (and are not heard by performers in any case). Yet through the subsequent words of critics, disapproval can still reach the star. Glenn Close, three times an Oscar nominee, has said, "Critics wait for you to fail. They can make you think you failed. I was crucified for *Maxie*. I don't understand it." Many performers behave the same way when criticized: they profess not to read the critics' accounts and will affect a lofty disdain, yet are nonetheless stung by the cutting appraisals. In one interview Eddie Murphy first pleaded ignorance of current criticisms, then proceeded to rebut them point by point.

The intermittently hostile attitudes that emanate from fans and critics, and that shadow all stars, can at times coalesce into a force mighty enough to propel the performer right out of Star Village. This is what happened to Charlie Chaplin, who was booted not only out of the symbolic community but out of the nation as well, when he was barred from reentering the United States. Bette Davis reflected that Chaplin's rejection was "an unconscious reaction to his dichotomous image—poor and good in movies, rich and bad in life." Similarly, when Ingrid Bergman moved in with Italian film producer Roberto Rossellini she lost the regard of the American audience, which had identified her with her wholesome roles. Both performers did eventually regain the affections of the public, however: Bergman after the piety of Americans began to wane, and Chaplin in a flood of nostalgia following his death.

A star can be vengefully and permanently destroyed, as happened to Eddie Fisher. The extraordinary public malice toward him was triggered by his two marital breakups in a decade when the ethos of family life was being upheld as never before. First he dared to leave Debbie Reynolds and ruin what the populace had perceived as an ideal union; then he proved to be not husband enough for Elizabeth Taylor. Taylor dumped him, and so did the nation. It was as if a trapdoor had opened beneath his niche in Star Village.

Another star sacrificed by the public was Tiny Tim. During the 1960s he earned $50,000 a week performing in Las Vegas nightclubs. When he married Miss Vicki on the "Tonight Show" in 1969, 35 million viewers were in rapt attendance. But not long thereafter he was reduced to playing lounges in airport hotels. Tiny Tim was an oddball associated by the public with the ascendant counterculture (an ironic linkage, since his own conservative beliefs were the antithesis of the hippies'). Discarding him, the audience was aggressing against cultural forces that made them uneasy.

A sports star suddenly rejected by the public was the champion hitter Roger Maris *(photograph 44)*. Despite his record of sixty-one home runs in a season, somehow he was not felt to be affable or boyish enough to inherit the mantle of the legendary Babe Ruth. As the 1961 season progressed, press accounts made his stolid, taciturn nature more visible, and popular sentiment turned against him. A few years afterward he left the Yankees. "Things had gotten so bad in New York, I had to get out," he told an interviewer. Decades later his recollection of the whole affair remained an unpleasant one: "Too bad it ended so badly. It would've been a hell of a lot more fun if I had never hit those sixty-one home runs. All it brought me was headaches."

The stars who come the closest to being sacrificed in the literal sense are those athletes who participate in contact sports. The audience urges them on and on, offering inducements of money and fame, until their bodies are completely broken down. In the name of delivering a good performance and rising through the ranks, leading boxers will come to suffer lifetime impairments. Muhammad Ali had his brain sufficiently jarred in his string of championship bouts that it caused a form of palsy; Sugar Ray Leonard suffered a detached retina. Professional football stars are also performance casualties, launching themselves play after play and season after season, ruining their bodies for spectators' amusement. The enormous physical mass and ferocious thrust of linemen invariably lead to a deterioration of the skeletal frame, particularly of the spine and knees. Among National Football League players some 400 knee operations are conducted annually. Hall-of-Famer Jim Otto, twelve years a center for the Cleveland Browns, found upon retirement that it would take him many minutes each morning before his racked back and knees were able to support him. In a 1988 survey of 440 retired NFL players, 78 percent said they had suffered physical disabilities related to football, and 66 percent expected shortened lifespans as a result.

But while some stars are destroyed in one way or another

per Joan Rivers's nightmare, by far the greater number of celebrity performers are separated from Star Village in a less dramatic manner. Sociologist Donald Harris pointed out that there are two ways sports stars are removed: by degradation (the forcible removal "which leads to identity destruction"), and by what he termed "cooling out": "Cooling out is the estrangement of the failed via alteration and adjustment of the role-identity of the failed. Professional baseball uses a form of cooling out by moving unwanted players down the ladder of success."[4] This second, more temperate way is the pattern for most stars, athletic and otherwise. Gradually they are eased out of their position. Without fanfare, the paths of performer and audience diverge. This kind of stepping down happened to Walt Frazier, a standout basketball player with the New York Knickerbockers in the 1970s: "They were real heady years, enough to make your head spin, but then I went to Cleveland, where I was just another ballplayer, and that brought me down to earth. It was a good thing that happened, because now I'm just an ordinary person making a living, and I am rid of any illusions that all my life I should be an idol."

The "cooling out" process for sports stars begins as fan fervor turns tepid, the mail drops off, and the requests for autographs become less insistent. Levels of performance may have been suffering, and trade talks could be in the air. When the player is not invited to training camp, or is shuttled off to a lesser team or league, the turn of events is obvious. For film stars the decline from glory is more attenuated, less explicit. The periodic nature of moviemaking is such that, until several vacant years have passed, performers cannot be absolutely sure they are on the downhill side. Their descent is never beyond reversal, even when signs of a slide abound. They will complain about not being sent good scripts, or enough of any caliber. If preliminary talks are opened, it is quickly established that producers are offering less compensation than before, because they do not see the declining stars as the drawing cards they once were, and perceive a growing apathy on the part of the audience.

For many television and music stars, the parting of performer and public is often characterized by neither the high drama of destruction nor the tapering process of dismissal, but

rather by simple curt abandonment. They receive wide exposure via broadcasting or recording technologies, get sacks of
mail and much press coverage, but then for some reason do not
repeat and are abruptly forgotten. Their popularity is as intense
as that of other stars, but their stay in Star Village is exceedingly brief. Their turn in the limelight resembles a one-night
stand of gigantic proportions.

Singers like Cat Stevens and Debbie Gibson produced a hit
song or two and a surge of popular interest, only to sink out of
sight. Peter Frampton was here and gone; so was Fabian. In the
sports world William "Refrigerator" Perry captured wide popular attention for two seasons and contracted endorsements for
over twenty products, but then he put on yet more weight, was
removed from the Chicago Bears starting squad, and quickly
lost altitude. On the television screen, too, some performers will
gleam brightly and then disappear. Max Baer, Jr., played Jethro
on "The Beverly Hillbillies" and then had few other offers; Adam
West found it difficult to get new roles after "Batman"; it was
downhill for Erik Estrada after "CHiPS."

Normally, stars' response to the disaffection of the public and
the loss of their place in Star Village is to fight back. They may
have been highly ambivalent about their spotlit occupation, but
the threat of termination removes all indecision. They will re-
double their efforts to reoccupy the lofty position they so recently held. In the career pattern of the star, this is the period of
comeback attempts.

Comebacks are integral elements of the mythology of stardom. The twilight of a star's career will be organized and retold
around this theme because the public is intrigued with the notion of regaining lost prominence. Over and over fans remind
each other that Joan Crawford, fired by MGM in 1945 after almost twenty years as a star, scrapped back, promoted herself
fiercely, signed with Warner Brothers, made *Mildred Pierce*, and
won an Oscar. Americans love success stories; here the protag-
onist, already well known, succeeds another time, and the audience experiences the thrill of triumph yet again. Then, too, the
comeback story appeals to the mischievous side of public interest, as acclaim is offered and then withheld before being
granted anew.

Such tales aside, the reality of comeback attempts is grim, and the prospects for retrieving success are bleak. Recovering stars work feverishly at their craft, for they can no longer take anything for granted. Onetime sports paragons will try to recondition and exert themselves to achieve the level of play that originally brought them fame. Johnny Unitas will try to catch on with the San Diego Chargers, Joe Namath with the Los Angeles Rams, O. J. Simpson with the San Francisco 49ers. Sugar Ray Leonard will come out of retirement, put himself through a punishing training schedule, and barely win one more bout.

Some comeback attempts do prove to be successful. Gloria Swanson came back briefly in *Sunset Boulevard*. Jerry Lee Lewis lost favor when the public learned he had married his thirteen-year-old cousin, but he eventually worked his way back into the audience's good graces. Often a successful comeback entails a slight change in persona, so that the public is shown a new facet of the performer. George Burns, once the befuddled spouse, returns as the aged roué. Tina Turner sheds Ike, comes back as a sizzling solo act, and achieves more renown than before.

Some of the best-known comebacks have been based on a change in the communications medium of the star's performance. The new vantage point offered to the audience can freshen the entertainer's image and stimulate interest. In perhaps the most famous comeback episode of all, Frank Sinatra had been losing his fans as his bobby-soxers grew up and turned away from his music. He then fought for the role of Maggio in *From Here to Eternity*, pestering studio executives and the producers until the part was his (although at a fraction of what his salary ought to have been). His success at that role reinvigorated his career and led to several decades of movie parts. When that side of his career declined, Sinatra's renewed attention to his singing kept him in the limelight for many additional years. A switch from acting back to singing also resurrected the career of Elvis Presley, who had devoted the 1960s to a series of films that produced a smaller and smaller gate as the decade wore on. By 1970 it was clear that he would have to return to live concert performances if he were to remain a star. This he did, with spectacular success.

Different media switches have resuscitated the careers of other stars. As a film actor Mickey Rooney was a self-acknowledged has-been, but when he took to the Broadway stage in the long-running *Sugar Babies,* it was stardom all over again. Joan Collins, a top film personality in the 1950s and 1960s, was collecting unemployment in the 1970s before she was able to regain entrance to Star Village as a television performer. Cybill Shepherd was also a failed movie actress—someone that nearly everyone had loved to ridicule—but she rocketed up from the depths when she switched to television and starred in "Moonlighting." "I absolutely deserve this," she said gleefully about her comeback.

Most comeback attempts, however, do not work. Theda Bara, Ginger Rogers, Buster Keaton, Jane Russell, Montgomery Clift, and Lucille Ball missed in their various comeback forays. Fabian was known to every teenager in 1960, his fame rivaling that of Presley, but shortly thereafter his celebrity was extinguished; he tried film roles, often playing psychotic killers, but it was to no avail. Carroll Baker attempted a return to Star Village with the 1965 film *Harlow,* a vehicle designed expressly for her, but received a cold shoulder at the box office. In the 1970s Paul McCartney thought he could regain lost glory with his band Wings, but failed. Donnie Osmond was not to make it back in the 1980s.

According to Richard Griffith, the most pathetic comeback campaign was waged by the onetime star Agnes Ayres.[5] She would seize on every possible means to place herself before the public, accepting all personal appearance opportunities no matter how minor or tawdry. Eventually a newsman discovered her working as a saleswoman in a Los Angeles department store, and reported her saying hurtfully, "When you see producers spending a million dollars trying to make some peasant into a star, while they ignore people who once had a name and a following, it's awfully hard not to ask 'why?'"

Why indeed? Just as performers have little understanding of why they were tapped to be stars, so they have an imperfect understanding of why their stay in Star Village is over. Searching for someone to blame, ex-stars consistently point to producers or team owners as the malefactors—these are tempting targets. Fading stars are afraid to recognize that those who brought them into the pantheon of fame are the same ones who have effected their removal: the public. Nelson Aldrich wrote,

"So the consumer [of celebrity performers] doesn't always get the performance she wants. Her control over the market is not perfect: it takes time to exert it, to banish the tired and bring on the fresh. But her discipline is relentless."[6]

The parting occurs because the public turns away, averts its gaze, and focuses elsewhere, but sometimes the star precipitates this. He or she behaves in such a way as to violate public perceptions of his persona, and he loses his audience's loyalty. This is what happened to Charlie Chaplin and Ingrid Bergman, who seemed to flaunt the disparity between their private lives and the innocent roles they played. Billie Jean King *(photograph 45)* incurred a double strike against her star persona—she stopped winning, and she was revealed to have been involved in a lesbian relationship.

Stars may cause themselves to be so narcotized and brain-numb that they can no longer function as performers. Errol Flynn's drinking rendered him increasingly unemployable. The alcoholism of John Barrymore drove him from films to theater tours and then even out of that; audiences would not show up anymore to watch him make a bumbling fool of himself. Montgomery Clift's multiple addictions ruined his career. David Crosby of the singing group Crosby, Stills, and Nash, identified by one interviewer as "the spiritual leader of the Woodstock nation," became a narcotics addict and was arrested four times in the early 1980s on drug and weapons charges. The interviewer recounted meeting Crosby in 1986: "Suddenly a door bangs shut, and a disheveled, unshaven figure walks into the living room. His stomach is bloated; thinning frizzy hair leaps wildly into the air. A few of his front teeth are missing, his pants are tattered, and his red plastic shirt has a gaping hole. The most frightening thing, however, is his pale, swollen face, riddled with thick white scales, deep, encrusted blotches that don't seem to be healing. Looking at him is painful."[7]

A less dramatic but equally decisive cause for expulsion occurs when a star gains excessive pounds. By putting on too much weight stars violate their image and the American mania for a trim figure. The press and the public fixedly study the body size of stars and are quick to notice any deviance. If Bette Midler or Elizabeth Taylor becomes fat, the audience will begin to recoil unless corrections are made. More tolerance is shown male stars, but complete license is certainly not granted. When Elvis Presley and Marlon Brando let their waistlines go, it was a matter of national concern; if they still wanted to perform, they would have to suck in their guts.

But the most emphatic way in which stars can alienate themselves from their audience is through the brutally simple, ineluctable process of aging. Each performer's niche in Star Village will have certain age parameters, and at some point it will become clear that the occupant has exceeded them. Mary Pickford found the age limit imposed on her to be low and definite, since "the public just refused to accept me in any role older than the gawky, fighting age of adolescent girlhood." For most sorts of stars the public demands at least a modicum of youthfulness and vitality; these characteristics reinforce the love or strength they personify for the audience. As the day draws near when the performer can no longer look sufficiently flush, he or she will grow anxious. Joe Esposito, road manager for Elvis Presley, recalled that "Elvis' fortieth birthday was definitely a crisis for him. He didn't like the idea, and it was after that his serious problems began. He saw himself getting older and it scared him."

Sports stars are the most unavoidably vulnerable to the scythe of time. Very few are going to endure as stars past the age of thirty; only a handful will see forty still in the limelight. The average professional athlete's career is short—about four years as a football player, five years in basketball, seven in major-league baseball—and stars in these sports do not last much longer. A common reaction among aging stars is first to deny that the passing years are taking a toll; pitcher Jim Bouton remarked that "the idea that you've lost your regular stuff is very slow in coming." But soon the wear and tear of daily play upon the body becomes undeniable. In his final season at age thirty-six, Joe DiMaggio found it painful just to get out of bed; once on the playing field, he could not stop his knees and arms from quaking.

Among Hollywood performers, women tend to be removed most decisively from Star Village because of age. Generally speaking, the audience tolerates older male stars more easily than female, perhaps because it prefers to see women in that stage of life when they are most available for romance and pairing off, while older male actors can illuminate another matter of interest to the American audience—the exertion of power and authority. In his study of the film industry, Leo Rosten observed that leading actors would continue to find work while leading actresses were being discarded from the corps of stars.[8] As Marilyn Monroe once predicted, "When my looks start to go, so will most of my fans."

Knowing that their careers are in jeopardy, most actresses are resentful about aging. Cher, turning forty, said, "I'm not like Jane Fonda or any of those other women who say how fabulous they think it is to turn forty. I think it's a crock of shit. I'm not thrilled with it." One actress who successfully prolonged her stay in Star Village was Angie Dickinson, but at passing the half-century mark she asserted, "Actresses who say being over fifty is great are lying. I may look good, but I looked better at thirty-two. No, it's not great being over fifty. It's like going to the guillotine."

The most plaintive instances of maturing out of their niche occur with child stars. Being so young, they are even less well equipped than their seniors to endure the finality of being discharged from the star role. Matthew Beard, who played Stymie in the *Our Gang* comedies, reflected about being replaced in 1935, "It felt very bad, because no one explained to me what happened."

Ousted from Star Village, discarded performers fall to earth. The individuals behind the image leave the star role and depart the circle of celebrity. No longer are eyes riveted upon them at work, no longer are they hounded after hours by the public and the press. Having once gone from obscure to famous, they now reverse the process. "The celebrity even in his lifetime becomes passé: he passes out of the picture. The white glare of publicity, which first gave him his specious brilliance, soon melts him away," decreed Daniel Boorstin.[9] The "has-been" stage now starts; post-star life ensues.

Those performers who found the burdens of stardom crippling may sincerely welcome this transition. They are delighted to get out from under and to be themselves once again. Kim Novak commented, "There are all those things you don't have to

deal with anymore, and that's a great freedom. As a child I was
shy and quiet, always staying behind the scenes. Now I can be
the person I always was." Jane Russell felt the same way. A similar sensation was reported by Roger Maris: "Getting out of
baseball is usually a tough adjustment. It's really hard, excruciatingly so, for most guys. It didn't hit me that way, since I was
happy to get out. The press gave me such a rough time I looked
forward to a quieter life." Mickey Dolenz, describing his enjoy-
ment of the period after his starring years, said, "The Monkees
were such a debilitating experience. I just partied, bought a
laser, and went hang-gliding."

But if Dolenz made the transition happily and successfully,
his fellow band member Peter Tork did not. For years Tork wan-
dered like a vagabond around the country, playing Monkees
tunes wherever he could get a gig for a day or two. Along the
way he married three times, worked at countless menial jobs,
and struggled with alcoholism. His difficult transition to post-
star life was more the norm than Dolenz's. A majority of celebrity performers have problems of one sort or another at the time
of their discharge from Star Village. In this book's study of 100
stars, of the fifty-three who entered into a life after stardom,
eighteen (such as Theda Bara, Babe Ruth, and Joan Crawford)
were judged to have had great difficulty with the transition,
eleven (Mary Pickford, W. C. Fields, and Joe Louis, for example)
experienced moderate difficulty, and the remainder had no noticeable distress. Hollywood agent Joan Scott told writer Mark
Litwak that "keeping on even keel when [celebrity] happens is
a very difficult thing. And keeping it when the acclamation is
removed is also very hard." [10]

It has proven especially difficult for child stars to weather
the transition. Their status as leading performers is altogether
clear to them even though they are so young, but when fame is
removed children have none of the interpreting and rationaliz-
ing faculties that can help an adult negotiate such a reversal.
Ex–child star Bobs Watson commented, "Unless you have someone who loves you and will help you get through it, you've got a
serious problem." The support of her parents apparently enabled Shirley Temple to shift from one status to another without
undue hardship. While most other child stars ended up in need

of psychiatric care, Temple went on (after one failed marriage) to a stable family life and a strong career in public service.

If the transition is unnerving for child stars, it is not much easier for a group that averages twice their age at the time of release from celebrity: starring athletes. To go abruptly from being a superordinate person to an ordinary one when about thirty years old is a disquieting experience for most sports figures. Until that point professional athletes have worked single-mindedly, their sole objective being to perform with excellence before spectators. "It was always a relief for me, getting in front of the public. As long as I could perform before them, I could feel strong and good," a retiring baseball player told sociologist Rudolf Haerle.[11] Haerle gathered data from 335 former major leaguers, and among other items asked them how they felt at the close of their playing careers. The majority admitted to sensations of regret and sadness. Mickey Mantle *(photograph 46)* once told a reporter, "It's tough to realize you're through. I don't think anyone gets over it, and I can see how it can kill somebody."

As well as remorse about leaving the excitement of the game and the adulation of fans, sports stars are likely to experience trepidation about what lies ahead for them. The skills they have worked so hard to perfect are generally not applicable anywhere outside the sport. Perhaps a tacit recognition of this fact dissuades most professional athletes from conscientiously planning for their eventual retirement. Jim Bouton, describing a teammate in his book *Ball Four*, could just as well have been describing himself: "Gary is a typical ballplayer in some ways in that he doesn't seem to have any plan for himself, nothing to fall back on. The day he's out of baseball is the day he'll start thinking about earning a living. And then it could be too late."[12]

The period of transition is therefore a stressful time for most sports stars. One confided to Haerle, "I thought it was the end of the world. My first year out I almost went out of my mind." To researcher Beverly Jean Crute one baseball wife reported that "one girl told me the first year her husband was cut it was the worst year of their marriage. He was depressed and he didn't know what he was going to do for the rest of his life. I think this is indicative of everyone that is through with ball. He

was taking some of his insecurities out on her, so it was a ter-
rible year." [13]

Hollywood celebrities, usually older than starring athletes
at the time they are discharged from Star Village, appear no
better prepared for the turn of events. Despite all the costs of
the star role, the thought of giving it up is usually anathema.
That the industry and the public would turn their backs on
them, after all the fine performances they have given and may
still be capable of delivering in the future, makes ex-stars resentful. As her career was ending, Carole Landis said, "You fight
just so long, then what have you got to face? You begin to worry
about being washed up. You get bitter."

After the initial dismay and anguish are weathered, former
stars from all fields will begin to look about for a second career.
Business opportunities may beckon. Some will go to work for
others: Jackie Robinson *(photograph 47)* became a vice president for the Chock Full o' Nuts restaurant chain, and Roger
Maris was given a chance by the Budweiser Company to take
over a distributorship. Other ex-stars will launch their own enterprises. Roger Staubach became involved in a number of ven-
tures, as did Lawrence Welk, who came to own a great deal of
southern California real estate. The business interests of Gene
Autry were especially successful, prompting him to say, "I have
had more fun with business dealings than I ever did with my
horse Champion."

An especially attractive second career, which does permit
some crossover from the world of entertainment, has proven to
be that of politics. A flair for public presentation, familiarity
with the workings of the press, established fame—these would
seem to be promising attributes for a neophyte public servant.
But while a star's performance used to be governed by the writer's words or the coach's plays, now the performance, verbal and
political in nature, must emerge directly from the individual—
a challenge most stars are unable to meet. Words and tact, the
lesser parts of their previous occupation, will be the greater
parts of the new one, should the jump be made successfully.
Some do manage: film actor Ronald Reagan became a governor
and then president of the United States; basketball star Bill
Bradley was elected a U.S. senator; quarterback Jack Kemp became a congressman and a candidate for the presidency.

For starring athletes, another second career of choice is sportscasting. Although only a sparse few will succeed at this occupation, which requires an articulateness and analytical ability that were in repose during their playing days, the appeal of broadcasting for ex-stars is clear. An athlete-turned-sportscaster can remain in public view—perhaps not in the spotlight, but at least in the reflected glow of younger players, which is felt to be better than not at all. He or she can stay close to the game that made him famous, and can bring a player's expertise to bear in his commentary.

Given the highly specialized nature of their skills, most leading athletes are compelled to find their initial post-star jobs in something allied to their sport. A study by sociologist Edwin Rosenberg determined that two-thirds of retiring major leaguers landed their first jobs somewhere in organized baseball.[14] Ted Williams found a home for several years as the coach of the Texas Rangers. The football star will also try to stay in the sport; Cleveland Browns quarterback Otto Graham became a coach at the U.S. Coast Guard Academy. And the basketball star is likely to try the same route; Bob Cousy was a coach at Boston College until he tired of the recruitment chicanery, then coached the Cincinnati Royals. If the star wanders from his sport, it may not be very far: Wilt Chamberlain went on to become president of the International Volleyball Association.

No matter what his performance field, the ex-star's stock in trade is the fact that some of his fame endures, that people will remember him. Should he start a restaurant, customers may be attracted; this worked for Jack Dempsey, although not for Clara Bow. Roy Rogers was not content with just one restaurant— only a whole chain would do. Books written by ex-stars may sell well, as they did for Errol Flynn and Gypsy Rose Lee. Or the onetime performer may become a highly remunerated product spokesperson, such as Cary Grant for Fabergé perfumes, Joan Crawford for Pepsi-Cola, and Joe DiMaggio for Mr. Coffee.

Once such second careers have been exhausted, the question becomes how to occupy one's final leisured years. For Douglas Fairbanks, Sr., the answer was travel; he spent most of the 1930s steaming hither and yon, while Mary Pickford simply stayed in her bedroom and drank. She was not alone at this pursuit; stars like Errol Flynn and Buster Keaton also spent their last years in an alcoholic haze. Betty Grable moved to Las Vegas so she could gamble full time. Golf was the preoccupation of Ty Cobb, while Ted Williams pursued hunting and fishing. Some have enjoyed their farms, James Cagney and Ginger Rogers among them. Doris Day *(photograph 48)* devoted her time and money to a foundation that protected stray animals, as did Brigitte Bardot. Some became so reclusive it was not known how their time was spent: Greta Garbo in New York, Ava Gardner in London, Bill Haley in Harlingen, Texas. Montgomery Clift stayed in New York, where he would sometimes solicit homosexual partners by shouting from his townhouse window.

Toward the end of their lives, many stars adopt a sour, resentful tone. In this respect perhaps they are not so different from elderly Americans in general. They have had enough of fans; "Go away," Norma Talmadge snarled at some autograph hounds, "I don't need you any more." Roger Maris observed, "Yeah, it was tough being Roger Maris then, and it's still difficult at times being recognized in public." Embittered, nasty, Bill Haley *(photograph 49)* would snap at people who dared to greet him. Katharine Hepburn called acting "an idiot's profession. I would've liked a more private profession. I would've loved to have been a painter or a writer." In Cary Grant's view, "Everyone tells me I've had such an interesting life, but sometimes I think it's been nothing but stomach disturbances and self-concern." Among former child stars, generalized Roddy McDowall, the common feeling was not fond recollection but rather resentment at having been hurtfully exploited: "They were wrong to take us children and do that with our lives, to twist our environment in that way and then leave it for us to sort out."

A representative post-star life was that led by Babe Ruth *(photograph 50)* following his retirement from the New York Yankees in 1934. The following year, when he was forty years old, lame, sick, and overweight, he made a comeback attempt with the Boston Braves, but only hit .181 and lasted just a few months. He was released by the Braves and, biographer Marshall Smelser reports, "on the way back to [his home in] New York Babe wept, feeling hopeless, desperate, desolate." [15] Ruth's ambition from this point forward was to become a manager of a major league club. According to his wife Claire, "From the end of the 1934 season until the day he died, Babe Ruth, figuratively speaking, sat by the telephone waiting for a call everybody but he knew would never come." In 1938 he briefly served as a coach with the Dodgers, but he squabbled with the other personnel and was let go; he was never offered a position of any responsibility again. From then until his death in 1948, he played golf whenever possible and whiled away the rest of the hours as best he could. "He was never emotionally disturbed enough to need psychiatric care," Smelser writes, "but in these years he was not a happy man." [16] One of his few diversions was to collect used flashbulbs from the photographers who occasionally sought him out; he would then take them to the roof of his apartment building in New York and bomb Riverside Drive down below. His Yankee number, no. 3, was retired in a ceremony on June 13, 1948. The famous photograph of Ruth standing at home plate before the stadium throng on that day was taken from behind; had it been taken from the front, it would have shown a dejected man, terminally ill, using his once prolific bat for a crutch.

Even after a onetime celebrity has departed Star Village, his or her hard-won image retains a half-life of its own, lingering on as an iridescence that tarries after the light source is removed. Through the memories of fans the star's image endures, but because the ex-star is aging and the image is not, when members of the public chance on the retired performer their response can be one of shock. Darla Hood, who played the little girl in the *Our Gang* comedies for almost a decade, commented about meeting people later in life, "I often felt that I had let them down by not remaining a child. They'd be dying to meet me and yet I could see their faces fall when I walked into the room. What do you say to someone whose fantasy has just been disturbed?" Betty Grable said she was impatient with those who invariably pointed out that she did not look the way she used to: "Who the fuck does look the way they used to? Am I supposed to walk around the rest of my life with my hand on my hip, looking over my shoulder?"

For a time the star's image will persist, but for all but a select few it will eventually start to decompose. New performances do not occur, new tidbits on the star's life cease to appear, and the image simply evaporates bit by bit. Once formidable personages such as Colleen Moore, William S. Hart, Red Grange, Alice Faye, Duke Snider, and Robert Taylor disappear from the mind's eye.

In her study of the public image of Betty Grable, Jane Marie Gaines described this twilight stage: "The jaded attitude characterizing the decomposition stage of the image begins to crop up in references to the star by her original name. Joan Crawford at this point became Lucille LeSueur and Billie Cassin. Rita Hayworth became the former Margarita Cansino in the later stages of her career."[17] Perhaps through such highlighting the public is being reminded of stars' mundane origins, in an ashes-to-ashes and dust-to-dust sort of reference.

The years go by and the end will draw near. Many elderly Hollywood players move to the Motion Picture Country House in Woodland Hills, California; Mae Clark, the actress on the receiving end of James Cagney's famous grapefruit, spent her last days here. Others, like Groucho Marx *(photograph 51)* and Fred Astaire, will remain at home, fortunate enough to have a companion to minister to them.

A terminal illness will ensue. Dying of cancer in a hospital but still able to walk, Betty Grable headed to a hallway lavatory and worried aloud about having her backside exposed through the slit in the hospital gown. "Don't worry," the nurse said offhandedly, "nobody's looking." The ex-actress retorted, "They would have once." A deathwatch may commence. As Liberace was expiring from AIDS, a crowd of between 50 and 150 journalists and fans waited uneasily outside his compound. On the avenue before the hospital where Babe Ruth lay dying from cancer in 1948, boys gathered in knots and spoke lowly.

10.★
DEATHS

The mythology that clings to the career arc of celebrity performers is probably nowhere denser than around the events of their dying. At their end stars are thought to combust in some grand way. Critic Martin Gottfried declaimed, "Stardom in show business invites an attention and a gratification for which the human ego is scarcely prepared. Is that why, in the modern show business of million-dollar one-night stands, the artist, ego inflating to the bursting, must die?"[1] A star's death is supposed to be spectacular, startling, rife with tragic themes. The nation is expected to gasp, the press to respond at a gallop.

It is easy to see why such a stereotype might arise. Even for ordinary citizens, the cessation of life represents a dramatic event. Continuities have been sharply terminated. All those who have been touched by the departed person will reflect on the passing. Stars, playing a larger role in the culture, should receive a commensurately greater response upon dying. Having been significant symbols when alive, in death they are certain to be significant losses. Their life stories as perceived by the public have been hammered into dramatic form around struggles, successes, setbacks, and comebacks; their deaths also tend to be reshaped into high drama, with details added or subtracted until the story line takes on a properly resounding conclusion.

But is it possible that, in thinking about how stars die, just a few atypical and histrionic deaths monopolize our attention? That the theatrical overwhelms the usual? In fact, wouldn't it be more likely that stars as a group would outlive the norms for Americans, given stars' financial resources for obtaining the best in health care? Wouldn't it be more probable that most stars would live to ripe old ages and expire in undramatic fashion?

This book's study of 100 stars offers mortality data that can be compared with those for the U.S. population as a whole. Of the 100 stars in the sample, seventy-four had died at the time the biographical information was collected. The median calendar year of their deaths was 1974—half the stars had died before that year (beginning with Rudolph Valentino and Harry Houdini in 1926) and half had died after. Mortality information for Americans in general in 1974, as tabulated by the federal government, was compared to that for the seventy-four deceased stars.

The initial and most striking conclusion of this comparison was that stars on average do indeed die much younger than the rest of the U.S. population. The average age at death for Americans was 71.9 years, while for the stars it was 58.7—a full 13.2 years younger. Here is confirmation that, just as the folklore would have it, stars do die younger than most Americans; those in this occupation have a life expectancy about thirteen years less than the average for people from other walks of life.

A second disquieting observation concerns a remarkable differential between the sexes. While both male stars and female stars expire younger than the norms for their gender in the general U.S. population, women fare much worse. In 1974 the average American man died at 68.1, and the male star on average at 59.8, for a difference of 8.3 years. The average American woman died at 75.8, while the average age at death for women included in the study of 100 stars was 54.3, for an astounding difference of 21.5 years.

To an awing extent, then, stardom must be considered much more hazardous for women than for men. Some portion of the explanation must rest with the fact that the star role is

harder for women to enter and to sustain. Those in the occupation are far more likely to be male than female; to illustrate, of
the seventy-four stars who had died, fifty-four (or 73 percent)
were men and twenty (or 27 percent) were women. There are
clearly more niches in Star Village for males. If the general population from which celebrity performers come is divided almost
evenly between the genders, and if the pool of aspirants is also,
then the competition is going to be stiffer among women for the
relatively fewer slots available to them. For those rare women
who do manage to become stars, their stay in the role is usually
much briefer than for males; few remain stars beyond their thir-
ties. So in addition to the pressures of fame that all stars must
confront, female stars must struggle harder both to become
stars and to last, only to face an early and inevitable dismissal.
It all portends increased stress and increased risk of untimely
death.

Of course not all female stars die younger than the averages
for the American people. Mae West lived to be eighty-seven, and
Mary Pickford, in spite of her reported alcoholism, was just a
year younger at death. But these are counterbalanced by the
larger number who died young. Jean Harlow was dead at
twenty-six, Janis Joplin at twenty-seven, Carole Lombard at
thirty-three, Jayne Mansfield at thirty-four, and Marilyn Monroe
at thirty-six.

In addition to comparing average age at death for stars and
for Americans in general, the various causes of death for the two
groups can be contrasted. When the official causes of death for
the seventy-four stars are set alongside the causes of death for
the overall U.S. population, several points stand out (see Table
1). Stars are noticeably less likely to expire from heart attacks
and strokes—probably the statistical effect of dying younger.
The most remarkable differences occur in the categories of accidents and suicides—two causes of death that do not result
from the internal breakdown of the body, but from lethal events
inflicted from outside. Compared to the general American population, stars are more than twice as likely to expire in accidents and over three times more likely to die by their own hand.

The reason behind stars' higher mortality rates from accidental deaths lies in the nature of their work. Stars are peripa-
tetic, spending much of their time journeying from one place to

Table 1
Causes of Death

	For Stars (%)	For the American Public (%)*
Diseases of the heart	28.4	38.2
Cancer	23.0	18.6
Cerebrovascular disease	5.4	10.7
Accidents	13.5	5.4
Influenza and pneumonia	4.1	2.8
Diabetes	1.4	1.9
Cirrhosis	2.7	1.7
Arteriosclerosis	1.4	1.7
Emphysema and asthma	0.0	1.4
Suicide	4.1	1.3
Homicide	1.4	1.1
Kidney disease	1.4	0.4
Ulcer	1.4	0.4
All other causes	12.2	14.3
Total	100.4	99.9

*U.S. Department of Health, Education, and Welfare, Public Health Service, *Vital Statistics of the United States 1974.* Hyattsville, Md.: National Center for Health Statistics, 1978. Table 1–5.

another. Doing so, they expose themselves to the perils of travel, and they are struck down accordingly. Four of the seventy-four stars died in automobile accidents, and three died in plane crashes.

Carole Lombard *(photograph 52)*, Metro-Goldwyn-Mayer star and the much-loved wife of Clark Gable, was one of the casualties of flying. In January 1942 she had enthusiastically agreed to launch the War Bonds campaign in her home state of Indiana. Gable had a film commitment and was unable to accompany her, so her mother went along. The tour was highly successful, and at the final performance in Indianapolis she sold over $2 million worth of bonds. As she led the audience in "The Star-Spangled Banner," she began to weep, so overcome was she by the emotion of the moment. Triumphantly she and her entourage boarded a TWA airliner that evening for the seventeen-hour trip back to Los Angeles. After refueling in Las Vegas, the plane took off on its final leg. Half an hour later it crashed into a remote mountainside, killing all aboard. It was said by many, including President Roosevelt, that the actress had given her life in the service of her country.

The three accidental deaths in the study sample that were not from plane or automobile crashes involved drug overdoses: Jimi Hendrix, Janis Joplin, and John Belushi. Overdoses also figured into the three suicides: Marilyn Monroe, Lenny Bruce, and Judy Garland. Some celebrity entertainers are so tormented by the demands of the star role that they try desperately to find relief by chemical means. They can narcotize themselves up to and then beyond the threshold of extinction.

Comedian Lenny Bruce killed himself in the summer of 1966 with a massive injection of heroin. His stage routine had become more daring and obscene over the years, resulting in numerous arrests and lawsuits. He found it harder to obtain bookings and grew more obsessed with his legal defenses. With him in his California home lived his daughter and mother, both dependent upon his shrinking income, plus several hangers-on. With every passing day Bruce became more despondent; he talked about death constantly. On August 3 he received a notice from his mortgage company that he was in arrears and that the house had been foreclosed upon. He went into his bathroom, liquified his stock of heroin, and shot it all into his arm; he was dead instantaneously.

Of the thirteen stars in the sample whose deaths were labeled as resulting from accidents or suicide, six were women. Females, who constitute only 27 percent of the total sample of deceased stars, thus represent 46 percent of the casualties from these two vicious causes of death. The excessive number of female deaths in these two categories does much to explain why the average age of death for female stars is so low; these six women died on average at 38.2, and they pull the average for their group of twenty women down to the previously mentioned 51.8 years. By one means or another, a surprising number of female stars manage to destroy themselves as their careers are ending. Monroe had predicted that her fans would leave her the moment she started to lose her looks; a way to maintain dignity in this situation was to leave them before they left her.

If the thirteen star deaths from accidents or suicide were set aside, then the remaining array would much more closely resemble the national averages. But properly included, these deaths produce the sorry mortality rates that characterize the occupation. At root, it is the demands of the role that produce these grim statistics. It is the job that kills stars.

The passionate display of public sorrow offers yet another indicator of how strong a hold stars have upon the emotions of the U.S. population. When a person as treasured as a child departs, the keening can be boundless. After John Lennon *(photograph 53)* was murdered in 1980 people soon began to gather outside his New York apartment building, some bringing flowers and holding candles. A vigil was organized across the street, where devotees could huddle together and commiserate. "I came here for John," one weeping fan said. "I can't believe he's dead. He kept me from dying so many times."

The grief can be so extensive as to grow out of control. This occurred upon the death of Rudolph Valentino in 1926. The thirty-one-year-old star, renowned for playing the great lover in a number of silent films, succumbed unexpectedly in New York City following surgery on his appendix. His body was laid out in a Manhattan funeral parlor, and preparations were made for his fans to pay their last respects. The throng was so large and unruly, however, that mounted police had to be summoned. A reporter stationed himself near the army of mourners and later wrote, "On one side, ten feet away, trudged the south-bound column, silent now except for a subdued moaning as it approached its grim goal. Across the street the mob was bigger and noisier than ever. The weeping and wailing were mingled with shrill imprecations directed at the mounted cops. Hysterical women, foiled in every rush by the hard-working horsemen, regarded them as personal enemies. 'Cossacks!' they screamed. 'Cossacks!'" The crowd did riot, and when the plate-glass windows of the funeral home were shattered several people were cut badly and hospitalized.

Five decades later, equivalent numbers responded to the death of Elvis Presley on August 16, 1977. By dawn crowds were gathering outside his home. That day Presley's songs were played round the clock on Memphis radio stations and throughout the nation. The following morning a file of mourners fifteen people wide extended for a mile from Graceland. The crowd became restless as the hours wore on. A teenage driver, gunning his car down Elvis Presley Boulevard, lost control and smashed into the milling fans, killing two. They had been sacrificed, not unlike the ancient Egyptian attendants selected to accompany a pharaoh into the afterlife.

If a star dies under ambiguous conditions, then rumors will spread through the populace as one explanation and then another is tried out. Far-fetched accounts will be aired in an effort to solve the mystery of the lost performer. No ordinary citizen, no matter how curious his or her death might be, would be subject to the same nationwide treatment. Thus rumors swirled when bandleader Glenn Miller's *(photograph 54)* plane disappeared over the English channel during wartime: that he was on a secret mission, that he was locked up in an insane asylum, that he had been killed by a lover. After rock star Jim Morrison was found dead from a heart seizure it was rumored that yes, he was dead but from drug use; and no, he wasn't dead but had made it appear so because he was tired of performing. The enigmatic details of Marilyn Monroe's death have kept the rumor mill going for decades. Through this process of spreading innuendos about departed stars, fans can mull over the demise and adjust themselves to the shock of losing someone significant in their lives.

The funerals of celebrity performers are among the most heavily attended of all twentieth-century funerals. After the death of Duke Ellington at age seventy-five from cancer, some 10,000 people attended his funeral in New York City. An estimated 33,000 came to the funeral of Humphrey Bogart, dead at fifty-eight from throat cancer.

When he died in an Alaskan airplane crash in 1935, Will Rogers *(photograph 55)* was the nation's top box-office attraction (having nosed out Clark Gable). To millions of Depression-stunned Americans, the Oklahoma-born entertainer had symbolized traditional values and wisdom. His wry and congenial words, served up in an offhand, beguiling manner, had reached the public not only through film but through other media as well—radio, newspapers, theater, the lecture circuit—until they had become familiar and welcome to all. The outpouring of grief upon his death was immeasurable, probably greater than for any other American since Abraham Lincoln. More than

50,000 people shuffled past his bier. At the service the pastor observed, "He has been the one figure in the life of our nation who has drawn to himself the admiration and the love of all classes of people. It is no exaggeration to say that no man has been so universally appreciated and loved as Will Rogers." In tribute to him movie screens were darkened briefly in 18,000 theaters across the nation, encouraging an estimated 10 million moviegoers to reflect on the lost star.

Perhaps the largest direct public response to the death of a star occurred in 1948, when Babe Ruth succumbed to cancer at age fifty-three. The next day, August 17, his body was laid out in Yankee Stadium, and until midnight and all the following day people filed by four abreast to pay their last respects—a total of 200,000 mourners by several estimates. Roughly 75,000 were in and around Saint Patrick's Cathedral for the funeral, and another 100,000 stood along the thirty-mile route to the cemetery, many weeping openly as the cortege passed by.

A star's funeral offers an occasion for other stars to appear in public. They were acquaintances of the departed, and may well have had fond feelings toward him or her. In attendance at the 1958 funeral of Tyrone Power were Henry Fonda, Yul Brynner, Gregory Peck, James Stewart, and Loretta Young (in an oriental costume she was wearing for a television production). When Nat "King" Cole died in 1965, those at his funeral included Jack Benny, George Burns, Johnny Mathis, Sammy Davis, Jr., Ricardo Montalban, Danny Thomas, Frank Sinatra, Peter Lawford, Jimmy Durante, Steve Allen, Milton Berle, Bobby Darin, and Jerry Lewis. At Liberace's funeral were Robert Goulet, Donald O'Connor, and Debbie Reynolds. In covering these ceremonies and reporting dutifully on the celebrity performers in attendance, the press once again strengthens the image of Star Village and gives the public a sense of a close community in which stars die in the arms of their fellow stars.

The body is usually interred. Clark Gable was laid to rest alongside his beloved wife Carole Lombard, who had died eighteen years earlier. Some stars are cremated. After Ingrid Bergman died in London in 1982 on her sixty-seventh birthday, her husband took her ashes to a private stretch of beach in Sweden, where along with flowers they were thrown into the surf.

The star may be dead, but that is hardly the end of it. There is certain to be an estate, and even if it is not large, it still has symbolic value and will be coveted. The will is probated, and if everything goes according to the star's wishes the estate passes smoothly to the heirs.

Occasionally things do not go smoothly. Errol Flynn's will was disputed in court by the star's last girlfriend, Beverly Aadland. She lost the suit, although even if she had won it would not have made any difference. The estate was declared insolvent after the IRS had raided it to settle a $2 million tax bill.

Upon the reading of her mother's will in 1977, Christina Crawford was shocked to hear that she and her brother had been disinherited "for reasons which are well known to them." She had thought herself to be on fine terms with her mother and knew of no cause to be left out of the will. As she later wrote about Joan Crawford, "She had tried to reach out of her grave and stop me one last time, just to prove who had really been in control all these years." Christina contested the will and two years later settled with the beneficiaries for a token sum of $55,000, to be split with her brother. The daughter may have been the winner in the end, for the royalties on her book *Mommie Dearest* approximately equaled the total value of the estate.

Rock Hudson's companion over the last year of his life, Marc Christian, blocked the probating of the actor's will with a $10 million claim in 1985. Like tens of thousands of other handsome young men, Christian had gone to Los Angeles following high school graduation to seek work as an actor and model. And like many others, he ended up bartending and waiting on tables. Hudson was fifty-seven and already infected with AIDS when he met and courted the man twenty-eight years his junior. Christian, installed in Hudson's home as the star's lover in 1983, later said, "I found out he had AIDS on the 6 o'clock news like everyone else." Left out of the will, he sued.

Following the death of most stars, their image will begin to deteriorate, if it has not done so already. Initially at a slow pace, then at an accelerating one, the public's awareness will dwindle until stars are forgotten in all but the archival sense. New generations will scarcely recognize departed performers or what they represented. The recollections of older citizens will begin to dim, too. New stars have quickly filled the ranks of Star Village.

But for a very select few, the public cannot let go. One form this possessiveness takes is the recurrent rumor that the star is not dead after all, but has become a recluse because of some disfiguring accident or to avoid the burdens of stardom. In 1988 Presley was said to be pulling up to drive-in windows at fast-food restaurants in Kalamazoo, Michigan.

For these unfading stars, anniversaries of their deaths become commemorative events. August 1987 was an important month for such tributes. To a ready audience the press relayed accounts of two ceremonies for long-dead performers. The first was on August 5, the twenty-fifth anniversary of Marilyn Monroe's death. Hundreds of her friends and fans convened at her grave site in Los Angeles, where a memorial service was conducted amid bowers of floral arrangements. The eulogy had been written by Lee Strasberg, her former acting coach, and was delivered by his daughter, actress Susan Strasberg, who wept as she read, "She had a luminous quality, a combination of radiance, yearning, that set her apart. I cannot say goodbye. Marilyn never liked goodbyes." The numerous admirers, including several Marilyn look-alikes, obviously agreed that they could not part with their adored star. Nor have the American people as a whole been able to. Almost every year since 1962 has brought forth a new biography or photograph collection. Her blond image appears and reappears, having become an icon.

A week later and half a continent away, Elvis Presley Tribute Week, August 13 to 21, commemorated the tenth anniversary of his death. A statue of the singer was unveiled in downtown Memphis; other activities included the Elvis Presley Karate Tournament and the Elvis World Impersonator Competition. On August 16, his day of dying, some 20,000 people visited Graceland, many carrying flowers as they filed past his grave. Traditional hymns broke out spontaneously as hundreds in the crowd clutched each other's waists and sang in unison. One man reverently told a reporter, "Everyone is entitled to have someone to look up to."

Another celebrity performer Americans cannot let expire is James Dean. Dean's tenure in the star role began, remarkably, *upon* his dying. Of his three films only *East of Eden* had come out before his life ended in an automobile crash; subsequently released were *Rebel Without a Cause* and *Giant*. For several years after his death on September 30, 1955, fans could buy publications declaring that he was simply hiding. His army of devotees was not going to readily relinquish him. Decades later, on each anniversary of his death thousands still gather at his grave site in his hometown of Fairmont, Indiana. After the brief memorial service is over and the crowd has scattered, a few will sneak back to the gravestone and bang away at it to chip off a souvenir piece. The stone had been considerably whittled down by 1983, when the remainder was stolen. This hunk was retrieved in 1987 some seventy-five miles distant, but by then a new stone had been placed on the grave and a new cycle of chipping had begun.

The clinging to dead stars reached some sort of extreme in the case of Harry Houdini. What added interest to his death from a burst appendix in 1926 was that he expired on Halloween, and that he had promised his wife he would attempt to contact her from the next world. With some fanfare she tried for a decade to reach him, and every Halloween since then others have made the effort. In a mock trial in 1987 a San Francisco municipal court judge said, "I do have some concern about letting him rest in peace," and ruled that Houdini should not be bothered by further attempts to contact him in the beyond. In the account of a wire service reporter covering the trial, "The blinds in the room began to rattle and the judge's gavel rose into the air and finally slid off the desk as the packed courtroom watched in silence and then began laughing nervously."

11.
RIPPLES

The American public is so fascinated by its celebrity entertainers that necks will crane and eyes will turn toward someone who is not exactly a star but is trying to evoke one. Through such impersonations the images of stars are duplicated and reanimated, and sent rippling again through the populace.

To bask in the awed glances of others, to share in the glory that is the star's, people will go to great lengths to make themselves resemble the original. They will attend costume parties decked out as Charlie Chaplin or Marilyn Monroe or Laurel and Hardy. Elvis Presley may well be the greatest favorite of impersonators, since imitations of him are tirelessly appreciated. At a July 4, 1986, celebration in New York City, some 200 Elvis look-alikes vied to be the closest approximation of the dead King of Rock 'n' Roll.

The value of stars extends to the best of their impersonators, and entrepreneurs have gladly capitalized on this. Look-alikes can make money by selling their ability to draw crowds to special events; they can also find work in advertising, films, and television. According to Ron Smith, the owner of a Los Angeles look-alike agency, 1987 payments to his stable ranged from a high of $100,000 for his best Burt Reynolds down to $200 for a Jimmy Durante double.

Since the American audience is eagerly receptive to these second-hand versions, some performers can even earn their entire livelihood doing impressions of stars. This has been Rich Little's stock in trade. Other entertainers may not deal exclusively in impersonations but find that one or two add flavor to their performances; in her nightclub acts Raquel Welch has imitated Bruce Springsteen and, of course, Presley.

Occasionally an impersonation is inspired by less than laudable motives, as when someone poses as a star in order to gain special favors. A man looking and acting like former football star James Brown can request and receive front-row seats at a Los Angeles Lakers basketball game. In 1985 in Trinidad, a Tom Selleck imposter caged numerous meals at restaurants and ran up an enormous hotel bill. Such deceptions are possible because others naively collude, their normal suspicions suspended in the urge to oblige a luminary.

Fraud aside, occasionally a look-alike and the original will encounter each other. It is invariably a touchy moment on the star's part, for both professional and personal reasons. He or she is meeting someone who is cashing in on the image he has worked so hard to establish. And, like someone who is startled when first hearing his voice played back to him, the star may experience a shock upon seeing his image as others see it. Pee-wee Herman reported about meeting a look-alike, "It was *so* bizarre, really frightening." Sylvester Stallone chanced upon an impersonator wearing a T-shirt that proclaimed "I'm him," and subsequently recounted, "I went up to him and I said, 'Are you? Then pay my rent.' Like, he shouldn't be that enthusiastic. It's not so easy."

The images of stars are promulgated in other ways and along other dimensions as well. The persona can ripple forward in time to engage a new series of audiences. A star's image can thus breach mortality and find an answer of sorts to humanity's age-old quest for everlasting life.

The perseverance of an image can be achieved in the most traditional manner, through statuary. A bronzed figure of Will Rogers stands in Oklahoma. A California bank commissioned a statue of John Wayne on horseback some twenty-one feet high.

Babe Ruth's image in bas-relief is stationed in Yankee Stadium's center field. But statuary, of course, is not the most potent form of perpetuation. The technologies of mass communication, which distribute performances far and wide, can also distribute them over time. The aging stage actress Sarah Bernhardt, captured on film in Adolph Zukor's *Queen Elizabeth,* exclaimed to the producer, "Mr. Zukor, you have put the best of me in pickle for all time." And indeed he had. Woody Allen once wisecracked, "I don't want to achieve immortality through my work. I want to achieve it through my not dying." While one wishes him well, it is inevitable that the twenty-first century is going to know Allen primarily through his films. Contemporary entertainers are fully aware that their best recorded performances will carry their images far into the future. Barbra Streisand remarked while working on *Funny Girl* that "this is for posterity. Everything I do will be on film forever."

In the estimation of James Cagney, "If you live long enough, they will bronze you." And rocker Jimi Hendrix once remarked, "Once you are dead you are made for life." But such observations apply to only an extremely limited number of stars. The images of most deceased stars sink beneath the surface of general indifference: Peggy Hopkins Joyce, Gilbert Roland, and Constance Bennett—they are virtually lost. In the posthumous contest of immortality only a few can be assured of finding future audiences. Bette Davis acknowledged this: "What I do believe is that, in death as in life, it is the survival of the fittest. That is to say, if what we do on earth is great enough, we live on in the hearts and memories of others."

For these immortal few, the image is freed from its originator and, purified, can soar across the years. In magazines and newspapers, still shots of the performer will appear every so often, stimulating memories and nudging the image forward to fresh generations. The star's reputation will be reinvigorated by the occasional replay of an old performance or the appearance of a new biography. As sociologist Orrin Klapp explained, "Once this intergenerational barrier has been passed, very possibly because a pure symbol has been perfected, there seems to be no necessary limit to the life of the symbol."[1] Charlie Chaplin's Little Tramp toddles on decade after decade, never to be extinguished.

A star persona endures when a succession of Americans continue to embrace it. The image is welcomed out of nostalgic feelings for what has gone before and, more fundamentally, from a basic need to sense continuity with the past. Legendary stars are signposts in the mists of time; their acceptance in a new age serves to link present and past, and to support the culture's passage through time.

Because Americans treasure these rare immortal stars, items associated with them take on unusual value. Buyers and sellers manage to set exorbitant prices on all sorts of mementos. The most costly autographs are those of James Dean and Greta Garbo—Dean because his career was so brief, and Garbo because she despised the practice and seldom signed. Items once possessed by stars are especially desirable. In 1985 a Rolls Royce Phantom V formerly owned by John Lennon was auctioned for $2.3 million. A year later at Sotheby's in London, Elvis Presley's 1963 Rolls Royce went for a paltry $143,800. One of Chaplin's many hat-and-cane sets brought $151,800 in 1987, while a pair of his black boots netted $70,840. The following year an anonymous bidder paid $165,000 at a Christie's auction for the ruby slippers Judy Garland wore in *The Wizard of Oz*. When Liberace's estate went on the block in 1988, the auctioneer gushed, "Bidding is way, way over our estimates." The first item, a pendant depicting Liberace's profile on a blue background, had been projected to sell between $10 and $100; it went for $3,500.

Even the mere likeness of a legendary star may maintain commercial value. In a lengthy 1980s campaign, for instance, IBM used Chaplin's image to market personal computers, trading on the respect and fondness with which the American public still regards the Little Tramp. Up until 1985 courts had held that the commercial rights to a star's likeness terminated upon his or her death. But that year the state of California adopted legislation that granted to a star's estate the ownership of the image, just like any other property. From then forward, the licensing of the images of deathless stars has become a sizable business.

Licensees now promptly pay 7 to 10 percent of their gross sales to make use of the public credibility that legendary performers have cultivated. A list of just which stars retain this power defines the truly immortal. In 1986 the two leading expired performers for commercial purposes were Elvis Presley, with approximately 100 different licenses, and Marilyn Monroe *(photograph 56)*, with about half that number of agreements. Every bottle of Love Me Tender shampoo sold, and every Max Factor compact with Marilyn's image, resulted in payments to the holders of these rights. Other deceased stars and their licensees in 1986 included Bing Crosby for Velamints, Groucho Marx and W. C. Fields for Tyson Chicken, Carole Lombard for Max Factor, Rudolph Valentino for Republic Airlines, and Babe Ruth for Coca-Cola. The few other stars who can sell merchandise from beyond the grave include Fred Astaire, Humphrey Bogart, James Dean, Clark Gable, Jean Harlow, Rita Hayworth, Buster Keaton, Will Rogers, John Wayne, Mae West, Laurel and Hardy, Abbott and Costello, the Three Stooges, and the Keystone cops.

The legacy of celebrated players consists not only in their recorded performances and lingering likenesses. Just as with ordinary citizens, stars leave behind their progeny.

To be the child of a star imposes particular difficulties. The strain between the son or daughter and the famous performer is potentially greater than that between most children and their parents. A star, surrounded by the mystique of public adulation, seems to approach superhuman perfection. A child, not famous and certainly imperfect, must struggle with the discrepancy between his lowly status and his parent's exalted one.

When a star's child is very young, he or she may well experience resentment as his needs come into conflict with the demands of his parent's professional life. As Michael Douglas commented about growing up in the household of Kirk Douglas, "What is hard to try to understand is the amount of public loving and praise that a personality gets and measure that against some of the deprivation that you feel." Speaking about his father, the singing cowboy Tex Ritter, John Ritter said, "There were times when I was really jealous of the public. I wanted more time with him. He was away about half my life on tour or doing radio or going to Nashville."

When the star is home, familial relations are frequently not as idyllic as the child might hope. Douglas Fairbanks, Jr.'s recollection of his famous father was this: "I always associated him with a pleasant, energetic, and agreeable 'atmosphere' about the house, to which I was somehow attached but which was not attached to me. He also seemed to be someone I did not know very well." Jane Fonda remembered that her father Henry "was not a demonstrative person, and never said, 'I love you,' and didn't hold you on his knees. In those days his major emotion was rage."

Naked exploitation is not inconceivable. Capable of supreme egoism, a star may take advantage of a child's eagerness to please the larger-than-life parent. Erik Preminger related how his mother Gypsy Rose Lee used him virtually as a maid to serve her and attend to her wardrobe. Christina Crawford was generally ignored by her mother except when the child was to be dressed and posed for photographs of domestic bliss. She was a publicity prop.

If in later life the star's offspring writes about such a life, as Christina Crawford did, there is invariably a resentful public response. Gary Crosby writing about Bing, and B. D. Hyman writing about Bette Davis, might have expected sympathy for the indignities of their childhoods, but instead they received scathing reactions. Why? According to Christina Crawford, "In writing about my mother I had exposed the ugly underbelly of the parent-child relationship—and it was something people didn't want to hear." Joan and Bing and Bette maintained firmly established images in the minds of the public, and when exposés jeopardized them, the audience became uneasy and then vindictive, choosing to see the children as abusers rather than the abused. That did not stop these accounts from being enthralling reading for Americans, however.

As stars' children progress through school, they will experience unremitting problems with their peers. Envy and malice will flow their way. Well into adulthood, Jamie Lee Curtis could not forget the hurtful taunts she endured when her father Tony was arrested with marijuana. Even without precipitating events, the parent's conspicuousness means that life is going to be difficult for the school-age son or daughter. When his boy was twelve, Sylvester Stallone remarked, "It's difficult for him to deal with broad team sports like soccer or football, because of the pressure on him to be a superboy." From this stage forward, the offspring will be endlessly plagued by variants of the question, "What's it like being so-and-so's child?" People are so intrigued by the star that they view the child primarily as a way to satisfy their curiosity. Seen as a means to an end, the child is denied an identity of his or her own.

Establishing identity, in fact, is probably more difficult for the children of stars than for most American youngsters. If children have suffered limited parental interest as well as little support from their peers, they will be handicapped in developing their own personalities. When Kathy Cronkite interviewed a number of children of celebrities, she discovered how common the problem of formulating identity was.[2] Maturing children must struggle to distinguish themselves from their prominent forebears; Jamie Lee Curtis remarked, "I used to say I had the longest middle name in the world. My name was Jamie Janet-Leigh-and-Tony-Curtis's-daughter Curtis. That's the way I was introduced."

As adults, the children of stars are frequently tempted to rely on the fame of their parents. The power of the celebrity is sufficient to open doors and create opportunities for the son or daughter, but this can undermine one's integrity as an individual. The potential for misjudgments and distress is great. Most negotiate this predicament warily, sometimes making use of the connection and sometimes shrinking from it. Kathy Cronkite found that almost all her interviewees had used an alias at least once.

No matter what a young adult's achievements might be, it is difficult to gain approval from others or even from oneself because the star-parent sets such an unapproachable standard. Producer Susan Newman, the daughter of Paul Newman and Joanne Woodward, commented, "How many actors are there who are as famous as my father? There are twelve or fifteen of them at the most. It's sort of like living up to the Joneses, but the Joneses are your own family. Whether or not you reckon with it consciously, it keeps coming up in your life. I think it's a tremendous burden."

When all these factors are taken into account—the distracted parent, the antagonism of peers, an elusive identity, enduring ambivalence—then it is easy to see why the children of stars might falter. And indeed, in the brief history of stardom, there is no shortage of failed progeny. A prototypical ne'er-do-well was Edward G. Robinson, Jr. An alcoholic from the age of eighteen, he made the news for his binges and his feuds with his parents. He was arrested for drunk driving, bad checks, robbery, and assault. His mother cut him out of her will for his "unforgivable" conduct, and he sued the estate. He succumbed at the age of forty in 1974, one year after the death of his famous father.

Substance abuse often figures in the dissipation of stars' children. Diana Barrymore, daughter of John, followed her father into alcoholism and died at thirty-eight in a littered apartment, three liquor bottles in bed with her. Paul Newman's son Scott died in a similar manner from an overdose of alcohol and Valium. Gary Crosby was an alcoholic; Desi Arnaz, Jr., was a confirmed drug addict; Carrie Hamilton, daughter of Carol Burnett, said that between the ages of thirteen and nineteen she took every drug she could get her hands on.

The litany of troubled descendants goes on. Peter Sellers's daughter Victoria was snared when police closed down on a drug ring with which she was linked. Ex-quarterback Don Meredith's son was arrested as a burglar. Johnny Carson's son Christopher was hauled into court for not supporting a child he had fathered in Florida; the mother, proclaiming that justice would have been done more quickly if she were white, had been living with the infant in a hovel. Natalie Cole, daughter of Nat "King" Cole, suffered a prolonged bout of depression and mental illness. Zsa Zsa Gabor's daughter, Francesca Hilton, was dispatched to a psychiatric ward after running amok in her Los Angeles neighborhood.

When young Griffin O'Neal had his two front teeth knocked out by his irate father, Ryan O'Neal, it was a highly visible sign of the waywardness of stars' children. Uncontrollable during his teenage years, addicted to Quaaludes, Griffin and his father had come to blows. Subsequently Griffin was arrested on manslaughter charges after a speedboat accident resulted in the death of a friend. O'Neal senior once mumbled, "I have this dream that someday my son will become president of the United States. He'd still be messing up my life, but at least he'd be getting paid for it."

As striking as accounts like these may be, however, they

misrepresent the norms for children of stars. The performers included in this book's study of 100 stars were parents of 209 children (a determination not easily or exactingly made, given the number of stepchildren as well as out-of-wedlock births). Of these only ten, or about 5 percent, could be judged to have had significant problems in being adequately adjusted citizens.

The reality is that most children of stars come to terms with their inherited situation. Jack Lemmon's son Chris said that "it *is* a hard fact to deal with, that you're a famous person's son, if you want to make it hard. I think that every child of a famous person faces it in one way or another; it's a question of how it's dealt with. You can either make it bad news, or you can simply realize what the situation is." As Stephen Farber and Marc Green concluded in their book *Hollywood Dynasties,* "Still, most of these star children would probably admit that the benefits of their lineage outweigh the drawbacks."[3] The majority of celebrities' children use the available wealth to obtain a good education and launch themselves on a solid career. Tyrus Cobb, Jr., became a doctor. Bette Davis's son Michael became a lawyer, as did Bob Hope's son Anthony. Fred Astaire, Jr., is a successful rancher, and Alan Ladd, Jr., rose to the presidency of a major Hollywood studio.

Of special interest are the children who want to succeed their parents in the limelight. They have seen the occupation from the inside and have a sense of its demands and dynamics. Yogi Berra's son Dale reported about his childhood, "I remember wandering around the locker room. I'd see Mickey Mantle shaving, Tony Kubek getting dressed. I decided that was the kind of life I wanted to lead." Edward Albert, son of Eddie Albert, grew up in a household where guests included Marlon Brando, Humphrey Bogart, and Spencer Tracy; his godfather was Laurence Olivier. Stardom became his goal. Vanessa Redgrave's daughter Natasha said about her ambitions, "When you've lived all your life as part of a family whose members are at the top of what they do, it rubs off on you."

"I want my kids to surpass me," Kirk Douglas has stated, "because that's a form of immortality." But most other starring parents dutifully warn their offspring against the attempt, stressing the constant rejection that is the lot of the neophyte performer. Alan Alda remarked, "I think that anybody who's gone through it would wish that their kids could find happiness doing something else," and Jane Fonda agrees: "I don't want my kids in show business. It's just not a happy business." (Ironically, both Alda and Fonda are themselves children of leading performers, and are thus giving advice they themselves would not have taken.)

Fonda's father had feigned nonchalance about her career. The responses of a number of celebrity parents to their children's starring ambitions range from disinterest to opposition, in part because the elders may have reached the point in their careers where they are feeling precarious. Comedian Ed Wynn ridiculed the acting successes of his son Keenan Wynn. Judy Garland was initially encouraging toward her daughter, but as Liza Minnelli achieved more renown the mother could not restrain her resentment. When Garland and Minnelli performed together at the London Palladium in 1974, to some observers they seemed to be fighting over the microphone; Minnelli admitted that "she became very competitive with me. I wasn't Liza. I was another woman in the same spotlight." Late in her life, Joan Crawford begrudged her daughter's work as a soap opera actress and maneuvered to replace her.

When Douglas Fairbanks, Jr., and his mother ran short of money, the young man began to audition around Hollywood. His father, who had divorced his mother to marry Mary Pickford and whose career was slipping, resented the upstart. After Junior landed one role, Fairbanks, Sr., called the director and urged him to renege, snarling, "There's only one Fairbanks." But increasingly that one Fairbanks was the son, who enjoyed a solid career through the 1920s and 1930s.

Fairbanks, Jr., was the first of Star Village's progeny to become a star in his own right. There have not been many. Simply being the son or daughter of a celebrity performer does not ensure success. Dale Berra, Edward Albert, and Natasha Redgrave have not made it yet, and never may. Being the child of a star can, however, position an aspirant among the other journeymen from whom the public makes its ultimate selection.

Of the few stars who were children of stars, the two most prominent examples are Liza Minnelli *(photograph 57)* and Jane Fonda. Additional examples include Candice Bergen, Jamie Lee Curtis, John Ritter, Isabella Rossellini, and Michael Douglas. By

forming the appearance of a dynasty, these stars define continuity and help Americans structure their sense of cultural history.

Stars are further amplified by the development of a mythology
about their profession. Most other twentieth-century occupations remain unexamined by all except their practitioners, but
this one is so pivotal to the conduct of American culture that a
body of folklore has evolved around it. Told and retold like ancient legends, these myths convey the star role across the decades.

The mythology usually takes the form of a curious, ellipti-
cal rendition of a typical star's career. Much is truncated; for
example, the ceaseless practice and rehearsal, the greater part
of the work of most stars, are indicated but abbreviated. Relations with the press and fans are rendered minor and innocuous.
Those who employ the star will scarcely make an appearance.
By diminishing the presence of audiences and owners, stars are
made to seem more independent than they ever could be in real
life.

And a great deal is simply omitted in mythic accounts. The
business aspects of being a star go unacknowledged. The performer's willing surrender to the crass demands of advertising
and merchandising is ignored, as is the flagrantly conspicuous
spending of the vast wealth that pours in. Slack periods, or the
drain of extended travel, have no place in the myth.

So that it can have impact and memorability, the mythology of the star must be dramatic, with career elements refash-
ioned into theatrical form. According to researcher Robert Milton Miller, who has analyzed over 125 dramatized versions of
show business careers, the story audiences most appreciate is,
at bottom, that of rise and fall.[4] This motif structures the
mythology of the star role, and all that does not lend itself to
the formation of such a tale is screened out.

The rise is almost always depicted as the result of innate
talent and determination, applied whenever opportunities present themselves. The performer in question is blatantly deserv-
ing. There is an inevitability to the ascent (or why else would
we be watching?). Forget the fact that a number of stars have
had no discernible talent. Forget the fact that many stars are

vicious and undeserving. Forget the fact that what is truly inevitable for virtually all aspirants is outright failure. Most especially, forget the fact that whatever the player brings to the effort counts for little in contrast to the wants and needs of the public, that the major dynamic in the creation of stars stems from the audience and not the performer. Forget all that. This is mythic territory, and the making of a star is being recounted with focus on the individual performer, not on vague sociocultural undercurrents. Consumers of the myth want a story about a person.

Likewise, the tumble from the top is more vivid in the mythology than could be documented by the study of 100 stars. Most stars in the study either died while in the role, were eased out, or eased themselves out. But the demands of drama call for another conclusion in which the star is brought to a devastating, heartrending end. It would not be an enjoyable story if it did not have a resounding denouement.

The mythology of the star role has reached an eager audience through a variety of media—through books *(The Day of the Locust* and *Hollywood Wives)*, through plays *(42nd Street)*, and through television series *(Fame)*. But the primary vehicle for the fictionalized star story has been the movies. Approximately 150 films have been made about stars, beginning with the 1915 silent movie *The Life of Buffalo Bill.* Performers from all sectors of stardom—actors and actresses, athletes, singers, dancers, comedians—have been featured in these recitations of the star myth.

A number of these productions were patterned upon the careers of actual stars. Almost invariably such films are criticized for their inexact depiction of the real life of the performer. Sidney Skolsky, producer of *The Jolson Story* and *The Eddie Cantor Story*, responded defensively, "You cannot put something on the screen as it really is, and in telling a life story in a film you cannot possibly cover all the points. The important thing is to arrive at the essence of your character, to decide what it is you want to say, and to do it within a dramatic framework."

The majority of films based on the lives of stars have turned out poorly, no matter what standards they are judged by. The life of Rudolph Valentino would seem to offer abundant raw material, but the 1951 film with hackneyed dialogue, untried actors, and a wayward plot turned out to be a sorry mishmash. A 1976 version by director Ken Russell, with Rudolf Nureyev in the lead, was idiosyncratic and fragmented to the point of being unwatchable, critics agreed. Two films titled *Harlow* were released in 1965, both structured along the rise-and-fall theme and both abysmal critical and box-office failures.

Movies founded on these "true" stories may be operating under a crippling disadvantage. The data of a performer's life may interfere with, rather than enhance, the tale that the public wants to see. The greater story is the general myth of stardom, not the partial version that any particular performer is bound to depict. Reality distracts. This, rather than an inattention to accurate biographic detail, may be the cause of the common dissatisfaction with such films.

The most prized and enjoyed films about stars are those that feature a composite character, one unfettered by the details of any single performer's life, free to sail on the fictive currents wherever they lead. Some of these films have emphasized the rising side of the star legend, some the falling, and some both. Not only one of the best movies about stars, but also one of the best musicals ever made, was the 1952 production *Singin' in the Rain*. Gene Kelly played a leading silent-screen actor, Don Lockwood, and Jean Hagen was his costar, Lina Lamont (described as "a triple threat: can't sing, can't dance, can't act"). Making a film, they are abruptly compelled to switch from a silent to a sound production, a transition Don can make easily, but Lina, with her reedy voice, cannot. Called in to dub her lines and songs is sweet young Kathy Selden (played by Debbie Reynolds), whom Don has fallen in love with. Kathy, a charming Hollywood newcomer, is the character designed to tug at heartstrings. At the premiere of their film, Lina unwisely accedes to the theater audience's call for an encore, and Kathy is quickly stationed behind the curtain to sing while Lina mouths the words. Don seizes the opportunity to pull up the curtain, revealing Kathy as the true entertainer that she is. Talent will out.

Critic Richard Schickel, who has an eye for the dark side of things, calls *Sunset Boulevard* (1950) the "best movie about movies ever made." Again the backdrop is the contrast between the silent-movie era and that of sound. Here the theme is not the rise of a star but the bitterness of life after the fall. It is all over for Norma Desmond (Gloria Swanson) and has been for twenty years. Unemployed scriptwriter Joe Gillis (William Holden) happens upon her baronial Hollywood mansion and, acknowledging her, comments, "You were big." Norma corrects him: "I *am* big. It's the pictures that got small." She is still dreaming of a comeback and hires Joe to work on her script. It is a doomed exercise.

Sunset Boulevard proved gruesomely fascinating for moviegoers. Observing the once-mighty brought low, they could wallow in the dramatization of a great career's pathetic aftermath. And they may have also sensed distantly their own power, for although Norma has money, a circle of friends, and the devotion of a man who was once her director and husband (played by Erich von Stroheim), she still wants the one thing she can no longer obtain: the adulation of the public. Her humiliation is inevitable; she visits a studio in the mistaken belief that Cecil B. DeMille (playing himself) wants to direct her, only to have him say, "Pictures have changed quite a bit, Norma." In the sordid finale she murders Joe and is arrested.

A film that combines the themes of ascent and descent, and does it in about even proportions, is *A Star Is Born*. In part because it allows its viewers to experience both an exhilarating rise and a dismaying fall, it has proven extremely popular and has been remade several times. An early imperfect version appeared in 1932 as *What Price Hollywood?*, to be followed in 1937 with the fully realized *A Star Is Born* with Janet Gaynor and Fredric March. In 1954 Judy Garland remade it with James Mason as a musical with the same title, and in 1976 Barbra Streisand's rendition with Kris Kristofferson centered on the world of rock stars.

In the classic version, Esther Blodgett (Gaynor) leaves her midwestern home to pursue a career in the movies. Her family discourages her, with the exception of her grandmother, who had come west on a prairie schooner and who now says, "There'll always be a wilderness to conquer, Esther. Maybe Hollywood's the wilderness now." Things do not go well for the pleasant Esther, however, until at a Hollywood party where she is working as a waitress she meets the well-known star Norman Maine (March). Maine gets Esther a screen test, and on the basis of it she wins a contract. Renamed Vicki Lester, her fortunes begin to rise. She and Maine marry, although his career is now on the skids. His drinking worsens, there is a series of calamities, and he is hospitalized. Acclaimed a star, Esther/Vicki remains steadfastly loyal to Maine, who eventually commits suicide by walking into the ocean.

Neither character is hamstrung by resembling too closely any particular real-life star. Vicki Lester fulfills a stereotype of the lovely young woman with shining values who deserves to rise because of her vision and virtue. Norman Maine, corrupt but not despicable, eliciting sympathy rather than contempt, is the victim of his alcoholism. His character is a composite of several well-known Hollywood figures, including John Barrymore, who displayed similar alcoholic and self-destructive traits, and John Bowers, who drowned himself when his acting career faltered. Both central characters in *A Star Is Born* became archetypes for the American audience.

Singin' in the Rain, Sunset Boulevard, and *A Star Is Born* have become treasured films because they give desired form to the prevailing notions about stardom. Through these classic fictions the star role lives on in the minds of Americans.

The role lives on in contemporary national life as well. It has become the axial occupation of American culture, and promises to remain so. Perhaps the most telling proof of the centrality of the role is that so much wealth is lavished upon those in it. No others are valued as much as stars. So important are the inhabitants of the role to us that, through the century, people have constantly complained about a paucity of current stars. The recurrent sentiment has been that recent stars are insufficient, that past stars were more ample. It is an erroneous perception— decades' worth of past stars are bunched together and compared to today's number, usually by those too old to appreciate the present crop—but it does reveal an important truth: that Americans retain an almost insatiable hunger for stars.

The prominence of the star role has been one of the most defining features of American culture as distinct from other cultures. During World War II combat, when shooting lulls descended upon American and Japanese troops, the GIs would needle their opponents by shouting, "Fuck Hirohito!" And the

Japanese would respond cuttingly, "Fuck Babe Ruth!" They knew the kind of eminent figures we idolized.

Observing the 1988 Academy Awards hullabaloo, a film journalist from the Soviet Union was dumbfounded by how fiercely the American press pursued stars: "If I were a famous actor or singer in this country I would go crazy. Everywhere you go, *paparazzi* and more *paparazzi*. You cannot take a swim in the ocean without some photographer hiding in the sand dunes. Nothing about your life is private anymore." Perhaps because this was his first trip to the United States, he was able to look freshly and insightfully at the phenomenon of stardom: "I think there is a certain cult of celebrity in the States you don't really find in my country. Because the TV is on so much and there are so many programs, I think there's a feeling that these celebrities are really a part of your family."

The American public's obsession with stars promises to continue strongly in the next century. The underlying conditions that gave rise to the role early in this century are not soon to disappear. If anything, they are becoming yet more prevalent. In particular, the institutions that had lent definition to human life during previous eras, and whose erosion led to the formation of the star role by 1920, have continued to decay as the century has worn on. The prescriptions of religious creeds have even less directive force in the lives of Americans; the percentage of people who affirm they are church members, or who say they have recently attended a religious service, has been on a lengthy slide. Communities do not command allegiance as they used to. The organizations and clubs that our forebears so proudly belonged to, we do less so. Statistics disclose that we are increasingly unlikely to join political parties or trouble to vote.

The most profound institutional decline has occurred with the family. Decreasingly marriage and family life serve to integrate the individual into anything beyond himself. Marriage rates have been dropping for three decades, while divorce rates have been rising. The size of the average family has been falling sharply and is now well below three people. American women, who in 1960 had an average of 3.6 children, now have half that—not even enough for a generation to replace itself. The evolution of American culture has reached the point that one-quarter of

all households consist of a person living alone. The traditional family is being shredded.

While these age-old institutions, once the determinants of existence, have been weakening, the mass media have been on the rise. Surveys over the years regarding how Americans spend their leisure time document increasing hours with the mass media and decreasing hours in face-to-face contact. Mass media use is now the third-ranked activity after work and sleep; the content of these media has come to occupy the greater part of Americans' recreational time. More than anything else, what we share as a people is this mediated material; the truth is that it comprises our new integrating institution. For the most part, the particular content we insist upon, and will continue to insist upon, is that of stars in performance.

If somehow the star role were eliminated from American culture, our lives would be much the poorer. We would be abandoned to swirl in the uncertain eddies of industrialized existence. The rejuvenation we now experience through stars' dramas, concerts, and athletic contests would be largely lost to us. We would have to feel our way along our paths without the benefit of idealized depictions of how to be and how to behave. Lacking a community of stars to observe, we would in all likelihood grow unsettled and uneasy. Other social institutions, perhaps more repressive ones, would have to rectify the situation. This sounds much like existence in the Soviet Union, an industrial but essentially starless society. Put stars back in the picture, and the resiliency of American culture returns. With the help of stars, our chosen beacons for the murky atmosphere of modern life, we move onward.

APPENDIX
The Study of 100 Stars

The Study of 100 Stars undertaken for this book was an objective and systematic investigation into the occupation of the celebrity performer. Its goal was to formulate norms regarding the lives and careers of stars. The research design was based on earlier occupational studies of notable people, including Rudolf Haerle's survey of former major league baseball players,[1] and the Goertzels' analysis of eminent people who were the subjects of book-length biographies.[2]

There were two major steps to the execution of this study: the definition of the parameters of the population of stars; and the identification of the particular star subjects and the collection of their biographical data.

The first step made use of *Current Biography* (the standard library reference work on those individuals who evoke general interest) to establish the composition of stardom. While *Current Biography* lists many types of noteworthy people, only performers were of interest in this research. Twenty years' (1966–1985) worth of the annual editions were consulted, so that short-term variations would be negated. A total of 433 popular performers

were profiled in these volumes; when sorted into performance
fields, they produced this distribution:

51%	Actors and actresses	14%	Athletes
18%	Musicians	2%	Other
15%	Comedians (in all media)		

Two-thirds of these performers were male, and 8 percent were
of minority racial origin. This information was accepted as a
definition of the general characteristics of the population of
stars.

It was decided to examine the lives and careers of exactly
100 celebrity performers. A sample size this large was necessary
to ensure representativeness. A larger number, however, would
have mitigated against the intensive investigation of each performer that was necessary for this research.

For several reasons, a subset of the performers listed in *Current Biography* was not appropriate. While people profiled in
that series are often at the height of their careers, the Study of
100 Stars was limited to stars whose careers were over, so that
norms for the later stages of the performer's life could also be
ascertained. Additionally, many of those mentioned in *Current
Biography* were not of such renown as to be considered unques-
tionable stars. For these performers of lesser rank, ample biographical information was not certain to be available.

For the second step, 100 individual stars were selected.
They were chosen for their indisputably high name recognition
value and starring status. The total sample was adjusted until
it matched the previously established distributions for performance field, gender, and ethnicity.

Then biographical information was gathered on each star,
in keeping with the attached inventory form. Sources for this
material were identified through *Biography Index;* every attempt was made to use only the most authoritative works. Once
the 100 biographical inventories were completed, numerical
norms were calculated for quantitative items, and common patterns were determined for nonquantitative questions.

A copy of the fifty-five-item biographical inventory form follows. Frequencies are given for those items that can be sum-
marized numerically.

BIOGRAPHICAL INVENTORY FORM

The Study of 100 Stars

1. This star's professional name: _____
2. Gender:
       __67__ Male
       __33__ Female
3. Ethnicity:
       __92__ Caucasian
       __7__ Black
       __1__ Other
4. Primary specialty:
       __51__ Actor or actress
       __18__ Musician
       __15__ Comedian
       __4__ Athlete
       __2__ Other

I. PRE-STAR LIFE

5. Professional name different from name at birth?
       __54__ No
       __46__ Yes. Name at birth was: _____
6. Country of birth:
       __83__ United States
       __17__ Foreign country: _____
7. If born in the United States, which state? _____
8. For those born in the United States, the place of birth was
       __17__ A farm or village
       __66__ A town or city
9. Birth order:
       __55__ Star was firstborn
       __45__ Other: _____ born of _____
             children
10. Father was
       __32__ Present during star's childhood, a strong figure
       __23__ Present during childhood, a weak figure
       __24__ Intermittently present
       __21__ Absent or dead
11. Mother was
       __37__ Forceful supporter of star's career
       __34__ Somewhat supportive of star's career

   _____13_____ Uninterested in star's career
   _____5_____ Opposed to star's career
   _____11_____ Absent or dead
12. Economic status during star's childhood:
   _____50_____ Poor
   _____41_____ Middle class
   _____9_____ Privileged
13. Was the star's family involved in show business?
   _____92_____ No
   _____8_____ Yes
14. The star's childhood was fundamentally
   _____49_____ Stable
   _____51_____ Unstable
15. A narration of the star's home life as a child (with attention to stabilizing and destabilizing factors):
16. A description of the star's relationship with parents throughout life:
17. Star's age at first clear desire to be a performer: ___13___
18. Highest year of education completed: ___11th grade___
19. Extensive training for work as performer?
   _____72_____ No
   _____28_____ Yes, as described:

II. LIFE AS STAR

20. A narration of the major "breaks" in this star's career:
21. A summary narration of the performance career of this star:
22. Which, if any, commercial accounts (advertising, endorsements, product lines, etc.) did this star have?
23. What political appearances, if any, did this star make?
24. What charitable or philanthropic services, if any, did this star perform?
25. Information about the financial remuneration of this star:
26. Indicators of fan devotion (letters, autograph-seeking, clubs, gifts, groupies, etc.):
27. Incidents of fan melees:
28. What was this star's attitude toward the press?
29. What did this performer feel about being a star?
30. A description of any discrepancy between the star's public image and the star's private nature:

31. A classification of this star as essentially
   ____34____ Introverted
   ____66____ Extroverted
32. How many times was this star married? ____2.31____
33. How many children did this star have? ____2.09____
34. A description of the relationship between the star and the star's children:
35. Were any of the star's children reported to be wayward or deviant?
   ____199____ No
   ____10____ Yes, as described:
36. What was the role of religion in this star's life?
37. Was this star involved in the practice of the occult?
   ____83____ None reported
   ____17____ Yes, as described:
38. What superstitions did this star have?
39. Did alcohol abuse figure in this star's life?
   ____15____ Chronic alcoholic
   ____24____ Not chronic alcoholic, but incidents of alcohol abuse reported
   ____61____ No abuse reported
40. Did the use of illegal drugs figure in this star's life?
   ____85____ None reported
   ____15____ Yes, as described:
41. A narration of any self-destructive or extreme behavior:
42. Hobbies and avocations:
43. Conspicuous spending and purchases:
44. Comeback efforts, both successful and unsuccessful:
45. Considering the years between the first starring performance and the last (excluding unsuccessful comeback attempts), how long did the performer's career last? ____25.3 years____

III. POST-STAR LIFE

46. Was this performer a star to the end of his or her life?
   ____47____ Yes
   ____53____ No
47. If this performer had stopped being a star at some point, what was the performer's response?
   ____18____ Great difficulty with transition
   ____11____ Moderate difficulty

_____14_____ No noticeable distress

_____10_____ Pleased not to be a star

48. If this performer stopped being a star at some point, was there a second career?

_____36_____ No

_____17_____ Yes, as described:

49. For individuals who retired, a description of their life during this stage:

50. Year of death: __1974 was the median year for this sample__

51. Age at death: __58.7 on average__

52. Cause of death:

53. If this star is dead, what noteworthy events surrounded the death:

54. If this star is dead, a description of the funeral:

55. If this star is dead, a narration of any continuing impact:

IV. LIST OF SOURCES

NOTES

Direct quotations attributed to stars, often taken from widely disseminated wire-service stories running in local newspapers, have not been referenced. More substantial and interpretive sources are cited in these notes.

PREFACE

1. Daniel Boorstin, *The Image: A Guide to Pseudo-Events in America* (New York: Atheneum, 1961), 273.
2. Orrin Klapp, *Symbolic Leaders* (Chicago: Aldine, 1964), 7.
3. Garth S. Jowett and James A. Linton, *Movies as Mass Communication* (Beverly Hills, Calif.: Sage, 1980), 76.
4. Leo Braudy, *The Frenzy of Renown: Fame and Its History* (New York: Oxford University Press, 1986), 9.

CHAPTER 1: STARRING

1. Philip Zimbardo, *Shyness: What It Is, What To Do about It* (Reading, Mass.: Addison-Wesley, 1977), 14.

2. Yoti Lane, *The Psychology of the Actor* (Westport, Conn.: Greenwood Press, 1959), 130.

3. Pamela Des Barres, *I'm with the Band: Confessions of a Groupie* (New York: Beech Tree, 1987), 28.

4. Wayne Harold Ault, "Show Business and Politics: The Influence of Television, Entertainment Celebrities and Motion Pictures on American Public Opinion and Political Behavior" (Ph.D. diss., St. Louis University, 1981), 119–20.

CHAPTER 2: A ROLE IS BORN (AND ENDURES)

1. Thomas Carlyle, *Heroes, Hero-Worship, and the Heroic in History* (New York: A. L. Burt, 1840), 14.

2. Leo Lowenthal, *Literature, Popular Culture and Society* (Palo Alto, Calif.: Pacific Books, 1961), 109–40.

3. Daniel Boorstin, *The Image: A Guide to Pseudo-Events in America* (New York: Atheneum, 1961), 61.

4. John Drinkwater, *The Life and Adventures of Carl Laemmle* (New York: Scribner's, 1932), 141.

5. Mary Pickford, *Sunshine and Shadow* (New York: Doubleday, 1954), 169.

6. Adolph Zukor, *The Public Is Never Wrong: The Autobiography of Adolph Zukor* (New York: G. P. Putnam's Sons, 1953), 170.

7. Charles Chaplin, *Charles Chaplin: My Autobiography* (New York: Simon and Schuster, 1964), 176.

8. Garth Jowett and James M. Linton, *Movies as Mass Communication* (Beverly Hills, Calif.: Sage, 1980), 69.

9. Quoted in Benjamin McArthur, *Actors and American Culture, 1890–1920* (Philadelphia: Temple University Press, 1984), 11.

10. Ibid., x.

11. Albert McLean, *American Vaudeville as Ritual* (Lexington: University Press of Kentucky, 1965), 53.

12. U.S. Department of Commerce, Bureau of the Census, *Historical Statistics of the United States: Colonial Times to 1970* (Washington D.C.: U.S. Government Printing Office, 1975), 11–12.

13. Ibid., 165.

14. Quoted in Russell Lynes, *The Lively Audience: A Social History of the Visual and Performing Arts in America, 1890–1950* (New York: Harper and Row, 1985), 2.

15. T. J. Jackson Lears, *No Place of Grace: Antimodernism and the Transformation of American Culture, 1880–1920* (New York: Pantheon, 1984), 280.

16. Warren I. Susman, *Culture as History: The Transformation of American Society in the Twentieth Century* (New York: Pantheon, 1984), 280.

17. John Richards Betts, "The Technological Revolution and the Rise of Sport, 1850–1900," *Mississippi Valley Historical Review* 40 (1953): 240.

18. Harold Seymour, *Baseball: The Early Years* (New York: Oxford University Press, 1960), 173.

19. Albert Mehrabian, *Silent Messages* (Belmont, Calif.: Wadsworth, 1971), 44.

20. Leo C. Rosten, *Hollywood: The Movie Colony, The Movie Makers* (New York: Harcourt Brace, 1941), 143.

21. Alexander Walker, *Stardom* (New York: Stein and Day, 1970), 251.

22. Edgar Morin, *The Stars* (New York: Grove Press, 1961), 32.

23. Walker, *Stardom*, 329.

CHAPTER 3: ASPIRANTS

1. Elaine Barrymore and Sanford Dody, *All My Sins Remembered* (New York: Appleton-Century, 1964), 19.

2. Betsy Borns, *Comic Lives: Inside the World of American Stand-Up Comedy* (New York: Fireside Books, 1987), 183.

3. Alfred C. Golden, "Personality Traits of Drama School Students," *Quarterly Journal of Speech* 26 (1940): 564–75.

4. Beverly Jean Crute, "Wives of Professional Athletes: An Inquiry into the Impact of Professional Sport on the Home and Family" (Ph.D. diss., Boston College, 1981), 44.

5. Anne K. Peters, "Aspiring Hollywood Actresses: A Sociological Perspective," in *Varieties of Work Experience*, eds. Phyllis L. Steward and Muriel G. Cantor (New York: Wiley, 1974), 39–48.

6. Hortense Powdermaker, *Hollywood: The Dream Factory* (Boston: Little, Brown & Co., 1950), 237.

7. Pamela Des Barres, *I'm with the Band: Confessions of a Groupie* (New York: Beech Tree Books, 1987), 220.

8. Penny Stallings, *Flesh and Fantasy* (New York: St. Martin's, 1978), 33.

9. M. K. and Rosemary Lewis, *Your Film Acting Career* (New York: Crown, 1983), 158.

10. Mark Litwak, *Reel Power: The Struggle for Influence and Success in the New Hollywood* (New York: Morrow, 1986), 141.

11. Benjamin McArthur, *Actors and American Culture, 1880–1920* (Philadelphia: Temple University Press, 1984), 22.

12. Diana Serra Cary, *Hollywood Children: An Inside Account of the Child Star Era* (Boston: Houghton Mifflin, 1978), 149.

13. Cathy Smith, *Chasing the Dragon* (Toronto: Key Porter, 1984), 118.

14. Muriel G. Cantor, "The Employment and Unemployment of Screen Actors in the United States," in *Economic Policy for the Arts*, ed. William S. Hendon (Cambridge, Mass.: Abt Books, 1980), 215.

15. Ibid., 213.

16. Mildred George Goertzel, Victor Goertzel, and Ted George Goertzel, *Three Hundred Eminent Personalities: A Psychosocial Analysis of the Famous* (San Francisco: Jossey-Bass, 1978), 11.

CHAPTER 4: STAR VILLAGE

1. John P. LaPlace, "Personality and Its Relation to Success in Professional Baseball," *Research Quarterly* 25 (1954): 313–19.

2. Gary Carey, *Marlon Brando: The Only Contender* (New York: St. Martin's, 1985), 68.

3. Leo Braudy, *The Frenzy of Renown: Fame and Its History* (New York: Oxford University Press, 1986), 589.

4. Irving J. Rein, Philip Kotler, and Martin R. Stoller, *High Visibility* (New York: Dodd Mead, 1987), 135.

5. Lura Beam, *A Maine Hamlet* (Augusta, Me.: Lance Tapley, 1957), 51.

6. Thomas Harris, "The Building of Popular Images: Grace Kelly and Marilyn Monroe," *Studies in Public Communication* 1 (1957): 45–48.

7. Richard Griffith, *The Movie Stars* (Garden City, N.Y.: Doubleday, 1970), 44.

8. James Robert Parish and Don E. Stanke, *The Glamour Girls* (Carlstadt, N.J.: Rainbow Books, 1975), 674.

9. Doug Warren, *Betty Grable: The Reluctant Movie Queen* (New York: St. Martin's, 1974), 79.

CHAPTER 5: INDUCTION

1. Leslie Raddatz, "Believe It or Not, He Can't Recall Donna Mills or Kate Jackson," *TV Guide*, 25 August 1984, 40.

2. Henry Edwards and Tony Zanetta, *Stardust: The David Bowie Story* (New York: McGraw-Hill, 1986), 184.

3. Edgar Morin, *The Stars* (New York: Grove Press, 1961), 102.

4. Albert Goldman, *Elvis* (New York: McGraw-Hill, 1981), 119.

5. Orrin E. Klapp, *Symbolic Leaders* (Chicago: Aldine, 1964), 43.

CHAPTER 6: STARS AT WORK

1. W. J. Weatherby, *Conversations with Marilyn* (New York: Mason/ Charter, 1976), 146.

2. Fred Lawrence Guiles, *Norma Jean: The Life of Marilyn Monroe* (New York: McGraw-Hill, 1969), 137.

3. Diana Serra Cary, *Hollywood's Children: An Inside Account of the Child Star Era* (Boston: Houghton Mifflin, 1978), 223.

4. Dick Moore, *Twinkle, Twinkle, Little Star* (New York: Harper and Row, 1978), xii.

5. Priscilla Beaulieu Presley, *Elvis and Me* (New York: Berkley, 1985), 279.

6. Joshua Meyrowitz, *No Sense of Place: The Impact of Electronic Media on Social Behavior* (New York: Oxford University Press, 1985), 46–49.

7. Martin Levin, *Hollywood and the Great Fan Magazines* (New York: Arbor House, 1970), 7.

8. George Eells, *Hedda and Louella* (New York: Putnam's, 1972), 21.

9. Kitty Kelley, *His Way: The Unauthorized Biography of Frank Sinatra* (Toronto: Bantam, 1986), 158.

10. Henry Edwards and Tony Zanetta, *Stardust: The David Bowie Story* (New York: McGraw-Hill, 1986), 158.

11. Leo Handel, *Hollywood Looks at Its Audience* (New York: Arno Press, 1976), 10.

12. Leo C. Rosten, *Hollywood: The Movie Colony, the Movie Makers* (New York: Harcourt Brace, 1941), 409–11.

13. Fred and Judy Vermorel, *Starlust: The Secret Life of Fans* (London: Comet, 1985), 248.

14. Marshall Smelser, *The Life that Ruth Built: A Biography* (New York: Quadrangle, 1975), 276.

15. Bob Greene, "Words of Love," *Esquire*, May 1984, 12–13.

16. John L. Caughey, *Imaginary Social Worlds* (Lincoln: University of Nebraska Press, 1984), 41.

17. Christina Crawford, *Mommie Dearest* (New York: Morrow, 1978), 73.

18. Guiles, *Norma Jean*, 213.

19. Donald Shepherd and Robert F. Slatzer, *Bing Crosby: The Hollow Man* (New York: St. Martin's, 1981).

20. Richard Schickel, *Intimate Strangers: The Culture of Celebrity* (Garden City, N.Y.: Doubleday, 1985), 128.

21. Hortense Powdermaker, *Hollywood: The Dream Factory* (Boston: Little, Brown & Co., 1950), 207.

22. Rosten, *Hollywood*, 53.

CHAPTER 7: WHAT STARS DO FOR THE PUBLIC

1. James Lull, "Girls' Favorite TV Females," *Journalism Quarterly* 57 (Spring 1980): 146–50.

2. Leo Handel, *Hollywood Looks at Its Audience* (New York: Arno Press, 1976), 144.

3. Timothy White, *Rock Stars* (New York: Stewart, Tabori & Chang, 1984), 23.

4. Fred and Judy Vermorel, *Starlust: The Secret Life of Fans* (London: Comet, 1985), 129.

5. Jeff Meer, "Loneliness," *Psychology Today* 19 (July 1985): 28.

6. Albert McLean, *American Vaudeville as Ritual* (Lexington: University of Kentucky Press, 1965), 19.

7. Edgar Morin, *The Stars* (New York: Grove, 1961), 73.

8. Hortense Powdermaker, *Hollywood: The Dream Factory* (Boston: Little, Brown & Co., 1950), 29.

9. Richard Schickel, *Intimate Strangers* (New York: Doubleday, 1985), 270.

10. Donald Horton and R. Richard Wohl, "Mass Communication and Para-Social Interaction: Observations on Intimacy at a Distance," *Psychiatry* 19 (1956): 222.

11. Pamela Des Barres, *I'm with the Band: Confessions of a Groupie* (New York: Beech Tree), 24.

12. Schickel, *Intimate Strangers*, 8.

13. Wayne Harold Ault, "Show Business and Politics: The Influence of Television, Entertainment Celebrities and Motion Pictures on American Public Opinion and Political Behavior" (Ph.D. diss., St. Louis University, 1981), 174–77.

CHAPTER 8: COMPENSATIONS

1. Richard Schickel, *Intimate Strangers: The Culture of Celebrity* (New York: Doubleday, 1985), 44.

2. Harold L. Vogel, *Entertainment Industry Economics: A Guide for Financial Analysis* (New York: Cambridge University Press, 1986), 92.

3. Mark Litwak, *Reel Power: The Struggle for Influence and Success in the New Hollywood* (New York: Morrow, 1986), 211.

4. Michael R. Real, "Understanding Oscar: The Academy Awards Telecast as International Media Event," in *The Critical Communications Review, Vol. 3: Popular Culture and Media Events,* eds. Vincent Mosco and Janet Wasko (Norwood, N.J.: Ablex, 1985), 163.

5. Cathy Smith, *Chasing the Dragon* (Toronto: Key Porter, 1984), 141.

6. Lyn Tornabene, *Long Live the King: A Biography of Clark Gable* (New York: Pocket, 1976), 153.

7. Beverly Jean Crute, "Wives of Professional Athletes: An Inquiry into the Impact of Professional Sport on the Home and Family" (Ph.D. diss., Boston College, 1981), 126.

8. Philip Norman, *Symphony for the Devil: The Rolling Stones Story* (New York: Linden, 1984), 176.

9. Philip Norman, *Shout! The Beatles in Their Generation* (New York: Warner, 1982), 345.

10. Tornabene, *Long Live the King,* 7.

11. Crute, "Wives of Professional Athletes," 213.

12. Smith, *Chasing the Dragon,* 124.

13. Litwak, *Reel Power,* 97.

CHAPTER 9: DECLINE

1. Nelson W. Aldrich, Jr., "The New Celebrity Class," *Vogue,* May 1986, 365.

2. Richard Schickel, *The Stars* (New York: Dial, 1962), 121.

3. Fred and Judy Vermorel, *Starlust: The Secret Life of Fans* (London: Comet, 1985), 249.

4. Donald S. Harris and D. Stanley Eitzen, "The Consequences of Failure in Sport," *Urban Life* 7 (July 1978): 183.

5. Richard Griffith, *The Movie Stars* (Garden City, N.Y.: Doubleday, 1970), 378.

6. Aldrich, "The New Celebrity Class," 365.

7. Edward Kiersh, *Where Are You Now, Bo Diddley?* (Garden City, N.Y.: Doubleday, 1986), 48.

8. Leo C. Rosten, *Hollywood: The Movie Colony, the Movie Makers* (New York: Harcourt Brace, 1941), 338.

9. Daniel Boorstin, *The Image: A Guide to Pseudo-Events in America* (New York: Atheneum, 1961), 91.

10. Mark Litwak, *Reel Power: The Struggle for Influence and Success in the New Hollywood* (New York: Morrow, 1986), 63.

11. Rudolf K. Haerle, "Career Patterns and Career Contingencies of Professional Baseball Players: An Occupational Analysis," in *Sport and*

Social Order, eds. Donald W. Ball and John W. Loy (Reading, Mass.: Addison-Wesley, 1975), 461–519.

12. Jim Bouton, *Ball Four* (New York: World, 1970), 142.

13. Beverly Jean Crute, "Wives of Professional Athletes: An Inquiry into the Impact of Professional Sport on the Home and Family" (Ph.D. diss., Boston College, 1981), 201.

14. Edwin Rosenberg, "Professional Athletic Retirement: Bringing Theory and Research Together," in *Career Patterns and Career Contingencies in Sport*, eds. Alan G. Ingham and Eric F. Broom (Vancouver: University of British Columbia, 1981), 447.

15. Marshall Smelser, *The Life that Ruth Built: A Biography* (New York: Quadrangle, 1975), 508.

16. Ibid., 528.

17. Jane Marie Gaines, "The Popular Icon as Commodity and Sign: The Circulation of Betty Grable, 1941–45" (Ph.D. diss., Northwestern University, 1982), 256.

CHAPTER 10: DEATHS

1. Martin Gottfried, *In Person: The Great Entertainers* (New York: Abrams, 1985), 246.

CHAPTER 11: RIPPLES

1. Orrin Klapp, *Symbolic Leaders* (Chicago: Aldine, 1964), 63.

2. Kathy Cronkite, *On the Edge of the Spotlight: Celebrities' Children Speak Out about Their Lives* (New York: Morrow, 1981), 21.

3. Stephen Farber and Marc Green, *Hollywood Dynasties* (New York: Delilah, 1985), 136.

4. Robert Milton Miller, "Show Business Biographical Drama in Film and Television: A Generic Analysis" (Ph.D. diss., Northwestern University, 1982), 246.

APPENDIX

1. Rudolf K. Haerle, "Career Patterns and Career Contingencies of Professional Baseball Players: An Occupational Analysis," in *Sport and Social Order*, eds. Donald W. Ball and John W. Loy (Reading, Mass.: Addison-Wesley, 1975), 461–519.

2. Mildred George Goertzel, Victor Goertzel, and Ted George Goertzel, *Three Hundred Eminent Personalities: A Psychosocial Analysis of the Famous* (San Francisco: Jossey-Bass, 1978).